MODERN ENGLISH

ITS GROWTH AND PRESENT USE

GEORGE PHILIP KRAPP

REVISED EDITION BY

ALBERT H. MARCKWARDT

PROFESSOR OF ENGLISH AND LINGUISTICS, PRINCETON UNIVERSITY

CHARLES SCRIBNER'S SONS

NEW YORK

Reviser's Foreword

It is now sixty years since George Philip Krapp's *Modern English* first appeared, published by a firm which miraculously in this day of change, bore the same name that it does today. The book has long since deserved republication: it was an important work then and still has much to say to the general reader for whom it was intended.

Unfortunately, an adequate sketch of the development of trends of thought about the English language over the past one hundred years, especially with reference to questions of grammar and usage, correctness and error, has never been written. Had it been, this book and its author would have been credited with giving a new direction to that thought, namely a definition of standard language based upon social utility rather than literary tradition.

From the turn of the century on, and even slightly before, scholars had recognized the extent to which the usage of cultivated writers and speakers could and did vary, and that there were historical and psychological factors which accounted for this variation. Nevertheless, they did not succeed in making a convincing case for their view of language. The general public for the most part believed firmly in a single, monolithic linguistic standard —the point of view expressed in such books as the long popular *English Words and Their Uses* by Richard Grant White. Some idea of the temper of White's linguistic judgments may be gained from his characterization of the word *practitioner* as "abnormal and indefensible," and his condemnation of *presidential, tangential,* and *exponential* as "a trinity of monsters which, although they have not been lovely in their lives, should yet in their death not be divided."

It was this kind of prejudiced and indeed overbearing approach to language problems that Krapp sought to overcome. The statement of purpose, to be found in the first two paragraphs of his Preface to the present work, is over-modest, falling far short of a reasonable assessment of the contribution of this book. True enough, many of the generalizations which appear throughout the work were—and still are—commonplaces of the historical study of language. But they were placed in a context and given a rationale which was quite new, namely a concept and definition of language based upon social utility rather than literary tradition. Krapp was among the first to recognize the uniqueness of the function of language and the nature of the linguistic standard in a democracy. He began and ended his book on this note, one which he was to repeat sixteen years later in his study of American English when he wrote, "A sufficient definition of the term standard will perhaps be found in the statement that speech is standard when it passes current in actual use among persons who must be accounted among the conservers and representatives of the approved social traditions in a community." This point of view, new in its time, still merits a hearing for its skill in combining the ideas of the operation of language in society, when that society is a democracy, with what is known about the history and development of English and with a carefully compiled and accurate record of current usage.

My own problem in revising the work has been to preserve its essential spirit and philosophy, but at the same time to update its references to the current state of English, and to restate in somewhat more contemporary terms what Krapp characterized as "the commonplaces in the historical study of the language." Naturally, some of these "commonplaces" have developed and matured in the past sixty years, just as certain uses of the language, moot in the first decade of the century, are accepted in the seventh, and others have quietly disappeared. I have attempted to make these changes as unobtrusively as possible and have retained the original reading to the degree that I could conceivably do so.

It is, however, the spirit in which the work was written, the broad view of language which it sets forth, which makes it still germane to the linguistic scene today. As W. Cabell Greet wrote, in an assessment of the author's work, "From his first book to his last, Krapp was engaged in clarifying, simplifying, purifying, in order to present truth—the facts of the English language, which had been confused by grammarians and pedants . . . He had a remarkable gift of viewing things without prejudice—a kind of blessed naiveté which in a very learned man is akin to greatness and genius."

It is this gift which makes of *Modern English*, sixty years after its composition, a book which may still be read with profit by the wide audience for whom it was written.

Albert H. Marckwardt

Preface to the First Edition

This book is not designed to do away with the necessity for using the dictionaries, grammars, and detailed histories of the English language, but to prepare the way for the more profitable and intelligent use of these books. The grammars and the dictionaries are the mines in which the crude materials, the natural resources, of the language are stored; the principles of development appearing in language, the opinions which men hold with respect to the use of language, these are the appliances and the machinery by means of which the riches of the dictionaries and encyclopedias of fact may be made available for effective command over language. Some of the more important of these principles and opinions it is the purpose of this book to present.

The generalizations here set forth are some of them the commonplaces of the historical study of language. For stating them again in his own way, the author does not feel that any apology is necessary. They are given as simply as possible for the advantage of those readers and students who wish to be informed as to the results of the modern scientific study of language, but who are not themselves professional linguists. The book is untechnical, but, the author hopes, not unscholarly. Attention is called in the brief bibliography at the end of the volume to representative works which may be consulted by those who wish to enter into the subjects treated more fully than the limits of this volume permitted.

Perhaps fuller citations of literary authorities may be expected in discussions of points of divided use than have been given. In general, however, it does not seem to the author that the appeal to literary authority is the proper method of attack in examining disputed questions of speech, spoken or written, and that very little is gained by an elaborate assemblage of examples from literary sources to confirm or to disprove a point of present use. Where there is a real difference of practice—and this, it may be pointed out, is relatively infrequent—nine times out of ten it would be as easy to support one side as the other by the testimony of literary authority. Past literary use is only one of many tests that must be applied in determining present use. The reading of literary English should strengthen the habitual and unconscious feeling for expression by which one acquires a large, a sure, and a varied sense of the possible values of language. It should suggest what may be done with language by showing what has been done with it.

Literary English, indeed, should be regarded in the same way as spoken English. Both are forms of expression which have to be reduced to natural and unconscious habit before they can be said to have been mastered. Now nothing hinders such mastery so much as a meticulous respect for the authority of literary practice. DeQuincey once said that authors are a dangerous class for any language. He meant, of course, that the literary habit of mind is likely to prove dangerous for a language. It is likely to prove dangerous because it so often leads a speaker or writer to distrust natural and unconscious habit, even when it is right, and to put in its stead some conscious theory of literary propriety. Such a tendency, however, is directly opposed to the true feeling for idiomatic English. It destroys the sense of security, the assurance of perfect congruity between thought and expression, which the unliterary and unacademic speaker and writer often has, and which, with both literary and unliterary, is the basis for all expressive use of language.

The source of authority in deciding questions of propriety in form, questions which naturally arise less and less frequently as one acquires a sure sense of the expressive value of language, lies not in past use, but in what might be called future use, that is, in the effectiveness of the expression upon the minds of those who are to be the receivers of it. But enough—perhaps too much—has been said upon this subject in the body of the book, and it may be left here with the statement that although good modern English derives much from traditional literary English, the final test of its goodness or its badness is to be found always in immediate and not in past use.

Contents

Illustrations

MODERN ENGLISH
ITS GROWTH AND PRESENT USE

1

INTRODUCTION

1 ▨ History and Politics

History, according to the saying of a distinguished modern historian, is past politics. To the contemporary observer, the practical measures supported and opposed by the various rival political parties seem of only passing significance because they arise out of the immediate daily problems and needs of actual life. Yet, when these same measures are viewed in the perspective of years, they are seen then not to be independent and unrelated. More or less unconsciously to themselves, the practical politicians advance or retard certain large principles of development in the life of a people. Thus, present politics is history in the making.

2 ▨ The History of Language

In the same way the history of a language is chiefly the record of the practical everyday speech of successive generations. Every person who speaks or writes a language, who hands on from one speaker to another any of the traditions of the language is, to that degree, a factor in the historical growth of the language. And the whole history of the language is made up of the sum of

3

the individual acts of all those who in past times have used the language in response to the immediate practical needs of life. Just as politics is history in the making, so present, everyday speech and writing is the history of the language in the making.

Another conclusion of the modern political historians is applicable to the history of language. Historians often maintain that one justification of the study of the history of past periods is to be found in the application of the results of such study to the conditions of life today. Man learns to know himself better, to conduct the affairs of his public and private life better, from having observed the consequences of the actions of men in other days. Similarly, by the study of the history of his speech he learns to adjust himself more wisely to the conditions of present speech. He learns that contemporary speech is not, on the one hand, a chaos of individual instances, nor is it, on the other, governed according to the decrees of a rigid, theoretical system. He perceives that it is a living thing, and that the principles which it illustrates in its growth have all the flexibility and variety of life. To enable a speaker or writer to realize this spirit, or life, of his own present speech is one of the main ends of the historical study of language.

3 ▨ The Function of Language

The effort to understand this spirit, to find out what the tendencies of one's native speech are, good and bad, is beset with many difficulties. The uncertainty of the bearing of present events always makes difference of opinion possible. If we knew exactly the future significance of an action, whether in politics, in personal conduct, or in speech, we should all be much more likely to hold the same opinion with respect to that action. But the future does not so easily yield up its secrets, and our only guides are inferences drawn from the observation of the past and the present. There is always one ground of inference, however, which offers a firm foothold. Our opinions with respect to an action are naturally determined by the value of that action in attaining the end towards which the actor is striving. Our attitude towards any question of language should consequently be determined by the purpose and the function of language, just as the value of any political action is determined by its serving or not serving the purpose for which the state exists.

What, then, is the function of language? Briefly answered, language is a form of social custom, and its function is the expression of social ideas. Language as social custom means that it has been slowly developed by mankind in the social relations of men to each other. It is closely paralleled in its development by other kinds of social custom. The laws governing rights of property, of individual liberty, of self-defense, the moral laws, such as those directed against lying, deception, and insincerity, the rules of conduct in minor matters, such as have to do with behavior and good breeding—all these have grown up as the result of the intercourse of man with man in social life. The habits, or the rules, of such intercourse, through a long succession of generations, have fixed themselves in the life of the people as their social customs. Whether they are reduced to writing, as is generally the case with criminal law, or are merely held as the traditional rules of conduct of a people, as in some of our conventional forms of polite behavior, they are always in their origins the customary rules of action which have arisen out of the practical exigencies of one man's trying to live on terms of social understanding with another.

4 ⊠ Speech as Social Custom

The special function of speech as social custom is the expression of social ideas. If men are to live with each other, if they are not to be like sticks and stones, then they must have some means of conveying to each other their needs, their desires, their ideas, their aspirations. This can be done by various means. So long as the ideas were simple and primitive, they might be conveyed very crudely. A brandished club could serve to indicate one's sense of the right of possession in a piece of disputed property. But it is one of the characteristics of man as man that the ideas which he wishes to convey to his fellowmen have not remained thus simple and crude.

The social intercourse of men has become extremely complex, both emotionally and intellectually, and corresponding to this complexity, there has been an equal growth in the variety and subtlety of the customs of speech. Out of the practical needs of communication has arisen the vast fabric of human language. Manifestly, then, the best language being that which most adequately realizes the function of language, that is the best which enables men to express themselves most fully and satisfactorily in their relations to each other. This is the ideal toward which language strives.

In the animal world we speak of degeneration when certain functions of the organism necessary to the preservation of its life and the existence of its species become weakened. In the same way we may speak of degeneration in a language when it changes in such a way that it becomes less capable of performing the functions for which language exists. On the other hand, we may speak of growth and improvement in language as it becomes more and more effective in enabling men to understand each other.

5 ▨ The Speech of a Democracy

The necessity of realizing in an ever-increasing degree this ideal function of language is peculiarly incumbent upon a democracy. The best national speech for a democracy is that which enables it to be most fully self-expressive. It is within itself that the fate of a democracy lies. From its own members must emanate all its laws, its ideals of conduct, of whatever nature. It must have confidence in the value of its united opinion; and its prime duty consists in such a free and liberal exchange of ideas that there shall be a united opinion. A democracy which is not self-expressive and self-determining is not a real democracy.

Anything in speech, therefore, which prevents the democratic nation from realizing itself as a self-determining body is harmful.

Thus the national speech of a democracy cannot be sectional. If there is not one uniform speech acceptable to the whole nation, then the speech of one region must have equal authority with that of another. The speech of a democracy cannot be a class speech. It cannot be a traditional literary speech, the so-called "best English" of a special limited academic or literary class. Its roots must go deeper. They must strike down into the region of the practical daily life of the citizens whose vote and whose opinion make the country what it is. If it is to have any enduring vitality it must rest upon the basis of national custom where national custom is made.

The duty of making tnese customs sound and good is one that rests on all alike. The welfare of the speech of a democracy can no more be left in the hands of a few preservers or regulators than its political destiny can be committed to a few self-appointed directors or dictators. In both language and government, a diffused intelligence is the prime requisite to a healthy national life.

6 ⊠ Speech and Education

The obstacles that stand in the way of the realization of the ideal of a democratic speech are confessedly numerous and great. It is difficult, in the first place, to determine just how much value should be ascribed to tradition. Old ways are not good merely because they are old; and of course the same can be said of new ways. It is a fair conservative assumption, however, that what has served man's purpose in the past will continue to serve it best in the present, until changed conditions demand new ways. But again one must take heed not to be so blinded by old customs as not to perceive when the conditions actually are changed.

In the second place, democracy works from the bottom up, and not from the top down. Consequently, popular education when it is diffused over the whole body of society, as society is at present constituted, is likely to be somewhat thin and inadequate. Thus, there are people who rest content with very imperfect education, who mistake the dry husks of rudimentary education for the kernel itself. Among them are many who think that the secret of good English consists merely in expressing themselves in a certain prescribed way, in using a particular voice intonation or a certain quality of vowel sound when they speak, or one form of phrasing, or even of spelling, rather than another when they write. They fail to realize that the conventional customs of speaking and writing, important as the knowledge of them is, are nevertheless the mere preliminaries, the elementary mechanics of a good use of language. English which is merely correct cannot claim very high praise.

Somewhat lower in the social spectrum, we may find that a man who has come from generations of ancestors who could not write is likely to think that the simple ability to write, or even to read, is an educational achievement of real magnitude. For him perhaps it is; and all that democratic education can offer to any large body of people at different stages of development is the opportunity for each to realize what at a given moment is the highest and best thing for him to do. The general level cannot be raised by a single act, or by the acts of a few, but only by the sum of all the acts of the people who make up the whole. In spite, therefore, of the modest ideals of certain members of the body politic, it must always remain the hope of a democracy that the average plane of its life will rise higher and higher from generation to generation. And so long as the life of the people remains vigorous, so long as their minds and their wills are energetic and stirring, this will remain a well-founded hope.

7 ▨ The Best Tendency in Speech

In speech, therefore, the ideal attitude of mind is that which leads the speaker to unite himself to those customs and tendencies which, in his opinion, make for the welfare of the national idiom in the most effective manner. If speech arises, as we have said, out of the immediate social relations of man with man, it will be seen that therein lies the final test of its value. It will be seen, also, that those tendencies of speech with which a speaker or writer wishes to unite himself are merely manifestations of general social tendencies. Shall our ideal social tendency be one that makes for exclusiveness, for the development of class distinctions? Or shall it be a broader and more liberal tendency, one that is democratic and generously inclusive? In speech shall we endeavor to cultivate refined and more or less arbitrary distinctions which shall enable us to make a strict division between conventional and literary English on the one hand, and what may be called natural and self-determining English on the other? Is the best English that which is acquired by learning and following an external rule, or is it the English which is acquired by following social custom, the best, as each views it, and as each is brought into contact with it in the actual processes of living, speaking, and writing? These are some of the questions which each of us must answer for himself.

Necessarily every speaker and every writer must follow some tendency of the speech of the community, whether this be conscious or unconscious. Every one of us is always following, at the same time that he is helping to make, custom. In what direction shall we throw our influence? Before we can answer this question we must have some knowledge of the conflicting customs and tendencies of our speech, and as this knowledge grows in breadth and certainty, the answer to the question will become, according to our sympathies, correspondingly easy and unhesitating.

8 ▨ Literary and Spoken Language

In all study of language as expression, it is now generally maintained, by those who have given much thought to the matter, that the spoken, as compared with the written or literary language, is of far greater importance. It is mainly in the speech of men and women as they come into direct social relations with each other that language develops and grows in a natural, untrammeled, and effective way. From one point of view, the language of literature is merely an approximate transcription, more or less remote, of the language of speech. It is from the latter that the language of literature is derived, and it must always return to its source to renew itself when, as it constantly tends to do, it becomes attenuated and outworn. From this it follows that the study of the spoken language is helpful not only for what it reveals about effectiveness in conversation, but for the clues it offers about effectiveness in literature as well.

Popular opinion is not usually in accord with this view of the relative importance of speech and writing. It is often believed that the language of literature is something different from and better than the language of speech. This latter, being the common possession of all, is looked down upon as somewhat loose and disorganized, or at least not admirable. Because it is familiar, it is not taken very seriously. It is supposed that the ability to use the English of literature is a special and acquired accomplishment, and that one learns the language of literature as one learns a new art, like playing the piano or painting. Being a special and higher accomplishment, the language of literature is thus often regarded as furnishing the model for the language of speech, and the theory is held that the latter should be made to conform as fully as possible to the former. One need only "talk like a book" to realize the absurdity of such a belief.

On the other hand it is no credit to the language of literature to read like a book. Literary language which is bookish we do not regard as admirable; on the contrary, when we want to praise an author's style, we say rather that it is true, natural, real. The fact is that literature generally endeavors to transcribe life, to give in the permanent form of words and sentences the passing experiences, thoughts, and emotions of men. To the degree that it does this the more directly and truly, the greater literature it is.

There is no need to prove that language is one of the most characteristic expressions of human life. It is as speaking beings that men think of themselves. The writer, therefore, who wishes to transcribe human life, must transcribe it in the forms of speech in which it finds its most immediate expression. His task is parallel to that of the artist. When a portrait painter wishes to paint a portrait, he must study the features of the human face and the lines of the human figure. When a landscape painter wishes to transfer his impressions of sea or land, he must go into the open and study clouds, trees, and atmosphere. Both are said to follow nature, because it is their impressions of the reality in nature which they endeavor to record. In the same way the literary artist must follow nature, not only by studying the inner moods and actuating motives of men, but also the ways in which these moods and motives find their most natural and effective expression.

It is true, of course, that literary language has customs and conventions, for example, meter in poetry, which are peculiar to itself. In the same way painting has certain devices, tricks of method, which in themselves are untrue to nature, but which are used because to the beholder they produce or heighten the effects of nature. The concern of many painters is to suggest the illusion of nature. So also, literary artists attempt to produce the illusion of reality in language. All that is appropriate to speech is consequently not necessarily appropriate to all forms of literature, and, on the other hand, some things are appropriate to certain kinds of literature which are not appropriate to speech. But whenever the customs and conventions of literature become so peculiar to it that they are purely literary, or academic, as we say, when they produce the effect of being untrue to, or remote from, nature, then they are appropriate neither to the literary nor any other language. It is to the natural, spoken language that we make our final appeal.

It is interesting to observe that just those periods of English literature have been greatest in which the language of literature stood nearest to the language of speech. Chaucer's literary style became more and more natural as he grew older, until in the *Canterbury Tales*, his latest work, we almost think we hear his characters speak. The language of Shakespeare is the language of the drama, and whatever conventions the language of the drama may have, its prime requisite is that it shall be true to life. The poets of a third great period of English literature, beginning with Wordsworth and Coleridge, made the imitation of the simple speech of daily life their first principle. The same principle was again invoked by the so-called New Poets in the second decade of twentieth-century America. Students of Greek tell us that much of the charm of Greek literature consists in the intimate dependence of the language of literature upon the language of speech. Greek literary style is not a special caste language for literary purposes, but rather an extension of the spoken language to written uses. Molière, the only Frenchman worthy to rank as the fellow of Shakespeare, owes much of his power to the naturalness of his style. Hating as he did hypocrisy and affectation in every form, we should expect to find him natural and real in his writing.

In short, it is a false standard of value to assume that the test of highest excellence is to be found only in printed and written words. These are merely makeshifts and substitutes for the reality. They serve, to be sure, an important purpose. For one thing, they preserve what otherwise might become lost if entrusted only to oral transmission. They perform a tremendous service to humanity also by extending the bounds of individual experience. In a library of books we can commune at will with the spirits of all ages and places. Indeed the ability to write is so highly regarded by mankind that perhaps no other kind of fame is so generally and so eagerly desired as literary fame. Yet this glory should not blind one to the fact that literature is not self-producing, but grows out of nature. The aspirant for literary fame must not only know letters; above all he must know life. If he wishes to write for his age, he must know how the men of his age speak.

He must not expend all his energy and admiration upon books, but must turn to that form of the language which, above the language of books, is the most wonderful, the most dignified, and the most worthy of respect, the flexible, subtle speech of men in the infinite relations of human life.

2

THE ENGLISH PEOPLE

1 ▨ Speech and Race

The English language is one of the most widely distributed languages of the modern world. Centered originally in the little kingdom of England, the speech has spread to all the four corners of the globe. It has become the speech of two of the most powerful nations of modern times. It is used more widely as a second or auxiliary language than any other of the world's tongues. In the course of its history, it has been adopted by peoples originally speaking many different languages and originally of very diverse racial origins; and although each new body thus incorporated has affected the whole to some extent, the stock of the language has remained essentially the same to the present day. It shall be our first task to make a survey of the history of the English language from this ethnological or racial point of view.

2 ▨ Celtic Britain

In the first century before Christ, when the island of Great Britain first became well-known to the Romans, who were then the most powerful as well as the most highly civilized nation

14

of Europe, it was occupied by a race of Celtic people, speaking a Celtic language. This race had been preceded in Britain by various different, prehistoric races concerning which little is known. It was one of these prehistoric races, however, which reared the great monoliths at Stonehenge on Salisbury Plain. The Celtic inhabitants of the island called themselves Britons. From this name of the people the country was called Britannia by the Romans, whence is derived our modern Britain.

The Britons were merely one branch of a large Celtic-speaking group of peoples who were spread over Gaul and Spain, the Celts of Gaul being the predecessors of the Franks, a Teutonic people from whom the country derived its modern name of France. On the Continent the Celts have been almost completely absorbed by the Roman and Teutonic conquerors of their countries. But in Britain to this day they have maintained a more or less separate existence, and their speech still survives in the Gaelic of the Highlands of Scotland, the Welsh of Wales, and also in the Irish Gaelic or Erse of Eire. Until comparatively recent times, Celtic speech was used in Cornwall and on the Isle of Man.

3 ⊠ The Roman Invasions

The first military invasion which the Romans, the world conquerors, made against the Celts of Britain was in the years 55 and 54 B.C. under the leadership of Julius Caesar. This was more in the nature of an excursion from Gaul, however, where Caesar was then campaigning,[1] than a settled attempt to conquer the country. The serious conquest of Britain was not undertaken until about a century later, A.D. 42, under the Emperor Claudius; and about the year A.D. 80 the country was organized as a Roman province under the command of the Roman general Agricola.

The portions of the country occupied by the Romans were chiefly those central, southern, and eastern parts which later

[1] See *Gallic War*, Books IV and V.

became the kingdom of England. The mountainous regions of Wales in the West and of Scotland in the North were sought out as places of refuge by the Celts who had been driven out of the more fertile regions of the lowlands. In these fastnesses they maintained an independent and hostile existence. As a protection against Celtic invasions from the north, the Emperor Hadrian (A.D. 120) built a wall, parts of which are still standing, between the Firth of Solway and the mouth of the river Tyne. A second wall was later built by Antonius Pius, extending from the Firth of Clyde to the Firth of Forth; and still later these walls were further extended by the Emperor Severus, who came to Britain in the year 208.

In the protected regions the Roman civilization in Britain was prosperous and highly developed. The ground was cultivated, and sheep and cattle were raised. The mines of Cornwall and of Northumberland were worked, and an extensive commerce with the Continent was carried on. The Romans built houses, temples, theaters, altars, and baths after the style of the buildings of their home country, and ruins and relics of these houses that have been preserved to modern times show that some of them must have been very luxurious. They also built highways, as for example Watling Street, extending the whole breadth of England from Canterbury to Chester, some parts of which are in use to this day. Our word *street*, derived from Latin *strata*, in the phrase *strata via*, "paved way," was borrowed from the Roman soldiers, both on the Continent and in Britain. These highways were built, in accordance with the usual policy of the Romans, as military roads to facilitate the passage of troops from one section of the country to another.

Walled cities were also established at various advantageous points in Britain, and many of these have likewise lasted to modern times, some of them still preserving parts of the old Roman defenses. They were called *castra*, and this word, in its modified forms, appears in the names *Chester, Winchester, Doncaster, Gloucester, Worcester, Exeter* (*Exanceaster* in its Old English form),

16

and in many other names of towns and places. The language which was spoken by the Romans in Britain was the Latin language in a popular or colloquial form, being the ordinary language of the soldiers and merchants who constituted the larger part of the population. It was like the language spoken in Gaul by the Roman conquerors of that country. If the Romans in England had continued in uninterrupted residence, as they did in Gaul, it is quite probable that the language of Great Britain today would be a Romance speech instead of English.

The Roman occupation of Britain, however, came to a sudden end. In the fourth and fifth centuries A.D., the pressures of the northern tribes upon Italy and Rome began to make itself felt, and Rome was compelled to strengthen her home defenses. To do this it was necessary to call in certain of the legions that were stationed in the provinces, and naturally the most distant were the first thus to be given up. In the year 407 the greater part of the Roman soldiery left Britain; in the year 410 the last Roman legion was withdrawn, and the Emperor Honorius sent a letter to the people of Britain in which he told them to take charge of their own defense. Since the Roman civilization in Britain had been altogether military in character, the withdrawal of the legions immediately prepared the way for the breaking down of the whole Roman system of government and for the next important and dramatic episode in the history of the island, the coming of the English.

4 ⊠ The Anglo-Saxon Conquest

Besides their hereditary enemies, namely the Celts of the mountainous regions of Wales and Scotland, the Romans in Britain had had another foe to contend with. These were certain Germanic tribes who were in the habit of crossing over from north Germany and ravaging the eastern coast of Britain, known as the Saxon Shore because it was exposed to the attacks of the Saxons. As long as the Roman soldiers were still stationed in

17

Britain these predatory bands of warriors could easily be held in check. With the departure of the legions, however, that state of affairs was altered.

The Celts of the highlands, finding that the defenses of the country had been weakened by the withdrawal of the Roman soldiery, swarmed down from their rocky fastnesses and, immediately began the task of regaining their ancestral kingdoms. It is probable that the town-dwellers, left behind after the departure of the legions, were an unwarlike population. The defense of the country had so long been left in the hands of a professional military class that when this group was removed there were none left trained in the arts of war to take its place. At any rate the inhabitants of the Roman towns and the dwellers in the Roman villas were no match for the rude and warlike Celts on the one side and the marauding Germanic tribes on the other. Thinking to seize the more favorable horn of the dilemma, they turned to the Germanic invaders and asked them to come over and help them subdue their enemies.

In response to this invitation, extended by Vortigern, king of the Roman Britons, tradition tells us that two Saxon chiefs, Hengest and Horsa, with their followers, landed on the island of Thanet on the coast of Kent in the year 449. True to their compact they first aided the Roman Britons in driving back the Celts, but the story goes that, observing the weakness of their allies and the richness of the land, they sent word back to their countrymen at home that they should come over and assist them, that they might together possess the land. The warriors who came in response to this request were of three tribes of north Germans: the Saxons, who lived in the region of modern Holstein; the Angles, who lived in the region of modern Schleswig; and the Jutes, who lived in the region of modern Jutland.

The story of the conflict between these Teutonic tribes and the Roman Britons, with whom the Celts now became united against the common foe, has been but imperfectly reported by history. We know that the struggle was stubborn, but it is plain

18

that the Britons were unable to stand out against their barbarous foemen. Battle after battle was fought, but always with the result that the Britons were driven further inland and up into the mountainous regions to which the Romans several centuries before had driven the original Celts. Later tradition has developed in great detail the story of King Arthur, the heroic leader of the Britons, and his twelve great battles against the Teutonic heathen. But there are no authentic records of these twelve battles, or of King Arthur, that would enable us to build up a connected story of the events. All we know is that out of the welter and confusion of these wars, a new Teutonic England, consisting at first of a number of separate kingdoms, arose from the ruins of the old Celtic and Roman Britain.

The first Anglo-Saxon kingdom to be founded was that of Kent. The first mention of a West Saxon kingdom occurs in 519, and 547 is the date of the first Northumbrian king. By the middle of the sixth century, therefore, we may say that the Germanic conquest of Britain was complete. This does not mean that the whole island was under the control of the invaders, for Wales and Scotland were still Celtic, as they had been all through the period of Roman occupation. From their retreats in the mountains the Celts continued to make frequent forays into the Saxon country, and the story of the complete reduction of Celtic Britain would carry us far down into modern times.

The three tribes who had thus become masters of the fairest part of the island of Britain settled in a separate region. The Jutes, the smallest of the three tribes, occupied Kent and the Isle of Wight. The Angles settled the regions north of the Thames to the Firth of Forth, exclusive of the region immediately north of the mouth of the Thames. The two main kingdoms of the Angles were Northumbria and Mercia. As the most numerous and best organized of the tribes and the one in which a literature was first developed, the Angles in time gave the name to the whole country, *Englaland*, "land of the Angles," and to the speech, *Englisc*, "English," or "the English speech."

The Saxons settled the regions south of the Thames, excepting those parts occupied by the Jutes, and the region just north of the mouth of that river. The chief Saxon kingdoms were Wessex, the kingdom of the West Saxons; Essex, the kingdom of the East Saxons; Sussex, the kingdom of the South Saxons; and Middlesex, the kingdom of the Middle Saxons. For a long time these various Anglian, Jutish, and Saxon kingdoms maintained separate existences. They were first united into a loose sort of confederation by Egbert, who came to the throne of Wessex in the year 802, but it was not until the beginning of the tenth century that the union became complete and lasting. This united people, as has been stated, called itself the English people. They are also known by the name Anglo-Saxons, a composite name made up of the two most important tribes that united to form the nation. This name, however, is an invention of scholars and historians of later times, and although it is a convenient descriptive term, it should be remembered that the Anglo-Saxons in their own time called themselves English and their country England. To bring out the fact of the direct sequence of the later periods of English history after the earlier, it is often convenient to speak of the Anglo-Saxon period as the Old English period, and of the language of the time as Old English. This terminology runs parallel to the succeeding Middle English and Modern English periods.

5 ♲ The Civilization of the Anglo-Saxons

At the time of their arrival in England the Anglo-Saxons were a heathen people, worshipping the gods Thor and Woden, and the many other divinities of the Teutonic mythology and religion. They were seamen and warriors, and gained a large part of their livelihood, like the Danes of a later period, by making plundering expeditions upon the coasts of neighboring countries. With their settlement in England, however, a great change came over this wild and barbarous people. Having now a rich and fertile land in their possession, they were no longer impelled to live by robbery and violence, but settled down to the peaceful occupations of farming and raising sheep and cattle. They soon became rich, and with this increase in wealth naturally came to a greater development of the arts and of the more humane aspects of life.

The greatest civilizing influence, however, to which they were subject was that of Christianity, introduced to them first by the Roman missionary Augustine and his assistants, who came to Kent in the year 597, and later by the Irish missionaries who, having come from Iona to found a monastery at Lindisfarne, made many converts in Mercia and Northumbria. The new faith spread rapidly during the seventh century, and by the end of it England had become Christian. Gradually, also, the newcomers worked out a political system, and from a disconnected group of tribal kingdoms or states, they developed, in the time of Alfred and successors, into a nation in the true sense of the word, with one king and a strongly centralized government to hold them together.

Their speech was, of course, Germanic—closely related to that spoken in Germany and other parts of northern Europe (see pp. 40–46). In the course of time this speech also became the vehicle for literary expression, both in verse and in prose. As is so often true of the beginnings of a national literature, the earliest records are in poetry rather than prose. As early as the beginning of the seventh century, Old English poetry was probably composed and written down in England, although all the manuscripts which have been preserved to modern times are copies which date from a period considerably later.

Most of this poetry is highly traditional in character. Although the Anglo-Saxons by this time had generally turned to quiet agricultural and pastoral pursuits, their verse is, nevertheless, very warlike in tone; and although they had long since ceased to follow the water extensively, the sea with its dangers and attractions is one of their most frequent poetic themes. This

21

applies not only to their native heroic poetry, as for example the great epic *Beowulf,* the most important literary monument of the Old English period that has come down to us, but also to the poetry of the school of Cædmon, written about the middle of the seventh century, and of the school of Cynewulf, written about the middle of the eighth. Both of these were strongly under Christian influence and had as their subject matter Christian story and legend, but they were generally cast in the epic warlike mold of the earlier native verse.

The explanation of this is to be found in the fact that all Old English poetry is popular in its origins. It goes back to the early warlike periods of the race when poetry was handed down by oral tradition and formula from minstrel to minstrel. And as poetry is always very conservative, it is natural that when the period of written literature began, the old poetic traditions and conventions should be preserved by the side of much that was new. The great body of Old English poetry is preserved in four volumes, or codexes, of miscellaneous content: Manuscript Junius XI in the Bodleian Library at Oxford; Cotton Vitellius A 15 in the British Museum; the Vercelli Book, found in the year 1822 in an out-of-the-way library at Vercelli, Italy, where it is still preserved; and the Exeter Book, the property of Exeter Cathedral in England.

Old English prose, on the other hand, the bulk of which was not written until the ninth century and later, is completely under the dominance of the new order of thought. There is nothing primitive and traditional about it. On the contrary, it is all distinctly Christian in tone and, for its period, very modern. It consists mainly of historical, philosophical, and religious or exegetical writings, and centers chiefly about the name of Alfred, who died in 901, and of Ælfric, who died near the close of the Old English period, about the year 1020. One of the most important prose documents is the Old English *Chronicle,* the earliest attempt at the consecutive writing of general history in the English tongue. It was probably compiled under the direction

The Old English *Chronicle*
From the Bodleian Manuscript, Laud 636, fol. 1ᵃ
(For description, see Appendix, p. 284)

of King Alfred about the middle of the ninth century, but it was continued in various forms by later hands, the Laud version, of which the opening is here reproduced, coming down as late as the middle of the twelfth century.

On the whole one must say that between the arrival of Hengest and Horsa in 449 and the close of the Old English period, with the coming of William the Conqueror in 1066, the Anglo-Saxons had developed a relatively high civilization. They were well governed; they had an enlightened religion; they cultivated learning and letters. In some of the arts, for example the making of enameled jewelry, they were famous, and the embroidery of ecclesiastical garments done by the Anglo-Saxon women had even a Continental reputation.

The people lived in comfort and often in luxury, some of the satires of the times showing that then, as always, extravagance in dress and the table accompanied prosperity. One must not think, therefore, of the Old English period as barbarous and uncivilized. It was indeed the period of the beginnings of English speech and English literature, but even in their beginnings our language and literature afford much that may and should be studied, not only for its historical interest, but also for its intrinsic wisdom and beauty.

6 ✍ The Danish Invasions and the Danish Conquest

In the midst of their peaceful development, however, the Anglo-Saxons were called upon to meet a great danger. History repeated itself. Just as the weakened Britons several centuries before had yielded to the attacks of the Jutes, Angles, and Saxons, so now these latter, also weakened by the refining influences of civilization and by the gradual decay of their warlike habits, were compelled to meet the advances of certain kinsmen of theirs from the Continent, the Danes.

The method of the Danish invasions was practically the same as that of the original Anglo-Saxon invasion. They first came on marauding expeditions, returning each time to their own country. About the year 850, however, they began a campaign of conquest and settlement. In a short time, they gained control of all England except the little kingdom of Wessex, south of the Thames, which was held and defended by the heroic Alfred. After Alfred's death in 901 his son and successor Edward and, after Edward, his grandson Æthelstan, were able to win back the greater part of England from the Danes. But this success was only temporary, for in the reign of Æthelred the Unready[2] (978–1016), the Danes and Northmen came over to England in ever-increasing numbers and gained possession of the entire land.

In the year 1017 Cnut became king of England, and a Danish king occupied both the English and Danish throne at the same time. Cnut was succeeded by his son Hardacnut (1039–1042), and Hardacnut was followed by Edward the Confessor (1042–1066), in whose long and peaceful reign the Dane and Anglo-Saxon in England became fused into one people. Closely related in blood and speaking languages which had much in common, the two peoples, conquered and conquerors, readily united. With that remarkable vitality which has always characterized it, the Anglo-Saxon language succeeded in crowding out the Danish. Though modified in some respects by the influences to which they had been subjected, it was an English language and an English people that arose again out of the Danish Conquest.

7 ⬚ The Norman Conquest

After the coming of the Anglo-Saxons to Britain in the fifth century, undoubtedly the event most far-reaching in its later effect upon the speech and the institutions of the people who inhabited the island was the Norman Conquest under William the Conqueror in 1066. The Danish Conquest had not

[2] *Unready*, a term first applied to Æthelred by historians of the sixteenth century, was intended to suggest "foolish, rash, incautious," rather than "unprepared."

been without its effect; but owing to the close relationship in blood and speech that existed between the Anglo-Saxons and the Danes, and the consequent ease with which they fused into one people, the Danish addition to the English population may be regarded rather as strengthening the original stock than changing it or turning it in new directions. The Norman Conquest, however, was entirely different; for it not only succeeded after a time in imposing a new social and political system upon the English people, but even in putting the English language into second place temporarily and in profoundly affecting it permanently.

The Normans who came to England in the train of William spoke Norman French, a dialect of the French language current in the provinces of Normandy. By birth and descent, however, they were not primarily Franks, but were closely related to those Teutonic Danish and north Scandinavian tribes who, in the reign of Æthelred, had become masters of England. The name Norman is merely a contraction of Northman, and the Normans were Scandinavian seafarers who had settled in northern France just as, and at the the same time that, the Danes and Northmen were settling in England.

Like their kinsmen in England, the Northmen in France gave up their native speech, and as the former had accepted English, so they accepted French. We have, therefore, the curious spectacle of a people of the same blood producing all the effect of a foreign race upon their kinsmen merely because of a difference in language—a striking illustration of the fact that speech is thicker than blood. But it should be remembered that with the French language the Normans had imbibed all the ideas and ways of thinking of the French, and consequently had become as much French as the Franks themselves.

The first effect of the Conquest upon England was to place Normans in the positions of authority in the country, and thus to make French the language of the court and the ruling classes. But there is no indication that William or any of his successors attempted to coerce the native English-speaking population into using French, and at first the growth of the Norman-French influence upon English was very slow. There is every reason to believe that if the relations between France and England had ceased with the Conquest, it would have been but a short time before the Norman French were as completely fused with English as the Danes had become. But the Norman-French influence upon English, although slow at first, increased gradually. French was not forced upon the English by any edict of law, but its use was encouraged by an even more powerful force, social custom. As the language of the ruling class, French came to be regarded as the polite and cultivated language. After a time, instruction was no longer given in English, but those who studied at all studied French and, if any other language, Latin.

Even when Normandy was lost to England in the year 1204, and later when, in the middle of the century, the separation between the two countries became more complete by the decrees of Kings Louis IX of France and Henry III of England, the latter prohibiting Englishmen from holding estates in Normandy, and the former prohibiting Normans from holding estates in England, the cultivation of French continued. In spite of these decrees, there must have been a continual freshening of the stream of influence by the passing back and forth of Frenchmen, not only Normans but Frenchmen of other parts of France, to and from England. The ties of blood could not be disregarded, even though political conditions had changed.

Another main reason for the increasing influence of French upon English is to be found in the way in which Englishmen themselves came to regard French. The great body of Englishmen, the plain people who were little influenced by matters of fashion or education, never spoke anything but English. In the middle and the higher social, literary, and educational life, however, French acquired a special distinction. As the language of the ruling class its authority was naturally great. It was, moreover, commonly regarded as the politest language of Europe. The University of Paris, founded about 1170, was a place of resort for the scholars of all Europe. The French language possessed a great and growing literature which other nations, the English especially, strove to imitate and absorb. French was also the language of polite intercourse, and the French capital was regarded not only as the seat of learning and of letters, but also of refinement.

Thus there grew up in England a sort of Gallophilia, as it may be called, a sense of respect and admiration for everything French because it was French. The height of this fashion was not reached until between the years 1300 and 1350, but it is this fashionable fad more than anything else that accounts for the powerful influence of French upon English in this early period. The French which was imitated in the fourteenth century was of course no longer Norman French, but the French of Paris. For it English was even in danger for a time of being given up altogether as the language of literature and polite conversation.

Those who continued to use English strove often to make it as much like French as possible. The imitation consisted in the borrowing of words and phrases, in the adaptation of French locutions and idioms to English usage, and even in such mechanical matters as spelling and handwriting. The use of French spelling and writing was in a way forced upon the English. Since instruction in English was no longer given in the schools, having been replaced by French, when one wished to write English the rules of French spelling and the style of French writing were simply transferred to English.

The extent to which this Gallicizing of the English language was carried may be seen from the usage of the writer of the collection of saints' lives known as the *Southern Legendary*, written about 1280. The author, or compiler, of this collection, judging from the sentiments he expresses, was undoubtedly a patriotic Englishman, but his patriotism did not prevent him from following French fashions. Thus, we find spellings such as *finguer* for *finger*, *bringue for bring*, *kingue* for *king*, and *doggue* for *dog*, presumably in imitation of the French practice in words like *langue* and *morgue* in which *u* is written after the *g* to indicate the hard or stopped quality of the sound. We still spell the Modern English reflex of—that is to say, the descendant or word derived from— Old English *tunge* as *tongue*. Had the spelling developed without foreign interference, it would have been *tung*, like *sung* and *lung*, which have a similar phonetic history. The *gu* spelling is used initially in words such as *guilt, guild, guess*, and *guest* none of which came into the language from French.

Toward the middle of the fourteenth century, however, this mad admiration for everything French began to suffer a decline, and English began to rise again in the ascendency. Thus in 1362 it was decreed that all pleadings in the law courts in England should be made in English and not in French. In the same year the English Parliament for the first time was opened with an English speech. French still continued to be cultivated as a polite accomplishment, as indeed it still is in some circles, but from this time on English came to be more and more the language of literature and scholarship, as well as of the higher official and court life in England. By 1500, the end of the Middle English period, French had long ceased to be a serious rival of English.

It should be remembered, however, that the English which thus came to the front again was very different from the literary English of the period before the French invasion. English had so long been neglected in favor of French that the feeling for it as a standard literary language had largely died out, although it served the people well as a popular or folk language. Consequently when English began again to rise into supremacy it was this popular transformation of the older English that gradually assumed the rank of the new standard speech. The new English of the Middle English period is therefore the Old English of the Anglo-Saxon period as this latter was modified, first by the influence of French, and second by its passage through the transforming bath of modern use.

8 ▧ Summary of the Influence of the Norman Conquest

The influence of the Norman Conquest and its consequences upon the English language and the English people was profound. The racial distinction between Norman and Englishman was soon lost; for the Norman when he had accepted England as his home, and even more when he had accepted English speech, became to all intents and purposes English. So completely were English and Norman assimilated that the third or fourth generation after the Conquest must often have been unable to distinguish between the two elements of the population.

It was, however, a new English and a different England that gradually emerged after the Conquest. The speech and the whole body of thought of the nation, as a result of the direct and indirect influence of the Conquest, had undergone a remarkable change. In the first place, from a comparatively highly inflected language, English became a language of few inflections (see pp. 66 ff.). The vocabulary of the language changed from a relatively "pure" vocabulary, that is, one made up of words of the same linguistic stock, to a bilingual vocabulary, a vocabulary made up of Teutonic and Romance elements. The influence of French extended also to the phrasing of English, the grouping of words in the sentence; and in many ways, direct and indirect, which are diffcult to follow, the new tendencies affected the whole tone of English thought and expression. The language after it had been subjected to the French influence was more supple; it became the vehicle for more varied forms of expression than it had been before. In this it was merely following the change in the intellectual life of the English people, which after the Conquest was richer and touched many more sides of life than it ever had in the Old English period.

This new spirit in English thought and letters received its fullest expression in the writings of Geoffrey Chaucer (1340?–1400). In Chaucer, we have one who was not only a consummate artist in the use of language, but one also who, in addition to the Old English themes of warfare and religion, could sound the whole gamut of human emotion, love, pathos, humor, chivalry, the dramatic instinct, the feeling for nature, in short all those shades of thought and feeling which the English heart is capable of experiencing or the English tongue of expressing.

9 ▨ Modern England

The England of the close of the Middle English period was never again subjected to foreign invasion or to any great external racial influences. The thought and language of the people followed in general a peaceful line of development, accompanying the intellectual, industrial, and political growth of the country and of the world as a whole. The periods in modern times that have been most important for the history of the language are the Renaissance period, which may be liberally interpreted as extending from about 1500 to 1640, in which the main purpose was that of "enriching" the language (see pp. 199 ff.); the so-called Augustan period of English literature, that of Dryden and Pope, Swift and Johnson, covering the Restoration and most of the eighteenth century, in which much thought and attention was given to "polishing" and "purifying" the language; and the most recent period of scientific, industrial, commercial, and political expansion with its remarkable extension of the bounds of human thought and activity. Of these later influences, perhaps the most significant are those which arise from the commercial and territorial expansion of the English-speaking people, and concerning these a word in especial may be said.

10 ▨ World English

History makes few appeals to the imagination stronger than that presented by the picture of the small kingdom of England reaching out step by step until now its speech and its culture are to be found on every continent of the globe. Beginning with the union of Scotland and England under one king in 1603, and the conquest of Ireland under Elizabeth, the three countries, which by later acts of union formed the kingdom of Great Britain and Ireland, entered on a period of territorial and linguistic expansion that almost passes belief.

As a consequence of the establishment of the first permanent colony at Jamestown in 1607 and the later settlements in other parts of this country, the national speech of the Continent of North America was determined as English, a fact assured by the victory of Wolfe over Montcalm in 1759. The separation of the colonies from the mother country in 1776 and the later opening of their gates to almost countless hosts of foreign immigrants have not availed to change the destiny of the English language in the United States. It is today as much the national speech of the country as it is of Canada or of England herself.

By the English settlement of Australia and New Zealand in the early nineteenth century, the speech of those Commonwealth Nations also became English. Other colonies, or offshoots of colonies, in which English is spoken include South Africa and the newly emerging countries in the British West Indies.

In India, which was first conquered by the English in the middle of the eighteenth century, English became the official language of that polyglot country. When India again became an independent nation, the Hindi language, though spoken by millions and one in which a great literature is preserved, was far from being universally understood and generally acceptable. Thus, despite a constitutional provision establishing Hindi as the official language, English continued to be employed in the Parliament and in commerce and education. Similarly, in many of the new African nations—Ghana, Nigeria, and Uganda, to name only a few—English is the official language and serves as the medium of communication among speakers of the many languages which exist in these countries.

The English language has made astonishing gains in countries which have never been under English domination. It is, of course, one of the five official languages of the United Nations, the others being French, Spanish, Russian, and Mandarin Chinese. It is to a large extent now the language of cosmopolitan intercourse in Europe, and there are few cities in which English is not sufficient on the main roads of travel to meet all a traveler's needs. English has thus gradually taken the place formerly filled by French. English is also, to a considerable extent, the language of international commerce. By international convention it has become the international language of aviation. Nautical and manufacturing terms, words derived from English social customs, from English and American sports and games, in Germany, France, and in other nations, are evidence of the growing prestige of English.[3]

In the Far East, English occupies a unique position as an almost pan-Asiatic language. A number of pidginized forms of it are spoken by merchants and sailors all along the coasts. To a considerable extent it is the language of diplomacy in that part of the world; even the Bandung Conference of some years back consisting of representatives of Asian and African nations and called for the purpose of castigating the Western powers, was conducted largely in English. Its teaching is obligatory in the schools of Japan, Thailand, Burma, and the Philippines.

English is the predominating native language of nine nations of more than a million inhabitants. It is spoken as a native language by two hundred and sixty million people—more than speak any other language natively with the exception of Chinese. The number who speak Hindi-Urdu is estimated at about one hundred and ninety millions. Spanish and Russian follow with about one hundred and forty and one hundred and twenty-five millions respectively. These languages are followed in descending order by Japanese, German, Arabic, Bengali, Portuguese, and French, the latter with about fifty-three million speakers.

[3] For lists of English words in German and French, see pp. 215–218.

33

The rate of increase of English since 1800 has been much greater than that of any other language. Since English is spread over such a wide extent of territory and is the language of rapidly growing and developing countries, it is altogether likely that this proportionate rate of increase will continue for some time in the future. Because of its relative freedom from complex inflectional paradigms and because of its composite lexicon, combining Romance and Teutonic elements, an elementary command of the language is acquired with relative ease. This explains in part the progress it has made toward becoming a world language. Even the traditional national vices of insularity and complacency contribute to this result. The English and Americans are among the greatest travelers of modern times, and the tenacity with which they hold to their native speech and native customs in foreign lands, while it often justly exposes them to the charge of naiveté and provincialism, at the same time makes them effective distributors of Anglo-Saxon ideas and traditions. If Mohammed will not go to the mountain, then the mountain must come to Mohammed.

That English will ever become the language of familiar daily intercourse in non-English countries is, of course, highly unlikely. There is no indication that any country will ever altogether give up its native idiom for another, except through the gradual method of complete national and racial assimilation. But certainly English has made notable strides toward becoming the language of international science, of international diplomacy, and of international travel and commerce. In the medieval period, the various European nations each learned one other language besides their native idiom for the purpose of international communication, and this second language was always Latin. Later the place of Latin tended to be taken by French. During the present century, however, French has yielded to English to a considerable degree, and, barring unexpected political and social upheavals, the nearest approach to a universal language of the future is likely to be English.

11 ⍰ Artificial Language

From time to time a great deal has been said about a universal language, and recently almost every decade has witnessed the launching of one or more projects of this nature. In all of them the attempt is to devise an artificial language which will be free of the defects of existing languages, and which, because of its reasonableness and economy, will either attain wide use as an international auxiliary language, or more optimistically, will induce the nations of the world to accept it in place of their native speech.

Artificial languages are by no means of recent origin. Such linguistic experiments have been made from the earliest times, some of them extremely ingenious, but none that ever realized in the slightest degree the hopes which their creators had for them.[4] In England the later seventeenth and early eighteenth centuries were productive of a number of artificial languages. One, as set forth by Sir Thomas Urquhart in a volume published in London in 1653, bore the alluring title *Logopandecteision, or an Introduction to the Universal Language digested into six books, published both for his own utilitie and that of all pregnant and ingenious spirits.* During the past hundred years various "ingenious spirits" have promulgated schemes of universal language, Volapük, Esperanto, Interlingua, and others, literally to be numbered by the dozen and all different.

Why have none of these experiments succeeded? In the first place the attempt to impose an artificial language upon a people, at least in terms of a replacement for the native language, runs counter to all the principles of development that have governed the growth of a people. A native speech arises in a community as the intimate accompaniment of all its social customs. It is a gradual and largely unconscious growth, arising out of the immediate experiences of life. No speech, as we shall have continual

---

[4] For a description of these various endeavors, see A. L. Guerard, *A Short History of the International Language Movement* (London, 1922), and H. Jacob, *A Planned Auxiliary Language* (London, 1947).

occasion to point out, has ever submitted to the systematizings of the theorist, no matter how reasonable and consistent these seemed to be. The attempt, therefore, to bring about the acceptance of an artificial language on reasonable grounds is not likely to succeed, because of the simple fact that a language is not directly under control of the reason. It is a common social possession, and a people fortunately does not, and cannot, change its social customs and habits by a sudden act of will.

One may doubt, moreover, whether an artificial language, the best that can be devised by an individual or a group of individuals, can ever be as good as a natural language. A natural language which has developed through thousands of years has acquired possibilities of expression, in thought and especially in feeling, which no language manufactured in cold blood can hope to equal. The wisdom of the nation is greater than the wisdom of an individual, and a national language sums up all the past wisdom and experience of the people.

Furthermore, a universal language, to remain universal after it had once been accepted by all peoples, must not be allowed to change. But if anything can be learned from the history of language it is just this, that all languages are continually subject to change, and that nothing can prevent them from changing. The advocates of a universal language must accordingly not only perform the initial miracle of getting their language accepted, but they must then perform the second miracle, a continuous one, of keeping that language permanent and fixed. In short, no artificial language, no matter how skilfully it is constructed, is likely ever to extend far beyond the small group of enthusiasts with whom it originates, and in some instances these will continue to pursue it only until their attention is attracted to some more diverting linguistic exercise. Of all the invented languages, Esperanto, launched in 1887 by a Pole, Dr. Zamenhof, has attracted the most converts; about one million and a half have been claimed for it, and this is surely a generous figure. Even so, it is less than one-twentieth of one percent of a global population of more than three billion.

J. R. Firth once wrote, "World languages are made not by amateur grammarians but by world powers." The reason why the English language is one of the most widely distributed of the modern world is that men who have spoken English have made their way to all corners of the earth, have carried with them their view of life and modes of conduct and along with this *Weltanschauung*, the speech in which it finds expression. Artificially constructed languages are well enough as challenges to "ingenious spirits," but a real language is formed in the market places and by the firesides of a living world.

If, on the other hand, an artificial language has as its aim primarily the expression of such impersonal ideas as might arise in international, commercial, or even scientific communication, then the matter becomes important to a much smaller number of people, and the possibility of acceptance increases. To some degree this has already occurred, through not so much the result of conscious effort as of natural process. The vocabulary of the sciences is a case in point. *Webster's Third New International Dictionary* wisely recognizes this by its use of *ISV* (International Scientific Vocabulary) as one of its etymological labels. Such a vocabulary does exist and is working tolerably well.

We must recognize, however, that language is much more than just vocabulary; it consists of sound and structure as well. Even granting that the vocabulary of the sciences has been widely adopted, this is code rather than language. Many of the projected languages, notably Esperanto and Interlingua, have been constructed on the basis of Latin. The reasons are not far to seek. Latin is, in one form or another, a natural inheritance of all southern Europeans. It is the basis for a large part of the English vocabulary. It is a language which many educated persons are likely to know or to have known. But the assumption that everyone knows Latin is hardly warrantable, especially if one thinks of the speakers of Chinese, Hindi-Urdu, Japanese, Arabic, and Bengali, amounting altogether to approximately one billion. Thus the international concept has remained Western oriented; it has not really become global in scope.

3

THE ENGLISH LANGUAGE

1 ▨ The Classification of Languages

One of the important results of the modern study of language has been the classification of the various languages of the world into groups according to their relationships. Although the science of language has not been able to arrive at any altogether satisfactory theory of the beginnings of speech, it nevertheless has done a great deal in discovering lines of evolution and development in those languages of which we have record. It has discovered that there has been a continual change and growth in language, that the languages of modern times are each of them a historic product which developed slowly and regularly out of preceding stages. Moreover, it has shown that many apparently dissimilar languages are really closely related and are the descendants of some original stock. It has thus divided languages into families.

2 ▨ The Indo-European Family of Languages

One of the largest and most carefully studied groups or families of languages is that known as the Indo-European or Indo-Germanic family. This group comprises certain of the languages of Asia and practically all the languages of Europe. The original unified Indo-European language from which they are all theoretically derived is no longer in existence. Its former existence is inferred, however, from the comparative study of the various Indo-European languages, since no theory serves so well to explain the many similarities which exist among them as the theory of a common origin.

It should not be forgotten, however, that the theory of a common original language from which the various Indo-European languages were derived does not carry with it the theory of a common and single racial ancestry of all the Indo-European peoples. In the course of its development the primitive Indo-European speech undoubtedly imposed itself upon peoples of widely different race, very much as the branch languages, French or English, have done in later periods. We accept, therefore, a common speech ancestry for the Indo-European peoples, but not necessarily a common race ancestry.

The period and place in which this common original language was spoken have been a matter of long dispute, but there is some ground for believing that the place was south of the eastern extremity of the Baltic, between the Vistula and the Dnieper rivers, and the time possibly as early as thirty-five centuries before the birth of Christ. Actually these are matters of comparatively slight importance. It concerns us much more to know the history, the changes and developments which have brought about the differentiation of the various languages of which we have specific knowledge. Careful study of these languages has enabled us to classify them according to their branches and subdivisions in an orderly fashion. The following is a list of the main members of the family, beginning with the languages farthest east in Asia and proceeding thence in order to the languages of western Europe:

Indo-Iranian. This branch is subdivided into 1. the Indian languages, including Sanskrit, the ancient literary language, and Prakrit and Pali,

39

contemporary vernaculars, and a dozen or more modern languages, including Hindi, Urdu, Bengali, and Gujarati; and 2. the Iranian languages, including Avestan, Scythian, and Old Persian among the ancient languages and Pashto, Persian, and Kurdish among the modern descendants.

Tocharian, an extinct language spoken in Central Asia. Its records, existing in two fragments, date from 600 to 1000 A.D.

Armenian, spoken in parts of Asia minor.

Anatolian. This family of languages includes cuneiform Hittite and its nearest relatives. Hittite was written in a pictographic script c. 1500 to 1200 B.C. in Anatolia and 1200 to 600 B.C. in Syria.

Greek, which may be subdivided into the various Greek dialects: Ionic, Attic, Doric, etc.

Albanian, spoken in Albania and in a few localities in Italy.

Italic, divided into Oscan and Umbrian, both with no known descendants, and Old Latin, from which the modern Romance languages are derived. These include French, Spanish, Italian, Portuguese, Provençal, Rumanian and several other less known languages.

Celtic. This branch may be subdivided into Gaulish, the language of the people of ancient Gaul, of which little is known; Goidelic, which included the languages of Brittany and of Wales; Brythonic, including the language of Britain prior to the coming of the Anglo-Saxons, Irish, Manx, Cornish, and Scots Gaelic, the language of the Scottish Highlands.

Teutonic or Germanic. This branch, the one we are particularly interested in, falls into three main subdivisions, as follows:

1. EAST GERMANIC, the main representative of which is Gothic, known chiefly from fragments of a translation of the Bible made in the fourth century by Ulfilas, the bishop of the West Goths.
2. NORTH GERMANIC, including Icelandic, Norwegian, Swedish, Danish, and Faroese.
3. WEST GERMANIC, including the following languages:
   a. *English*, in its various periods of Anglo-Saxon or Old English, Middle English, and Modern English.
   b. *Frisian*, in the two periods of Old and Modern Frisian.

    c. *Franconian*, the chief modern representatives of which are the languages of Holland and Flanders.

    d. *Low German*, in the two periods of Old Saxon and Modern Plattdeutsch.

    e. *High German*, in its three periods of Old High German, Middle High German, and New High German, the language of Germany and Austria. The German spoken in Switzerland, Yiddish, and Pennsylvania German also belong in this category.

Balto-Slavonic. This branch falls into two main divisions: 1. the Baltic languages, including Old Prusisan, Lithuanian, and Lettish; and 2. the Slavonic languages, including Polish, Czech, Serbo-Croatian, Bulgarian, Russian, and Ukranian.

3 ▨ The Principles of Classification of Languages

    The question arises, How do we know that these languages are related? What are the points of difference and resemblance which justify us in holding together the languages of the Indo-European family in a single group and at the same time in dividing this group into the ten branches indicated above, with their further subdivisions? In answering the question, it should be noted, first, that the Indo-European family is constituted a group apart from the other languages of the world by certain features which all the languages of the family have in common, but which are unknown to languages outside the group.

    Thus, first of all, the languages of the Indo-European family are all inflectional in structure, that is, they indicate the relations which words bear to each other in the sentence by the use of case, gender, number, tense, voice, and other endings. This seems to those whose native speech is inflectional such a natural characteristic of language that it is often supposed that all languages make use of this device. Such is not the case, however, and there are certain languages, like the Chinese, which have no inflection at all, and others, like Turkish, which employ a type of word composition or agglutination that is so different from our kind of inflection that it has to be put into an entirely separate class from it.

In the second place, it has been found that the languages of the Indo-European family have a considerable number of words in common that are not found in other languages. The number and the character of these words are so significant as to lead one almost necessarily to the inference that they are a common inheritance from a common original stock. The study of the languages of the Indo-European family from the point of view of their sounds and of their syntax confirms the results of the study of vocabulary and inflection, and makes unavoidable the conclusion that we have in them a group of closely and mutually related languages.

The method by which the division of the family into its branches has been obtained is similar to that which determined the classification of the family as a whole. It has been found that, although all the branches of the family have certain characteristics in common, which hold them together as a family, at the same time each branch has its own individual characteristics, due to the special development it has followed and the special influences to which it has been subjected. It would carry us too far at present to attempt to show all the special characteristics of each branch, for example, how Greek differs from Latin and how Celtic differs from both; all we can do is to point out the main characteristics which distinguish the Germanic or Teutonic branch, the one in which our special interest lies.

4 ▨ The Germanic Languages

The main characteristics which the Germanic languages have in common as features distinguishing them from the other Indo-European languages are four: (a) a regular shifting or change of consonants, known as Grimm's Law; (b) the Germanic classification of the verb as strong and weak; (c) the twofold declension of the adjective as strong and weak; (d) the Germanic system of word stress. The last three of these characteristics need only a word of explanation, but the importance of Grimm's Law makes it deserving of a more extended discussion, and we shall therefore leave it to the last.

A comparison of the Modern English verb, which is representative of the Germanic verb in general, with the Latin, as representative of the original Indo-European verb, will show the distinguishing features of the Germanic verb system. The English verb consists of two classes, the weak, or regular verb, which forms its past tense by adding *d* or *ed* (sometimes assimilated to *t*) to the present or infinitive stem, as for example, *call, called, called*; *walk, walked, walked*; and second, the strong, or irregular verb, which forms its tenses by an internal change of the radical vowel of the word, as in the verb *sing, sang, sung*. The Latin verb, on the other hand, falls into a number of different classes, dependent to be sure on the formation of the principal parts, but in which can be found no such simple principle of tense formation as that which distinguishes the English verb.

The twofold declension of the adjective has been lost in Modern English, inasmuch as the declension of the adjective (except for comparison) has been lost altogether. In the Old English period of the language, however, the full declension of the adjective was still maintained, as it is in High German to this day. The principle behind it may best be characterized by the phrase "economy of distinctive form," and it works out in the following manner: when the adjective is preceded by a demonstrative pronoun or a definite article, either of which would be highly distinctive of case, number, and gender, it is declined in a non-distinctive or weak manner. When, on the other hand, the adjective is not preceded by a demonstrative pronoun or a definite article, the so-called strong endings that are applied to it serve to distinguish case, number, and gender. Thus the phrase *These young boys* would take the weak form of the adjective in Old English, *þās geongan cnapan*; but the phrase *Young boys* would take the strong form, *Geonge cnapan*. Latin, like modern English, would take the same form of the adjective in both phrases.

The Germanic system of word stress is well illustrated by Modern English usage. The rule there is that words of native origin usually take the stress on the root syllable, and this root syllable, except in the case of prepositional compounds, is almost always the first syllable of a word. Moreover, the stress of English words is *fixed*, that is, a noun has the same stress, no matter what its case or number may be, and a verb keeps the same stress through all its various inflections. Latin, on the contrary, which typifies the non-Germanic members of the Indo-European family, has what is called *free* or *variable* stress, changing with the various forms of a word. Thus the nominative is stressed *imperátor*, but the accusative is *imperatórem*. The English derivative word, "emperor," has fixed stress on the first syllable.

5 ▨ Grimm's Law

In the year 1822 the German scholar Jacob Ludwig Grimm formulated a series of nine rules relating the consonants of Germanic to the other Indo-European languages. Grimm who, along with his brother Wilhelm Carl, is best known perhaps as a collector and writer of fairy tales, was also a philologist of great industry and learning. The set of sound correspondences which he devised is often referred to as a law, but the term is applicable only in an empirical sense. That is to say, by observation the discovery was made that a definite set of linguistic phenomena operated in a certain way, and the generalization drawn from this observation was formulated as the law, or rule, of the phenomena. This kind of law does not imply that the language *must* act in a certain way, that there is a compelling lawgiver or power back of the law, which controls its action. It simply states what does happen, or what appears to our observation to have happened. The ultimate explanation of the cause of the series of correspondences known as Grimm's Law is one that, so far, has escaped the scientific students of language. We accept the facts as they are because we observe them, but no satisfactory theory in explanation of these facts has as yet been brought forward.

The phenomena, that is to say the facts upon which Grimm's Law is based consist of certain regular changes in sounds. It was observed that where Indo-European words (as represented say by Greek or Latin) appeared with certain consonants, the same word in the Germanic languages appeared with different consonants, always, however, according to a regular scheme of equivalents or correspondences. Thus, Indo-European *p* became regularly Germanic *f*, and *d* regularly became *t*; the relation of English *foot* to Greek πoδ-oς (*pod-os*) is therefore obvious. Other illustrations of the change of *p* to *f* are Latin *pater*, English *father*; Latin *piscis*, English *fish*. The change of Indo-European *d* to *t* is further illustrated by Latin *dent-is*, English *tooth*; Latin *decem*, English *ten*.

Another regular change, which has been illustrated by the word-pairs Latin *pater*, English *father*, and Latin *dent-is*, English *tooth*, is that of Indo-European *t* to Germanic *th*. Further illustrations are Latin *tres*, English *three*; Latin *tenuis*, English *thin*; Latin *tu*, English *thou*. A third change, also involving a voiceless stop, is that from Indo-European *c* to Germanic *h*, as in Latin *corn-us*, English *horn*; Latin *can-is*, English *hound*; Latin *coll-is*, English *hill*. Illustrations of these changes might be increased indefinitely. Instead of adding others, however, it will suffice to make a general statement of all the consonants affected by the law and their correspondences. They may be grouped as follows:

The Indo-European voiceless stops *p*, *t*, and *k*, became the corresponding voiceless fricatives *f*, *th*, and *h*.

The Indo-European voiced stops *b*, *d*, and *g*, became the corresponding voiceless stops *p*, *t*, and *k*,

The Indo-European voiced aspirated stops *bh*, *dh*, and *gh*, became the corresponding voiced fricatives *b*, *ð*, and *ʒ*.

It should be understood, of course, that this is a very general statement of Grimm's Law, and that, as thus expressed, it is open to numerous exceptions and to the qualifications of some important sub-laws. Moreover, it should be remembered when we trace back English words to their cognates in the other Indo-European languages which are not subject to this shifting of consonants, such as Latin for example, that these other languages may also have had their own peculiar consonantal developments which may serve to obscure the simple operation of the law.

It is also apparent that only those English words which are of native origin, that is, only that half of our bilingual language which is Germanic and not borrowed Romance, can be subject to Grimm's Law. Despite its various restrictions and qualifications, this statement of the first consonant shift is one of the most valuable linguistic principles which we possess. It enables us not only to group the Germanic languages together, but also often to determine the history and etymology of the vocabularies of the various Germanic languages, to tell what words are native and what are foreign. Moreover, the study of Grimm's Law has carried and continued to carry in its wake the discovery of many other linguistic laws and principles which are of the greatest interest and importance.

6 ▨ English and German

The exact relation between Modern English and Modern German should be clearly understood. First of all, one is not derived from the other, as is so frequently the popular belief. The number of words in the English language which have been directly borrowed from German is comparatively small,[1] most of them having been taken over of recent years, and the same is true of the English words in the German language. The two languages are, however, of the same stock, and they resemble each other because they, like the other Germanic languages, are derived from some common original Germanic or Teutonic mother speech, which is no longer in existence and which has left no written records, but the existence of which we infer from the

---

[1] For a list of these words, see pp. 216–218.

comparative study of the various Germanic languages, just as we infer the former existence of a parent Indo-European speech for all the different Indo-European languages.

German and English, therefore, have much in common because they inherit their language from a common ancestral speech. They differ, on the other hand, from each other, because throughout centuries of development each has followed its own course and has been subject to its own special influences.

The most important special development of German, which differentiates it from English, is what is known as the second shifting of consonants. English and German alike are subject to Grimm's Law, or the first shifting of consonants, but the Germanic consonants which resulted from the operation of Grimm's Law underwent a further change, producing a series of consonant correspondences which is peculiar to High German, and which is one of the things which justifies the linguist in setting off that language as a special subdivision of the West Germanic languages.

Thus, where English has *p*, German usually has *f* or *pf* in cognate words, as in English *pound*, German *pfund*; English *help*, German *helfen*; English *sleep*, German *schlafen*; English *ship*, German *schiff*; English *sheep*, German *schaf*; English *sap*, German *sapf*. Likewise, where English has *d*, German usually has *t*, as in the following pairs of words: *dead, tot* (formerly spelled *todt*); *deaf, taub*; *deal, theil* (the *h* being silent in pronunciation); *do, thun*; *cold, kalt*; *hold, halten*; and so with many others. English *t* frequently appears as German *z* or *tz* (pronounced *ts*) as in *to, zu*; *tin, zinn*; *tooth, zahn*; *tongue, zunge*; *write, ritzen*; *cat, katz*; *sit, sitzen*. English *v* appears in cognate German words as *b*, as in *over, ober*; *leave, (er-)lauben*; *grave, grab*; *shove, schieben*; *love, liebe*; *knave, knabe*.

7 ⌾ Periods of English

From the seventh century, the earliest period of which we have any knowledge of recorded forms of English, the language has been subject to constant change. In this it merely partakes of

47

the nature of language in general, for speech, so long as it is living in actual unconstrained use, is continually growing and developing. It is only in the so-called "dead" languages that language can be drawn up into a system once and for all. From the earliest Indo-European times, therefore, down to the present day, it is safe to say that the language which we now know as English has been ceaselessly, though often imperceptibly, dropping old and assuming new forms. Since this process has been unbroken from the beginning, it is in a way illogical to divide the history of the language into periods.

There have been, however, certain times at which changes took place more rapidly than at others, owing to the special attendant circumstances. As long as we keep always in mind that the dates by which we divide a language into periods are more or less arbitrarily chosen, they will serve the convenient purpose of indicating roughly the large general divisions in the development of the language. In this way we may indicate three major divisions in the history of English:

1. The Old English or Anglo-Saxon period, beginning with the coming of the Jutes, Angles, and Saxons to England and ending with the Norman Conquest in 1066—or better, about 1100.

2. The Middle English period, extending from 1100 to the beginning of printing in England in 1475—or roughly 1500.

3. The Modern English period, extending from 1500 to the present time.

The language in each of these periods is distinguished by developments which are to a large extent characteristic of the respective periods. These developments affect all the various sides of the language—sounds, inflections, words, and syntax, and in some instances even spelling. It will be the purpose of the following chapters to give an account of the changes in the language from these several points of view.

4

ENGLISH INFLECTIONS

1 ◩ The Nature of Inflection

It has already been pointed out (pp. 41 ff.) that inflection is one of the distinguishing characteristics of the family of Indo-European languages. The extent to which these various languages make use of inflection differs greatly. There is often considerable variation, as with English, even in the periods of one and the same language.

Broadly defined, inflection is the change or variation in the forms of a word for the purpose of indicating corresponding variations in its meaning and use. The definition implies that there is a certain root element which remains constant, but which is given specific application and meaning by additions to this element. This concept, however, is too broad for the traditional use of the term inflection, since it includes not only the formal changes for person, number, gender, tense, and so forth, but also such word-changes as *swift*, adjective, to *swift-ly*, adverb. A term frequently employed to designate a change such as that of *swift* to *swiftly* is derivation. Like the inflectional endings, the *-ly* of *swiftly*, the *-dom* of *kingdom*, the *-ness* of *kindness* are not separate words; they have no independent existence. They appear to have

49

somewhat more meaning as independent elements in the word than true inflections, as for example the plural -*s* of *books,* the preterit ending -*ed* in *differed,* and the participial ending -*en* in *spoken.*

At the other extreme of the combining process is composition or compounding, the placing together of two word elements each of which has a separate and independent existence—free forms, in contrast to the bound forms of inflectional and derivative elements. *Houseboat, bluegrass,* and *bookmark* are compound nouns; *to babysit, to overspend, to underwrite* are compound verbs. It is not always easy, in fact it is not always possible, to draw a clear line between composition and derivation because such derivational elements as the -*dom* of *kingdom,* the -*hood* of *knighthood,* and even the -*ly* of *swiftly* are weakened forms of words that were originally independent.

In precisely the same manner the line of demarcation between derivation and inflection is often hazy. One distinction which is often made is that inflection includes only those variations or changes in the form of a word which do not alter or affect its part-of-speech function; when the part of speech is changed, then we have derivation. It is immediately apparent, however, that, as far as English is concerned, the distinction will not hold. *Manhood* and *kingdom* are clearly derivational products, yet they are nouns, just as are *man* and *king.* On the other hand, -*ing,* usually regarded as an inflection, serves to convert a verb into either adjective or noun. We can only conclude that these processes run into each other imperceptibly, and that a hard and fast division between them cannot be made.

It is best, perhaps, to limit the application of the term inflection to the plural and the genitive forms of nouns and pronouns, the object forms of pronouns, the comparative and superlative forms of adjectives, the forms for present and past tenses of verbs, including the third singular, and the participle-gerund. This leaves derivation as the combination of one free form and one or more bound elements other than those which have already been specified as inflectional suffixes, and compounding as a process involving only free forms.

2 ◙ English as a "Grammarless Tongue"

The history of English inflections has been one of continuous loss. As far back as we can go in the history of the English language we can trace a gradual breaking down of the inflectional system. And even when we arrive at the earliest periods of Old English, there are sure indications that the language is already in a transitional stage, and that the tendency toward inflectional loss in English is one that goes far back into the prehistoric periods of the language.

This tendency toward inflectional loss is not to be regarded as a degeneration of the language. The language of relatively primitive peoples and eras is often more elaborately inflected than the language of a more highly developed people and civilization. Thus today the language of certain tribes in Africa who have had relatively little contact over the years with the rest of the world is infinitely more complex in grammatical structure than that of any of the European nations.

The development in the English inflectional system has, of course, been altogether unconscious, so far as the users of the language are concerned. The language changed to meet the needs of those who spoke it, and no conscious theory of improving the language by getting rid of unnecessary inflections has ever been in operation. To say that inflections were lost is merely to say that, in the practical use of the language, men tended to express themselves as briefly as possible.

In English, furthermore, the language has developed freely and unrestrainedly from the earliest times down to the Modern English period. This would not have been the case, at least with literary English, if in the Old English period we had had a great classic literature which was set up and retained as a model for all later periods, as classical Latin literature became the model for all later generations of Romans. If that had taken place our language would now probably have the comparatively elaborate Old English inflectional system instead of the present Modern English one, which is almost completely devoid of inflection.

The number of Modern English inflections is so small that they may be very briefly summarized. The only parts of speech which are capable of inflection are the noun, the pronoun, the verb, and for the single characteristic of comparison, the adverb and the adjective, although comparison is often classified as a derivational rather than an inflectional feature. Of these the noun inflects for number, singular and plural, and for one case, the genitive, singular and plural, the other cases being all alike. The personal pronoun inflects for three persons, for three genders, for two numbers, and in some forms for three cases, nominative, genitive, and objective.

The verb inflects more elaborately than the noun, but less elaborately than the personal pronoun. The present tense usually has two forms, one for the third person, singular number, and another for all other uses of the present. There is a distinctive form for the past tense, which is the same, however for all persons and both numbers. The past participle sometimes has a distinctive form (*see, saw, seen*), but usually it is the same as the form of the past tense (*differ, differed, differed; bind, bound, bound*). In a few instances, that is, *be* and *were*—the present and past of the verb *to be*—and the third person singular of the present tense of other verbs, there are special forms for the subjunctive mood; but these are rarely used.

So few are the inflections of Modern English as compared with those, for example, of Latin or Greek, or even of Old English, the earlier stage of its own language, that it has been characterized as a "grammarless tongue." This characterization is approximately true of course only if we think of grammar as meaning the same thing as inflection, and we shall come to see later that it involves many other things as well. In the Greek and Latin languages, grammar, that is to say inflection, or accidence as it is sometimes called, does play a large part. In fact, inflection and the rules of concord were the two important divisions of classical grammar.

Through its loss of inflections, however, English has also simplified its rules of concord, and consequently it does not present the same kind of grammatical system as the classical languages. That it is a "grammarless tongue," however, in the true sense of the word grammar, is not at all true. The language has its structures and its rules of right and wrong, and it is as necessary to observe them as it was for speakers of Greek and Latin to observe their inflectional systems and rules of concord.

3 ⊿ The Inflections of the Old English Period

It is convenient to divide the history of English inflections into three chronological periods, corresponding to the three great stages in their development. The first is the Old English period, from the earliest records to about 1100; this is the period of *full inflections*. The second is the Middle English period, from 1100 to about 1500; this is the period of *leveled inflections*. The third is the Modern English period, from 1500 to the present time; and this is the period of *lost inflections*. The periods of course pass over into each other gradually, although at the two main dividing lines, 1100 and 1500 respectively, changes took place more rapidly than during the central portions of the periods. There is, therefore, both in the Old English and in the Middle English period, a fairly stable and fixed central or classical form of the language which we shall briefly describe.

The Old English is called the period of full inflections because the inflections of the language at that time were not only relatively more numerous than they were in later periods, but were also pronounced with a full and distinct sense of the values of the various vowels in the inflectional endings. Since the inflectional endings bore no accent, it will be seen that this method of pronouncing the inflectional vowels is very different from the tendency of Modern English (or even of Middle English), where we regularly obscure final unaccented syllables in pronunciation.

One or two illustrations will suffice to make this point clear. In Old English a noun in the nominative singular might end in -*a*, as *hunta*, 'hunter'; or -*e*, as *tunge*, 'tongue'; or -*u*, as *sunu*, 'son'; or -*o*, as *wlenco*, 'pride.' Now these various endings were all given distinctly and clearly the values of the vowels -*a*, -*e*, -*u*, and -*o*, and were not obscured and slurred as they would be in our Modern English pronunciation. The same principle holds true when the inflectional syllable consists of a vowel followed by a consonant or consonants. The noun *stān*, 'stone,' had a genitive singular *stānes* and a nominative and accusative plural *stānas*, each of which was clearly distinguished by the value of its vowel. In short, we may say that inflectional endings received far more attention in the Old English period than in later periods. There was more feeling for them and consequently a stronger tendency to preserve them.

The tendency which kept the vowels of the inflectional syllables full and clear served naturally to prevent the loss of inflectional endings. The extent of inflection in the Old English period may be briefly indicated, choosing for this purpose the West Saxon dialect in the early West Saxon period, that is English between the years 800 and 900, in the central and southern parts of England. The noun inflected for three genders: masculine, feminine, and neuter. Gender in Old English was still grammatical and not natural or logical, as it has become in Modern English. Thus, Old English nouns ending in -*a* are masculine, and this includes names of such inanimate objects as *mona*, 'moon'; *steorra*, 'star'; *naca*, 'boat.'

This distinction between the grammatical gender of Old English, based upon the forms of words, and the natural gender of Modern English, based upon the meanings of words, should be clearly apprehended. In Old English, adjectives, like nouns, have gender since they are inflected in such a manner as to agree with the nouns they modify. With the loss of inflections,

Modern English has given up the distinctions of grammatical gender and employs this category now for the much simpler and what appears to us the more natural purpose of indicating sex. This explains why native speakers of English often find it difficult to understand why the possessive pronoun must be feminine in a French sentence like *Il a perdu sa femme,* 'He has lost his wife.' But the possessive *sa* is an adjective, and as such it must take the feminine form when it modifies a feminine noun, no matter what its antecedent may be or what its logical meaning may be.

The noun was inflected also for two numbers, singular and plural. It was inflected for four cases: the nominative, genitive (from which is derived the modern possessive), accusative (the modern objective), and a dative-instrumental case, lost in Modern English. Furthermore, it inflected for class or type of declension, there being two main types of noun declension, the strong and the weak, and each of these types or classes consisted of several subtypes or classes. This somewhat complicated state of affairs may best be represented by the following table of the different inflectional endings which the nouns of the various genders and types may take. Words which appeared in certain cases without any inflectional endings are indicated by the sign ø, which symbolizes zero. Since the instrumental is always the same as the dative in the noun, it is not mentioned specifically in this table.

	SINGULAR		PLURAL
NOMINATIVE	ø, –u, –a, –e	NOMINATIVE	ø, –as, –u, –a, –e,– an
GENITIVE	–es, –e, –an	GENITIVE	–a, –ena
DATIVE	ø, –e, –an	DATIVE	–um
ACCUSATIVE	ø, –e, –an	ACCUSATIVE	same as the nominative

An examination of this table will show that the inflectional system of the Old English noun is not distinctive for all uses. The same ending sometimes has to do duty for various values of the noun. Thus, the ending -*e* may appear in any case of the singular as well as in the nominative and accusative plural. There are other endings also which serve a multiple purpose, -*an* being used five times. The most distinctive and characteristic endings are -*es*, which appears only in the genitive singular; -*as*, which is used only for the nominative and accusative plural of certain masculine nouns; and -*um*, which is always the ending of all nouns in the dative plural. It will be seen later that these endings are of primary importance in the further development of the inflectional system.

The declension of the strong masculine noun *stān*, 'stone'; the strong feminine noun *lār*, 'lore, learning'; the strong neuter noun *hof*, 'court'; the weak masculine noun *steorra*, 'star'; and the weak feminine noun *tunge*, 'tongue' may be cited in illustration of the declension of five large groups of Old English nouns, although these five are not exhaustive of all the different Old English declensions. The declensions of *stān* and *steorra* are typical of by far the greatest number of nouns in Old English.

Strong

	SINGULAR			PLURAL		
	Masc.	*Fem.*	*Neu.*	*Masc.*	*Fem.*	*Neu.*
NOMINATIVE	stān	lār	hof	stānas	lāre	hofu
GENITIVE	stānes	lāre	hofes	stāna	lāra	hofa
DATIVE	stāne	lāre	hofe	stānum	lārum	hofun
ACCUSATIVE	stān	lāre	hof	stānas	lāre	hofu

Weak

	SINGULAR		PLURAL	
	Masc.	*Fem.*	*Masc.*	*Fem.*
NOMINATIVE	steorra	tunge	steorran	tungan
GENITIVE	steorran	tungan	steorrena	tungena
DATIVE	steorran	tungan	steorrum	tungum
ACCUSATIVE	steorran	tungan	steorran	tungan

There are various minor declensions of the noun in Old English besides the above five types, but most of these have been more or less completely assimilated in later English to the type forms represented by *stān* and *steorra*. Only one has left considerable traces in Modern English, nouns in which the plural number was formed by mutation of the radical vowel. For example, Old English *fōt*, *gōs*, *mūs*, *brōc*, etc., formed their plurals *fēt*, *gēs*, *mȳs*, *brēk*, corresponding to Modern English *foot, feet; goose, geese; mouse, mice*. The word *brōc* has disappeared in the singular in Modern English, which should have *brook*; its plural is retained, however, in *breeches*, which has the old mutation of the vowel to indicate the plural, but which has also added the regular plural -*s* ending of nouns like *stān*. Some other words which in Old English belong to this class of mutation plurals have been attracted completely into the larger class of regular nouns. Thus Old English *bōc*, *bēc* should give regularly Modern English *book*, with the plural *beek*, like *goose, geese*. But by analogy to the large class of plurals in -*s* without mutation of the vowel, *beek* was changed to *books*.

The Old English adjective differs from the Modern English adjective in that it inflects for all those forms for which the noun inflects—for gender, number, case, and type or class—as strong and weak.[1] The rules of concord also demand that an adjective shall agree in its inflection with the gender, number, and case of the noun which it modifies. The main inflections of the adjective for all genders and types are as follows:

	SINGULAR		PLURAL
NOMINATIVE	ø, −u −a, −e	NOMINATIVE	ø, −u, −a, −e, −an
GENITIVE	−es, −re, −an	GENITIVE	−ra, −ena
DATIVE	−um, −re, −an	DATIVE	−um
ACCUSATIVE	ø, −ne, −e, −an	ACCUSATIVE	same as the nominative

With the adjective should be grouped the definite article, for this part of speech in Old English is a real adjective, inflecting

---

[1] For the use of the strong and weak declensions of the adjective, see p. 43.

like the adjective and like the Modern German article, for gender, number, and case. The inflections of the article are as follows:

	SINGULAR			PLURAL	
	Masc.	*Fem.*	*Neut.*	*All genders*	
NOMINATIVE	sē	sēo	þæt[2]	þā	'the'
GENITIVE	þæs	þære	þæs	þāra	'of the'
DATIVE	þǣm	þære	þǣm	þǣm	'to the'
ACCUSATIVE	þone	þā	þæt	þā	'the'
INSTRUMENTAL	þȳ	þære	þȳ	þǣm	'by or with the'

The Old English personal pronoun differs mainly from the Modern English in that it has preserved remnants of an old dual number, the only survival in any period of English of an inflection which probably, in prehistoric stages of the language, appeared also in the noun, the adjective, and the verb; and secondly, in that it has only one form for the second person, *ðū*, Modern English 'thou,' with its various case forms. The dual number survives only in the personal pronoun of the first and second persons. The inflections of the Old English personal pronoun, followed in each case by its Modern English derivative or equivalent when it has one, are as follows:

FIRST PERSON SINGULAR			SECOND PERSON SINGULAR		
NOMINATIVE	ic,	'I'	NOMINATIVE	ðū,	'thou'
GENITIVE	mīn,	'mine'	GENITIVE	ðīn,	'thine'
DATIVE	mē,	'me'	DATIVE	ðē,	'thee'
ACCUSATIVE	mec or mē, 'me'		ACCUSATIVE	ðec or ðē, 'thee'	

DUAL		DUAL	
NOMINATIVE	wit	NOMINATIVE	git
GENITIVE	uncer	GENITIVE	incer
DATIVE	unc	DATIVE	inc
ACCUSATIVE	unc	ACCUSATIVE	inc

[2] The characters þ (thorn) and ð (eth) were used interchangeably and were both equivalent to *th*. The character æ (called the digraph) has the sound of Modern English *a* in *hat*, the value of Old English *a*, as in *stān*, being the same as in Modern English *father*.

PLURAL			PLURAL		
NOMINATIVE	wē,	'we'	NOMINATIVE	gē	'ye'
GENITIVE	ūre or ūser, 'our'		GENITIVE	ēower,	'your'
DATIVE	ūs,	'us'	DATIVE	ēow,	'you'
ACCUSATIVE	usic or ūs,	'us'	ACCUSATIVE	ēowic or ēow, 'you'	

THIRD PERSON SINGULAR

	Masc.		*Fem.*		*Neu.*	
NOMINATIVE	hē,	'he'	hēo,	'she'	hit,	'it'
GENITIVE	his,	'his'	hiere,	'her'	his,	'its'
DATIVE	him,	'him'	hiere,	'her'	him,	'it'
ACCUSATIVE	hine,	'him'	hīe,	'her'	hit,	'it'

PLURAL

	All genders	
NOMINATIVE	hī or hīe	'they'
GENITIVE	heora	'their'
DATIVE	heom	'them'
ACCUSATIVE	hī or hīe	'them'

These forms of the personal pronoun were simplified in several ways in the Middle English period. In the first place the dual forms disappeared, and with them the last traces of the dual number in English. The form *ic*, since it generally occurred in unstressed position, tended to assume a weakened form, which later became conventionalized in spelling as capital *I*.[3] The genitives *mīn*, *ðīn*, persisted as *mine*, *thine*, but there also developed forms without final -*n*, that is, *my*, *thy*, which were used before words beginning with a consonant, the full forms being used

---

[3] The use of the capital for the pronoun of the first person, nominative case in English, a custom not shared by any other European language, is due to purely mechanical reasons. The custom arose in the late Middle English period, when in order to distinguish the letter *i* in cursive writing, which as a single stroke of the pen might easily be mistaken as part of another letter, it was commonly written as J or I. With the invention of printing, the form *I* was carried over from writing as the symbol for the letter when standing alone, although in the early days of printing both the capital and the small letter were used. Gradually, however, with the establishment of fixed conventions in printing and writing, the capital letter came to be the only recognized form for this purpose.

before vowels and in absolute constructions. The dative and accusative fell together under the original dative forms *me*, *thee*, *us*, and *you*. Like the first person singular, because it was in the unstressed position, Old English *ūs* developed a weak form with short vowel, Modern English *us*, although in most words Old English *ū* became Modern English *ou* (Old English *hūs*, Modern English *house*, etc.).

The forms of the third person were variously modified. The dative and accusative singular were simplified under one form, for the masculine *him*, the old dative, for the feminine *her*, likewise the old dative—the same development which had taken place somewhat earlier with the pronouns of the first and second persons. The neuter dative-accusative form became *hit*, 'it,' the old accusative. The old dative *him* was not used here as in the other genders because of its identity with the masculine form. The genitive singular of the neuter, *his*, was also gradually discarded because of its identity with the genitive singular of the masculine, and in its place there developed a new genitive singular neuter, formed by adding the regular -*s* ending of genitives to the uninflected form of the nominative.

In all these instances it will be seen that the tendency was towards a limitation of the number and also towards a stricter definition of the value of forms. Old English permitted identity of forms in different grammatical categories, *his*, for example, for both masculine and neuter genitive. The tendency, at least, of later English development has been in the direction of a single form for each grammatical category.

This tendency was helped in the present instance by the change from grammatical to logical gender. So long as gender was a purely grammatical distinction, as in Old English, one might use the same form for masculine and neuter; but when gender came to mean a real difference in the nature of the objects designated, as in Modern English, there was a movement toward the development of distinctive forms for the different genders. The plural forms did not persist because of their similarity in form to singulars. *Hī* occurred in both singular and plural and was not readily distinguishable from *hē*. *Hīere* and *hēora* were much alike, as were *him* and *heom*. For the Old English forms were consequently substituted the forms *they, their, them*, probably under the influence of the Scandinavian forms, which began with *th*. The first person singular of the feminine became *she*, probably representing a development of the Old English feminine article *sēo*, since the Old English pronoun *hēo* might, in many dialects of Middle English, have been confused with the masculine *hē*.

The adverb in Old English does not differ greatly from its use in Middle and Modern English. In all three stages of the language it was susceptible of inflection only for the purpose of showing degrees of comparison. Various inflections, however, which were lost in later English, were used in Old English with the power of forming adverbs. Thus the instrumental (originally a locative) singular ending *-e*, added to an adjective formed an adverb, e.g., *sōft*, adjective; *sōfte*, adverb. The dative plural ending was similarly used, e.g., *hwīl*, 'time,' Modern English *while*, with the dative plural inflection, *hwīlum*, was used with the sense of Modern English 'at times, from time to time.' The genitive singular ending *-es* also often had adverbial value, as in *dæg*, 'day,' *dæges*, 'by day.'

With the gradual disappearance of inflections, these inflectional adverbs ceased to be used, their place being taken largely by the compositional adverb with *-ly*. The adverb in *-um* persists, however, in the archaic form *whilom*. The *-es* adverb of genitive origin is not now distinguishable from the plural form. But in constructions like "Evenings is the best time to see him," the word *evenings* is a direct survival of the old genitive adverb construction. With the loss of final inflectional *-e*, adverbs like *softe* could no longer be distinguished from the adjective form *soft*. This type of adverb formation also persists in Modern English in adverbs without ending, as in constructions like "Go *slow*"; "He fought *hard*, but there was no hope for him"; and very

61

commonly in Biblical and poetic English in phrases like "*exceeding* glad," and "the sun shone *cold* upon the earth."

The inflection of the Old English verb differs from that of the Modern English verb only in having a larger number of specific forms for the various persons, tenses, and classes or conjugations. There was considerable variety among the dialects of Old English in their treatment of the inflections of the verb, the most conservative dialect being the West Saxon, which is the basis of this description. In Old English, verbs fell into two main categories, weak and strong. Weak verbs formed the past tense and the past participle by the addition of an inflectional ending containing either a -*t* or -*d*; with the strong verbs there was a change in the stem vowel. (See p. 43.)

In addition, Old English verbs were inflected for three persons, for two numbers, and for three moods—indicative, imperative, and optative or subjunctive, the last mood being used much more extensively in Old English than it is in Modern English. There were also inflections for the participles and the infinitive and, as we have seen, for two tenses, the present and the past. The forms of the present tense are also used to indicate future time. Besides the simple inflectional tenses, there are, as in Modern English, a number of phrasal verbs formed with the auxiliaries *habban*, 'have,' *sculan*, 'shall,' *willan*, 'will,' *bēon*, 'be,' joined to the infinitive of the main verb.

Old English, like Modern English, has no real inflectional passive, but only a compound or phrasal passive, formed either with the help of the verb *bēon*, 'be,' or *weorðan*, 'become,' joined to the past participle of the verb. The infinitive ends usually in -*an*, *singan*, 'to sing,' but occasionally also in -*ian*, *endian*, 'to end.' The preposition *to* is not used in Old English merely as the sign of the infinitive, as in Modern English. When it is used, it is followed by the inflected form of the infinitive, in the dative case, the whole being virtually a prepositional phrase indicating purpose, e.g., *tō singanne*, 'for the purpose of singing,' *tō endianne*, 'in order to end.' This construction is usually classified as a gerund. The past participle of strong verbs ends in *-en: sungen,* 'sung,' of the weak verb in *-ed, -od,* frequently carrying also the prefix *ge:- ge-fylled,* 'filled,' *ge-endod,* 'ended.' The present participle ends in *-ende, singende.*

The personal endings are few in number. For the present tense indicative singular they are *-e, -est, -eð: ic singe, ðū singest, hē singeð.* All persons of the plural end in *-að: wē, gē, hīe singað.* But most verbs whose infinitives end in *-ian* have *-að* in the third person singular, and *-iað* in all persons of the plural. In the optative or subjunctive all singulars end in *-e* and all plurals in *-en.* In the past tense the first and third persons of strong verbs have no endings: *ic sang, hē sang.* The second person, however, has the ending *-e,* and likewise in the root of the word, it takes over the radical vowel of the plural: *ðū sunge.* The plural has the ending *-on* for all persons: *wē, gē, hīe sungon.* In the weak verb the second person singular of the past tense has the *-est* ending of the present, *ðū fylledest;* the first and third are *ic fyllede, hē fyllede,* and the plural *wē, gē, hīe fylledon.* The subjunctive forms are the same for the past as for the present, *-e* for the singular and *-en* for the plural. The only other forms which need be noted are those of the imperative, which appear in the singular either without ending or with the endings *-e* or *-a,* and in the plural with the endings *-að* or *-iað.*

4 ◙ The Inflections of the Middle English Period

The language of the Middle English period underwent a vast number of changes, affecting not only inflections, but also vocabulary, sounds, and the whole structure of the language. The causes of this development, this thoroughgoing reconstruction of the language, are very complex. As far as inflections go, however, one of the main causes was pretty certainly a change in the way words were accented in the Middle English period. At this time apparently the stress of words began to become more like that of Modern English, placed strongly and heavily on the root syllables of words, with a consequent obscuring and weakening of the later syllables, particularly the inflectional suffixes.

A second main cause of inflectional change in the Middle English period was the tendency for certain inflectional patterns to extend their spheres at the expense of others. Thus the genitive singular ending in -es, which belonged to the masculine and neuter strong nouns, was extended to the feminine strong nouns and to weak nouns of all genders. Genitive singulars in -e and -an became fewer and fewer as time went on. Similarly the -es (earlier -as) of the masculine nominative-accusative plural of strong nouns became the generally established inflection of all plurals. The process by means of which such a development occurs is called analogy.

A final factor which must be taken into account is the condition of general social and political unrest which accompanied the period of the Danish Conquest, and, a little later, the Norman Conquest. The result of these two invasions was the complete overthrow of the English social and political system. For a period of several generations there was a time of great confusion; the standards, the traditional rules and habits of the English people of Britain, in speech and in other matters, were forgotten and broken down. The result was that the constraints of rigid social custom, of conventional education and good breeding, being to a considerable extent removed, the language developed in an untrammeled and popular way. The usages of the unconventional, the ignorant, and uneducated part of the people were not held in check. The result was that when English began to reassert itself, it was no longer the English of the Old English period, but an English that had been modified by passing through a period of popular and natural development.

The situation was very much as though what we now call "good English" should for some reason or other be given up, say as a result of a Cambodian conquest of America. For a time Cambodian would have the upper hand. Americans would all try to learn Cambodian, to talk Cambodian, to act like Cambodians, because the Cambodians would give tone to everything and would be the controlling power in the country.

English would no longer be taught in the school or the home, and the only persons who would use English would be the populace, who would not, of course, come into close contact with the new ruling civilization of the country. They would speak their natural speech, the English of the people and the old "good English" would become extinct and would be crowded out by the "incorrect English" of the uneducated and heedless part of the population. All who spoke English at all might then say "You was," instead of "You were"; "He ain't," instead of "He isn't"; perhaps "He done it," instead of "He did it"; and a thousand similar uses which are now unacceptable according to the standards of careful English would become general. For a time, then, we should all together be "uneducated" and "popular."

But suppose now that after several generations this Cambodian invasion and the prestige of things Cambodian should pass over, and that English should begin to reassert itself. Soon the educative and conservative instinct would set to work. The more thoughtful part of the people would again construct a system of the language. Again we would have rules of grammar, a correct speech at the side of an incorrect one. But the new correct speech would be based simply upon the usage of the people of this later generation, and consequently it would contain much that the earlier generation regarded as incorrect. After the language had passed through the popular stage and had emerged again into a cultivated stage, "You was," "He ain't," and "He done it" might very well be the only possible correct forms.

This, as has been said, is what happened in the Middle English period. The old standards of conventional propriety and correctness were more or less forgotten. The language followed the free and unregulated impulses of the people. Consequently, when it rose again to the position of a stable and classical literary language in the time of Chaucer and his predecessors, it was a very different language from what it had been in the time of Alfred and Ælfric.

It is not necessary, however, or even reasonable, to regard the language of the Middle English period as a corrupt and degenerate form of Old English, for these terms suppose that the language of

65

the latter period is less admirable and effective than that of the earlier. It is better to speak of it as a development from, or an evolution out of, Old English. It does not follow, by any means, that the popular dialect of a language is any less capable of doing all that language is expected to do than is the conventional "correct speech." It often happens that it is more capable, and one of the main sources of strength in the English language is the frequency and ease with which it renews its vigor by drawing from the living and ever-flowing well of popular speech.

The inflections of the Middle English period are largely the inflections of the Old English period in a disappearing stage. Owing to the change in word stress which has just been mentioned, the final syllables of words, which often consisted of inflectional suffixes, tended to become weak and indistinct in pronunciation. This tendency, already apparent in the late Old English period, manifested itself first in the ending -*um* of the dative plural of nouns and of adjectives, in the time of Ælfric. The ending gradually became vague and uncertain, appearing in the various forms -*un*, -*on*, -*an*, -*en*, the last two predominating by the end of the Old English period.

The most important inflectional development, however, of the early Middle English period consisted in the levelling of all unstressed end vowels under the vowel -*e*, pronounced like the second syllable of *tuba*. The effect of this change upon the inflectional system of the noun, for example, will be seen by substituting this vowel -*e* for the various vowels given in the table of noun endings in §3 p. 55. The result would be the following scheme of noun inflections in Middle English:

	SINGULAR	PLURAL
NOMINATIVE	ø, –e	ø, –e, –es, –en
GENITIVE	–e, –es, –en	–e, –ene
DATIVE	ø, –e, –en	–en
ACCUSATIVE	ø, –e, –en	ø, –e, –es, –en

Several important consequences followed this levelling of the

66

distinctive Old English vowel endings under the neutral vowel -*e*. In the first place, the grouping of the nouns into classes or types of declension had largely to be given up, for the characteristic feature of this classification was the difference in vowel ending. The two classes which remained were the class of the strong and weak nouns, the strong nouns being those that formed their genitive singular and nominative-accusative plurals in -*es*, the weak nouns those that used the ending -*en* for these and other forms.

Moreover, with the breaking down of the different classes of declension, grammatical gender also became inoperative. All inflections being levelled under the general inflections -*e*, -*es*, -*en*, there was no longer any reason, or indeed any means, for keeping up the distinctions of grammatical gender. Words came to be used as they are in Modern English, without gender, except in so far as they indicate, by their logical meaning, the sex of the objects which they designate. The inflection of a typical strong noun in Middle English is that of *ston* (the vowel *ā* having changed to *o* in the Middle English period), of a typical weak noun, that of *sterre*, 'star,' in the following paradigms. Letters which are enclosed within parentheses are such as are sometimes dropped in the early Middle English period and are altogether dropped in the later Middle English period.

SINGULAR		PLURAL	
NOMINATIVE	ston	NOMINATIVE	stones
GENITIVE	stones	GENITIVE	ston(en)e, stones
DATIVE	ston(e)	DATIVE	stonen, stones
ACCUSATIVE	ston	ACCUSATIVE	stones

SINGULAR		PLURAL	
NOMINATIVE	sterre	NOMINATIVE	sterren
GENITIVE	sterre(n)	GENITIVE	sterr(en)e
DATIVE	sterre(n)	DATIVE	sterren
ACCUSATIVE	sterre(n)	ACCUSATIVE	sterren

67

ⅼhe tendency of all nouns was to fall into these two groups, the *ston-stones* group, and the *sterre-sterren* group. The *ston-stones* group, as the more numerous, tended to impose itself upon the *sterre-sterren* group, so that besides these forms and contemporary with them are often found the forms *sterre, sterres*.

The loss of grammatical gender in the noun naturally led to the loss of agreement in inflection between the noun and its adjective, so far as gender is concerned. The same leveling of inflectional endings took place in the adjective as in the noun; the only one which persisted after the loss of those indicative of gender was the vowel *-e*, which served to mark the plural number and the weak inflection of the adjective. The inflection of the Middle English adjective *god*, 'good,' would, therefore, be as follows:

Strong

SINGULAR	PLURAL
All cases and genders	*All cases and genders*
god	gode

Weak

SINGULAR	PLURAL
All cases and genders	*All cases and genders*
gode	gode

An example of a strong singular would be the phrase *A yong Squyer* (from Chaucer's Prologue to *The Canterbury Tales*, l. 79); a strong plural would be *and smale fowles* (*ibid.*, l. 9; it should be remembered that every vowel is pronounced in Middle English); a weak singular is the phrase *The yonge sonne*, and a weak plural, the phrase *The tendre croppes* (both *ibid.*, l. 7).

In the case of the definite article, the forms with initial *s*, that is *sē* and *sēo*, gave up this *s* for þ (th), by analogy to the majority of the forms of the article, which begin with þ. This gave for the nominative singular forms þe, þeo, þæt. But by a regular phonetic development, the vowel of þeo became the same as that of þe,

68

The Beginning of Chaucer's " Pardoner's Tale "
Ellesmere Manuscript, fol. 144ʳ
(For description, see Appendix, p. 287)

This item is reproduced by permission of The Huntington Library,
San Marino, California.

and with the loss of grammatical gender in the noun, the separate neuter form *þæt* was given up as an article, its place being taken by the form *þe* of the masculine and feminine.

No longer needed as an article, the form *þæt* itself persisted with changed value as a demonstrative pronoun. Having gone as far as this, analogy then operated still further, and the single fixed form *þe* (the) established itself for all genders, numbers, and cases of the article. The main principle, therefore, which operated in the simplification of the definite article is that of substitution, one single form crowding out all the dozen or more inflections of the Old English article.

Inflection of the verb as strong and weak, or irregular and regular, persisted in the Middle English period, but from early Middle English times there was a tendency on the part of strong verbs to become weak, for example Old English *wēpan, wēop* beside Middle English *wepen, wepte*, 'weep, wept.' This tendency, which was developed still further in the Modern English period and which is still operative, was due to the fact that the weak verbs were the more numerous, as well as being the simpler and more readily apprehended manner of tense formation. The weak verbs thus tended to become the type form, crowding out by analogy to them many old strong verbs and attracting to their class virtually all new verbs that entered the language.

Upon examining the description of verb inflections for the Old English period given on pp. 62 and 63, we can readily see that the general neutralization of inflectional vowels under the vowel *-e* affected a considerable number of verb forms. The endings *-að, -iað* of the present plural became *-eð*, like the third singular. The endings *-e, -a,* and *-að, iað* of the imperative became respectively *-e* and *-eð*. The infinitive endings *-an, -ian, -anne* became *-en, -enne*. In the preterit plural the *-on, -don* endings became *-en, -den*, making the indicative and subjunctive identical.

Other changes were due to different causes. The ending of the present participle *-ende* tended to fall together with certain verbal nouns which ended regularly in *-ung, -ing*, e.g., *langung,* 'desire, longing.' In Old English these were distinctly felt as nouns and not as parts of the verb. Their similarity in form and meaning, however, attracted the present participle to these nouns. As a result, the -*ende* participial inflection was given up; the verbal noun and the present participle became indistinguishable in form, both with the ending -*ing*.

Another simplification that occurred affected the preterit tenses. In the Old English strong verb, the preterit plural stem was frequently different from the preterit singular, and the past participle often differed from both. In Middle English the three preterit stems tended to become alike, to simplify under one form, just as the forms of the article all tended to simplify under the type form *the*. Thus the Old English verb *bindan, band, bundon, bunden*, became in Middle English *binde, bound, bound*. This leveling never became complete, as in the case of the article, and we still have in Modern English verbs like *sing, sang, sung; drive, drove, driven*. The simplification, however, affected a considerable number of verbs.

5 ▨ The Inflections of the Modern English Period

Although the Modern English period is called the period of lost inflections, it should be understood that this term is used with relative, and not absolute, meaning. All inflections have not been lost in the Modern English period, but compared with those of the Middle English of the Old English period they have dwindled to a very small number. Nevertheless the language still remains an inflectional language, and for the expression of certain ideas no other means than inflection has been devised. The developments in the Modern English period arise from the further carrying out of the two tendencies of the Middle English period, first the tendency towards obscuring the vowels of inflectional syllables, and second, the tendency towards simplification by the substitution of one type form in the place of a variety of forms.

In the passage from the Middle English to the Modern English period, the language did not again become merely a popular dialect which later was elevated to the dignity of a standard literary language, as had occurred in the transition from the Old English to the Middle English period. On the contrary, from the end of the Middle English time to the present day the language has been watched with increasing care and vigilance. It has been systematized, regulated, purified; in short, it has tended to become more and more an established and settled literary and conventional language. The changes, consequently, which have taken place in the Modern English period have been comparatively slow and comparatively few in number. The difference between the English of the year 1900 and the year 1500 is less than that between the English of the year 1250 and the year 1000. The Modern English has been a regulating, refining, systematizing period, rather than a revolutionizing, reconstructing period.

The final result, in the early Modern English period, of the weakening of inflectional vowels was, as has been stated, their complete loss. Thus starting with the Old English dissyllabic noun *nam-a*, 'name,' we get in Middle English the form *nam-e*, still a dissyllable; but in Modern English we have *nam(e)*, a monosyllable, the final *-e* having no other value than to indicate the length of the radical vowel. Likewise the Old English plural *stān-as*, the Middle English *ston-es*, becomes Modern English *ston(e)s*; and the Old English genitive *stan-es*, Middle English *ston-es*, is Modern English *ston(e)s*, with an apostrophe as a mechanical device to distinguish the possessive from the plural.

With the loss of the final *-e* disappeared also the last remnant of concord between the adjective and its noun. For where Middle English indicated agreement in plural number and indicated the weak inflection of the adjective by means of the final *-e*, Modern English, through the loss of this inflection, lost also the grammatical distinctions, and uses now only one adjective form in all situations. The definite article, in which the invariant *the* replaced all other forms, had already in the Middle period developed as far as possible. The verb underwent the same changes in the loss of final syllables that other words experienced: thus the Old English infinitive *wēp-an* became Middle English *wep-en*, and this by the loss of the final syllable and the regular change in the radical vowel became Modern English *weep*.

As important as these changes due to inflectional loss, are those which were brought about by substitution. At the outset of the Middle English period there was a tendency for the many Old English noun declensions to be subsumed under two general types, strong and weak. The strong declension formed its plural by means of the *-es* inflection. The weak nouns, employing the *-en* inflection, tended more and more to move into the strong category, which included a greater number of nouns. The result was that where Chaucer wrote *treen*, 'trees,' *been*, 'bees,' *shoon*, 'shoes,' and so on with a great many other nouns, we now use the common *-s* ending for all plurals. The only exceptions to this rule (aside from a few words like *tooth*, *teeth*, which form their plurals by internal change) and the only survivals of the old weak inflection in Modern English are the words *ox-en*, plural of *ox*, *children*, and *brethren*, plurals of *child* and *brother*.

Substitution affected the genitive case, which frequently but not always indicates possession, in a remarkable way. The genitive ending *-es* in Old English was the mark of the genitive singular, masculine and neuter, of the noun. It then became a type form for all genitives, feminine as well as masculine and neuter, in the singular. The genitive plural inflection for all genders in Old English was *-a*, *-ena*, which in Middle English became *-e*, *-ene*. Had only the normal loss of unstressed vowels operated upon these forms, the genitive plural would have had no ending in Modern English. This is the case with such substandard forms as *forty mile*, *six year*, in which the noun is historically a genitive plural. In Standard English, however, the *-s* inflection became typical for all cases of the plural, thus rendering the genitive singular indistinguishable from the plural, and the genitive plural indistinguishable from all other cases of the plural.

In the course of time the apostrophe was adopted as a means of distinguishing the genitive, singular and plural, from other uses of the plural. It was placed before the -*s* in the singular (*stone's*) and after it in the plural (*stones'*), although the phonetic value of the word is the same in the genitive singular and all cases of the plural. This use of the apostrophe as a mechanical device to indicate the genitive is of comparatively late origin. It became established only at the end of the seventeenth and in the early eighteenth centuries as a result of the growing influence of printing and of printers' rules. It is of course a device for the eye and not for the ear.

Before the use of the apostrophe, however, another method of indicating the genitive had become fairly general in writing, the use of the pronoun *his* instead of the genitive ending -*s*, as in *God his wrath* for *God's wrath*. This pronoun *his* was never given its full stress in actual speech. Like the apostrophe it served merely as a visual symbol to indicate the genitive relation. In proof of this the remark of the Elizabethan versifier, Gabriel Harvey, the friend of Spenser, may be cited. Harvey is complaining that the English spelling of his day was misleading to the poet, because often words were spelled as dissyllables but pronounced as monosyllables, and continues thus: "But see what absurdities thys yl fauored Orthographye, or rather Pseudography, hathe engendred, and howe one errour still breedeth and begetteth an other. Haue wee not *Mooneth* for *Moonthe*, *sithence* for *since*, *whilest* for *whilste*, *phantasie* for *phansie*, *euen* for *evn*, *Diuel* for *Divl*, *God hys wrath* for *Goddes wrath*, and a thousande of the same stampe." [4]

Modern English has developed special forms of the genitive pronoun when it stands in absolute position, that is, when it is not immediately followed by the noun which it modifies. Thus we say, "This is my hat," or, in the archaic form, "This is thy hat"; but "This hat is mine, thine." In their origins the

---

[4] Gabriel Harvey, *Of Reformed Versifying*, written in 1579–1580, and reprinted in Smith, *Elizabethan Critical Essays*, I, 120. Notice in this passage how freely and inconsistently Harvey uses the final -*e*, e.g., *hathe, howe, moonthe, whilste, thousande, stampe*. Of course none of these final -*e*'s were pronounced. At the close of the Middle English period when the final -*e*'s had lost all phonetic value, they were often retained in spelling, but also often dropped, and even were indiscriminately added to the spelling of words to which they had never really belonged.

thine, mine forms of the possessive are direct survivals of the Old English genitives, *ðīn, mīn*. Formerly, that is, in the Middle English period, these full forms were retained before words beginning with a vowel sound, as they are still in Modern English poetry, e.g., "Mine eyes have seen the glory of the coming of the Lord"; but the abbreviated forms *my, thy*, tended to become general, especially before words beginning with a consonant. When special forms were required for the possessive in absolute position, the full forms *mine, thine*, were naturally chosen, and *my, thy, his, our*, and *your* became the only forms for the possessive in adjective position.

Moreover, the forms *his, her, our, your*, and *their*, in absolute position, also underwent a change. In Old English there were not two forms of these pronouns, the same form being used in both the adjective and absolute positions. In Middle English the unchanged forms continued to be used for some time, as in the Wycliffe-Purvey Bible, Luke vi, 20: *the kyngdom of God is youre*. But apparently a distinctive genitive ending for these absolute possessives was felt to be necessary, and thus two forms came into use. The first was made by adding the regular *-s* genitive ending, as the type indication of the possessive relation, giving *ours, yours*, and of course *his*, which needed no addition. But by analogy to the *mine, thine* forms, possessives with an *-n* ending were formed, giving *mine, thine, ourn, yourn, theirn*, etc. Examples of this second kind of formation are found in the Wycliffe-Purvey Bible, as in Mark xii, 7: *the eritage schal be ourun*; Matthew v, 3: *the kyngdom of hevenes is herne*. This form of the absolute possessive persists in Modern English only in substandard speech, the standard or conventional use having become *yours, hers, theirs*, etc.[5]

---

[5] Some of the dialects of England have carried this method of possessive formation over into the nominative, e.g., *shisn*, composed of the nominative *she*, to which are added first the possessive *-s*, and then the absolute possessive *-n* endings. See Wright, *English Dialect Grammar*, p. 275. The *Oxford English Dictionary* cites the following example from the Hampshire dialect: "Let thee and I go our own waay, and we'll let she go shisn." Another analogical formation, sometimes heard in the language of children, is the possessive *mies* for *my*; *mies* is to *my*, as *yours, theirs* are to *your, their*.

Substitution affected also the forms of the personal pronouns in an interesting way. In the first person, the correspondence between Modern English and the earlier periods is close, Modern English *I, mine, me,* and *we, our, us,* being the direct representation of Old English *ic, mīn, mē,* and *wē, ūre, ūs.* In the second person, however, the difference is great. This change started with the nominative plural, Old English *gē,* which gave our Biblical English *ye,* as in *What went ye out for to see?* For this *ye,* however, was early substituted the form *you,* which was the form for the dative and accusative, derived from Old English *ēow.* The possessive form was also *your* from *ēower,* and the preponderance of the spellings *you, you-r* may well have led to its substitution in the nominative, giving *you.*

In the singular old forms *ðū, ðīn, ðē* gave regularly our Biblical English *thou, thine, thee.* In the late Middle English period, however, the *thou, thine, thee* forms tended to be given up for the *you, your, you* forms of the plural. The substitution was brought about through the influence of the French language, in which the plural form of the pronoun was the polite form, even in addressing a single individual, a convention which apparently grew out of the use of the plural as a pronoun of respect in fourth-century Latin. The singular pronoun was used only in familiar address, in the conversation of intimate friends or the members of a family. Both forms of the singular have persisted to modern times, but the forms *thou, thine, thee* are now used only in poetry and elevated discourse; the real singular is now *you, your, you.* In some dialects, especially in England, the *thou, thine, thee* forms also persist in popular spoken use.

In the earlier Modern English period, in the time of Shakespeare, and as late as the early eighteenth century, the two forms *thou* and *you* existed in good English side by side. They could be and were employed in current colloquial speech with good effect. The form *thou* was used in the conversation of friends, or of a husband and wife, the transition to *you* indicating a slightly more formal tone in conversation. Thus, for example, in the comedies of Etherege and Vanbrugh, two men friends or two women friends (but not a man and a woman, unless they are husband and wife), usually address each other as *thou*, but to others they are *you*. In Etherege's *She Would if She Could*, Sir Frederick, a boisterous swashbuckler, noisy and familiar, uses *thou* to Mrs. Rich, the effect being one of a sort of friendly, good-natured impertinence, Mrs. Rich being his only friend and therefore properly to be addressed by *you*.

In speaking to servants and those of inferior social rank, and in giving orders, *thou* was also the form used. It was likewise used in contemptuous language, as in Sir Toby's advice to Sir Andrew Aguecheek, "If thou thou'st him some thrice, it shall not be amiss" (*Twelfth Night*, III, 2). All this is what we should expect, for the language of familiar intercourse, of friendship, and of contempt is all on somewhat the same plane—that is, it is all the language of strongly colloquial and familiar color.

It is interesting to observe that the forms *thou*, *thine*, and *thee* have been at all periods the ones used in prayer and generally in elevated discourse; this is true even of those periods in which *thou* is used as a mark of familiarity or of contempt. The polite forms *you*, *your*, *you* have never been used in addressing the Deity, probably, first of all because there was originally a feeling of incongruity in using what was fashionable or courtly language for this purpose. Now, of course, *you* is no longer courtly or fashionable, but too familiar to be used for lofty purposes. Moreover the language of poetry and prayer is always strongly traditional and conservative; it would consequently tend to preserve the old historical usage of the English tongue. Once the use of *thou* was fixed in sacred language, as in the prayer book and the English translation of the Bible, it would naturally be very influential in maintaining that usage through later periods.

This feeling for *thou* as the only proper form to be used in addressing the Deity is well brought out in a passage of a sixteenth-century work, *A Dialogue against the Feuer Pestilence*, printed in

1564.[6] A beggar, Mendicus, appears at a door and recites part of the Lord's Prayer as follows: "Our father whiche art in heauen, hallowed be your name, your kyngdom come, your will be dooen in yearth as it is in heauen," etc. For this he is ridiculed by Civis and Uxor, the gentlemen from whom he is soliciting alms, one of whom remarks, "Me thinke I doe heare a good manerly Beggar at the doore, and well brought up. How reuerently he saieth his Pater Noster! he thous not God, but you[s] him."

The contradiction inherent in the plural form *you* as a word of address to a single person disturbed greatly the peace of mind of the founders of the Society of Friends or Quakers. They observed that the Bible, meaning of course the English translation, always used *thou* to one and *you* to many. They thought it not fitting, therefore, that men should use a more dignified form of expression in addressing each other than they used in addressing the Lord. Moreover *you* as a word of address to a single person was not consistent with the traditional grammatical conception of *you* as a plural, and therefore on that score also its use as singular was wrong.

⟩ This is just the kind of linguistic crotchet which we might expect to stick in the mind of a half-educated person like George Fox, the founder of the Society of Friends; and it is not surprising to see him come forth in defense of *Thou* to *One* and *You* to *Many*, to use his own battle-cry. He published a work called "*A Battle-Door*[7] *for Teachers and Professors to learn Singular and Plural;* You *to* Many, and Thou *to* One: *Singular* One, Thou; *Plural* Many, You," which was printed in London, for "Robert Wilson and to be sold at his Shop at the Signe of the Black-spread-Eagle and Wind-mil in Martins le Grand, 1660."

In this pamphlet Fox takes the teachers and professors of his

---

[6] Early English Text Society, Extra Series, Vol. LII, p. 5.

[7] A battle-door, as the word is used here, means a primer. Literally the word means a wooden bat, shaped somewhat like a tennis racket. But it is used in this metaphorical sense because the early primer, or horn-book, consisted of a cardboard with the ABC, etc., on it, surrounded by a wooden rim with a handle, and covered with a transparent piece of horn, the whole being shaped somewhat like a flat bat or racket.

day to task in the following fashion: "Do not they speak false English, false Latine, false Greek, false Hebrew, false Caldee, false Syriack, and Arabick, false Dutch, false French; and false to the other Tongues, that followes here in this Book, that doth not speak *thou* to *one*, what ever he be, Father, Mother, King, or Judge; is he not a Novice and Unmannerly, and an Ideot and a Fool, that speaks *You* to *one*, which is not to be spoken to a *singular*, but to *many*? O Vulgar Professors and Teachers, that speaks Plural when they should Singular, *lapis*, a stone, *lapides*, stones, that is, more than one. Come you Priests and Professors, have you not learnt your Accidence?"[8]

This avoidance of *you* as a pronoun of address in the singular has persisted to this day among the Friends. But the old, and historically correct, form *thou* as nominative has been given up for the type form, *thee*, used for both nominative and objective, as in "Thee will have to get thee another coat." In thus using the objective *thee* as the type form, the Friends have done exactly what the standard language has done, since the nominative here is historically *ye* and the objective is *you*, from Old English *gē* and *ēow*, the two forms being simplified under one, the objective form *you*.

Substitution also contributed significantly to the simplification of the Modern English verb system. The limiting of the principal parts by reducing the past tenses to a single form has already been mentioned. The personal inflections have also been simplified, especially in the present tense. Here, through the combined influence of inflectional leveling and loss, and of substitution, working through several dialects of the Middle English period, all forms have been reduced to a single type, e.g. (*I, you, we, you, they*) *sing*, with the exception of the third singular, (*he*) *sings*, which has an inflectional *-s*. The elevated language has been more conservative, preserving the special forms for the singular (*I*) *sing*, (*thou*) *singest*, (*he*) *singeth*, but the plural is the same in both elevated and normal style.

[8] Fox, *A Battle-Door for Teachers*, pp. 2–3.

6 ⊠ Conclusions

The general effect of inflectional loss and substitution has been to change to a considerable extent the structure of the English language. From a language in which words representing at least the major parts of speech tended to be united by agreement in grammatical form, that is to say a synthetic language, English has evolved into a language in which the words, so far as formal agreement goes, are almost altogether free and independent. The language has developed type forms which can stand in virtually any position, their relationships being indicated largely by the order of the words as they are put together rather than by inflectional elements.

This kind of language is called analytic, because in its structure it is made up of independent units which may easily be detached from each other. In the synthetic structure, the language binds the word group into a whole in which all the words are mutually dependent for their form on their place in the group. A simple illustration will help to clarify the difference. The adjective *old* in our modern analytic language may modify any noun of any gender, number, or case. It is a wholly free, universal word-unit. In a synthetic stage of the language, however, as in Old English, the adjective *old* had to take on various forms according to the gender, number, and case of the noun, and according as it was inflected strong or weak. Thus the Modern English phrases *the old man* and *the old men* change only the word *man*, the other words being type forms that modify the plural as well as the singular. In Old English, however, we should have to change all three words, *sē ealda man* for the singular, and *þā ealdan menn* for the plural in the nominative case alone, to say nothing of a series of different modifications for the other cases.

It will be seen from this example that the modern analytic language has in many respects gained in economy over the older synthetic language, at the expense, perhaps, of a certain kind of flexibility. By the use of type forms, the modern language avoids a great deal of repetition. Thus in the two Modern English phrases cited in the preceding paragraph, the ideas of singular and plural are each expressed once by *man* and *men*, and need not, so far as power of conveying thought is concerned, be expressed by the modifying words. But in Old English not only does *man* express the singular idea, but it is expressed also by the inflections in *sē* and *ealda*; and in the case of the plural, the idea of plurality is indicated three times as well, once by *men*, once by *ealdan*, and once by *þā*.

Although there are some advantages to a degree of redundancy in a language, it must be conceded in this instance that little is gained by the threefold repetition of the idea of plurality. Certainly Modern English is much the simpler in allowing it to be assumed that when one uses the noun *men*, adjectives which limit this noun are plural also. In the same way the synthetic language has to repeat the idea of gender and of case with each new modifying word, whereas in Modern English this repetition is likewise avoided by the use of type forms for all genders and cases.

One further illustration of the change from synthetic to analytic structure may be cited, the example being taken from Modern English and Latin, the latter a more highly inflectional, and therefore more synthetic, language than any recorded form of English that we have. The English relative pronoun *who* is a type form, expressing merely the interrogative idea without limitation of gender or number. In Latin, however, the English sentence *Who did it?* has not one but four equivalents: *Quis hoc fecit?* the pronoun being the singular masculine interrogative and the verb singular as well; *Quae hoc fecit?* the pronoun being the singular feminine; *Qui hoc fecerunt?* the plural masculine and corresponding plural verb; and *Quae hoc fecerunt?* the pronoun being ambiguous as to number but the verb signalling plurality.

The person who utters such a sentence is requesting an identification and presumably does not know what the answer is going to be. Therefore he may often be unaware of the number of persons involved or of their sex. Consequently, it seems some-what more convenient to have a general type form for the question than to be compelled to make it specific as to gender and number as the Latin speaker had to do. To us, at least, the English analytic form of expression answers more exactly to the logic of the situation.[9]

The question naturally arises whether Modern English has carried the process of simplification and regularization as far as it can, and if not, whether it is likely to carry it further. As to the first half of the question, it is obvious that there is room for further simplification in the English language.

Such simplifying substitutions are indeed carried out in strata of the language which do not feel the restraining force of the conventional and standard speech. We have all observed that children strive to substitute the type plural in -*s* for those few irregular plurals that survive in English, giving thus *foots, tooths,* for *feet, teeth,* etc. It is a general tendency with children also to substitute the regular weak forms for all the irregular or strong forms of the verb, giving *grow, growed, growed,* for *grow, grew, grown*; *drive, drived, drived,* for *drive, drove, driven,* etc. These usages of child language are often paralleled by usages of uneducated adults, since children and the uneducated are on the same plane so far as the restraining power of rule or convention in language is concerned. Thus the very common tendency of the uneducated to use only one form for the past tense and past participle of the verb, as in *He done it,* and *I seed* (or *seen*) *him,* is precisely this process of type substitution.

Logically, or even psychologically, there is no reason why we should have more than two principal parts in the verb, one for present (or more accurately non-past) and one for past time: *I do,* and *I did,* or *done, I see,* and *I saw, seed,* or *seen,* with which the auxiliaries can then build up the various compound tenses and

---

[9] For the expression of an earlier view, which held that analytic languages were generally superior to synthetic, see Jespersen, *Progress in Language,* pp. 30–31. Linguists today are inclined to be somewhat more relativistic in their judgments.

forms. The regular verbs, like *walk, walked, walked*, and many of the irregular have had only two principal parts for centuries. The substitutions of *seed* for *saw* and *done* for *did* are exactly similar in kind to other substitutions which took place in earlier periods, and which have been accepted into the standard language. Thus the verb *cling, clung, clung*, historically should have three parts, *cling, clang, clung*, like *sing, sang, sung*; *ring, rang, rung*, etc. So also the verb *shine, shone, shone* is derived from the Old English verb *scīnan, scān, scinon, scinen*, which should have given regularly *shine, shone, shinnen*, like *ride, rode, ridden*; *write, wrote, written*, and numerous other verbs. Instead, however, it has substituted a type form for the past tenses, using for this purpose the regular form of the preterit singular.

But the question whether or not Modern English will carry out further these simplifications by type substitution is one which does not depend upon precedent or to any considerable extent upon the reasonableness and advantage of such changes. The English language of today has become relatively fixed by long use, to some degree by the systematic statements of it which have been made by the grammarians and rhetoricians, and by the conventionalizing tendencies which have accompanied the ease and spread of communication characteristic of most European cultures. As a result, changes in such obvious features of the language as inflection find it extremely hard to make their way into good use. To the extent that they continue in use, the popular dialects will continue to grow and develop in a freer and less trammeled way. The cultivated speech, on the other hand, though no less subject to continuous change, is more likely to change in subtler ways than by the direct substitution of one form for another.

5

ENGLISH SOUNDS

1 ◪ The Study of English Sounds

Although it did not develop until fairly late in the nineteenth century, the study of sounds, or phonetics, to give the subject its technical name, has been most productive of valuable results. The reconstruction of the sounds of past periods has made the science of etymology possible, and has been one of the chief means of determining the relationships of languages. Grimm's Law, for example, is a statement of a series of phonetic correspondences. The history of the sounds of a particular language often reveals patterns of phonetic development.

The study of contemporary sounds also is helpful in various ways. It is of great practical value to all who have anything to do with foreign languages, or with the earlier stages of their own language. There is no quicker or more certain way of mastering an unfamiliar sound than by observing by just what positions and movements of the vocal organs it is made, and then by repeating these positions and movements for one's self. Another reason for the study of the sounds of contemporary speech is based on the general principle that we all owe it to ourselves to be aware of what we do.

It might seem that it could be taken for granted that everyone naturally knew just how his speech sounded, without giving any special attention to the matter. Experiment and observation have shown that this is far from being true. One who has not given considerable attention to the study of speech sounds is not likely to hear his own speech accurately and justly. Time and again it has been shown that a person thinks he says one thing when actually the sound which he utters is quite different. As a general rule, when one's speech is recorded on disc or tape, it is not recognized and may often be disclaimed by the person who uttered it.

The practical bearing of all this is obvious. Pronunciation and grammar are without doubt the most generally applied and, to a degree, the simplest and most effective tests of education and cultivation. George Bernard Shaw made use of this principle in his play *Pygmalion,* better known perhaps in its musical transfiguration, *My Fair Lady.* As Oliver Wendell Homes, Sr., wrote in *The Autocrat of the Breakfast Table,* "a movement or a phrase often tells you all you want to know about a person." No doubt there is danger of drawing too sweeping inferences from the speech of others, a danger to which most of us are liable. Nevertheless, in the end speech remains the surest and most convenient index of the social habits and the intellectual life of the person who uses it.

It behooves all, therefore, to take cognizance of their speech, especially of the subtle and elusive matter of pronunciation. Every person owes it to himself to know what the facts of his pronunciation are and how these facts impress other persons with whom he is thrown into contact. When he has a just appreciation of all these facts, he can then order his conduct as seems wisest and best to him. Before we can proceed, however, to the intelligent discussion of historical sound changes or of specific questions of contemporary pronunciation, it will be necessary first to describe briefly the organs of speech and the manner of sound production. In addition, we must settle upon a terminology and a mode of representation by means of which the various sounds may be accurately designated and distinguished.

85

2 ▨ The Production of English Sounds

Sound, so far as we are concerned with it in the study of language, may be defined as the sensation of hearing produced by the modifications of a column of air in its passage from the lungs through the organs of speech. The specific character of the sound varies as the column of air is variously modified by the different articulatory organs through which it passes. The production of speech sound, therefore, is essentially not different from the production of musical sound in a wind instrument, as a horn or a clarinet.

Phonetics, however, which is the study of the sounds of language, is not concerned with all the sounds which the human organs of speech are capable of producing, such as shrieks, cries, groans, and so forth. Generally it is restricted to a consideration of articulate sounds, namely those sounds which are joined together, or articulated, for the formation of syllables, then of words, phrases, or sentences. Moreover, a language, English for example, does not use all the possible articulate sounds which the voice can produce, but makes a selection from a potentially much larger number, which becomes then the sound material of the language.

Different languages make a choice of different sounds. We have sounds in English which are not used in French and German; French and German, on the other hand, have sounds which we do not use in English. Yet we know from the fact that Englishmen learn French and German, and Frenchmen and Germans learn English, that everyone, with practice, is equally capable of producing all the sounds of the various languages. Each particular language, therefore, makes what seems to be an arbitrary choice of a certain number of possible sounds. Consequently, we may define English phonetics as the study of the sounds used in English utterances.

The organs mainly concerned in the production of speech sound are the lungs; the larynx, in which are the glottis and the vocal folds; the cavity of the mouth, in which the tongue, the palate, the lips and the teeth are important modifiers of sound; and the cavity of the nose. The lungs are concerned with the production of sound only in that they send forth the column of air which later is modified by the more special organs of voice so as to produce sound. When one produces sound by playing a wind instrument, the column of air passes unmodified by the speech organs into the more distant modifying agent, the horn or flute or whatever the instrument may be. Under normal conditions it is only the expiratory column of air that is used in the production of speech sound, the inspired or drawn-in air being productive of sound only in the case of sighing and a few interjections.

The larynx, or voice box, is the first place at which the air from the lungs on its passage outward may meet with any obstruction. The larynx is really a part of the windpipe, or trachea, and leads from the rear end of the opening of the nose and mouth to the lungs. From the back of the mouth a second tube, the gullet, or esophagus, leads into the stomach. The common space at the back of the mouth from which these two canals branch is called the pharynx. The entrance to the trachea is provided with a valve or lid, called the epiglottis, which can be lowered in the act of swallowing so as to prevent food from passing down the trachea. When for any reason the epiglottis fails to work, as it does sometimes, and portions of food or water make their way into the trachea, we perform the operation popularly known as "swallowing the wrong way."

The larynx itself is a circular, or nearly circular, and tubular combination of cartilages and muscles. The largest of these cartilages, the thyroid or shield-like cartilage, forms the main structure of the larynx. It can be felt from the outside of the throat and is commonly known as the Adam's apple. Another important cartilage is the cricoid, or ring cartilage, which forms the base of the voice box or larynx, and to which the vocal folds are attached. The muscles of the larynx pass from one cartilage to the other and have as their chief function the contraction and loosening of the vocal folds.

The folds are two in number, and they are attached to the base of the larynx, passing approximately over the middle of the opening of the larynx. They are not to be thought of as cords like violin strings, as the popular term *vocal cords* suggests, for one side of each is completely attached to the sides of the voice box. The vibrating part is only the free outer edge of each, which, as has been stated, can be tightened or loosened by the aid of certain muscles.

The space between the two outer edges of the vocal folds, which varies of course in width according to the tension of the folds, is called the glottal rift, or *rima glottialis*. When the edges of the folds are relaxed, allowing a wide rift between them, the breath from the lungs passes through this space without setting the folds in vibration; consequently, no sound is produced *in the larynx*. This last qualification is important, because the air from the lungs may still meet with some obstruction from the organs of the mouth or nose, in which case sound would be produced. If it does not, it passes out of the nose or mouth almost noiselessly, and the process is simply that of breathing.

When the rift is narrowed, however, by the stretching of the vocal folds, the passage of the air makes the folds vibrate, and the sound which we call *voice* is produced. It should be clearly understood that the word *voice* is used here in a restricted and special sense. It does not mean any sound produced by the organs of speech, but only those sounds in the production of which the vocal folds are set in vibration. Such sounds are called voiced *sounds*; others are *voiceless*. In whispering, voiceless sounds are produced in the same way as when they are given their full resonance. In the whispering of voiced sounds, however, the vocal folds do not vibrate, or vibrate only slightly, although they are made tense, and the glottal rift is accordingly narrowed, as in the production of the full-voiced sounds.

We may now pass to those organs above the larynx which are

important for the production of speech sound. They are the pharynx, the cavity of the mouth, and the cavity of the nose. Together, these three spaces are known as the *resonance chamber*. They are of the greatest importance in the production of sound, because no column of air can proceed from the lungs which is not modified in some way by the resonance chamber. In fact, all voice as it comes from the vocal folds would be the same except for differences in loudness and softness; it is the resonance chamber which determines the specific value of a sound as one vowel rather than another. By changing the shape of the resonance chamber, the speaker gets different vowel effects, just as the musician gets different tone effects from a tuba and a cornet, because the two instruments have resonance chambers of different shapes and sizes. After the breath from the lungs has passed through the larynx and into the pharynx, it may then enter the cavity of the mouth, or of the nose, or both together. We shall consider, first, the cavity of the mouth, and second, the nasal cavity.

The roof of the mouth is divided into two parts, the soft palate, or velum, at the back part of the mouth, and the hard palate at the front part. The hard palate is fixed and motionless, except as it moves with the motion of the jaws. But the velum (a Latin name meaning 'veil') may be raised or lowered. When it is raised, it closes the entrance to the nasal cavity; when lowered it permits the air from the lungs to pass out equally through the nose and the mouth. Within the mouth the most important of the movable muscles is the tongue, consisting of the tip, the blade, the front (really the center portion) and the back. Beside the palate and tongue, the teeth, gums, and lips are also used in the production of sounds.

The nasal cavity or passage is a membrane-lined channel with no movable or muscular parts. It leads out from the pharynx and is narrower at both ends than at the middle, thus forming a good resonance chamber. The passage is divided in the nose by a septum or partition, into a right and left portion. As has been stated, the entrance to the nasal passage can be closed by raising the velum, in which case all breath passes out through the mouth. "Talking through the nose" is a popular misconception of the facts. The truth is that when one "talks through the nose," one doesn't talk through the nose as one does under normal conditions. Instead, the velum is raised, or the entrance to the nasal passage is closed because of swelling due to a cold or some other disturbance of normal conditions. The unpleasant effect which results is due to the lack of that resonance which the sound should have received by passing through the nasal chamber. The difference between the closed and the open nasal passage may easily be observed by first imitating the speech of one suffering from a cold and then speaking with the full quality of sound which characterizes the ordinary use of the voice.

It is a general principle that the more resonance sounds are given, the more pleasing they are likely to be. Insufficient resonance, either in the mouth or nose, or both, is likely to give a flat, unmusical quality to the sounds thus produced.

3 ◙ Voiced and Voiceless Sounds

Having described the main organs of speech, we may proceed now to some account of the modifications of sound produced by these various organs. The first important distinction is that between voiced and voiceless sounds. Voiced sounds (also called sonant sounds) are those in the production of which the vocal folds are set in vibration. Vowels, for example, are all voiced; without exception they are produced by the vibration of the vocal folds. The differences between vowels are caused by the modifications of the sound produced by these vibrations through changing the configuration of the resonance chamber. Some consonants are voiced; others are voiceless. Examples of voiced consonants are *g* in *go*, *b* in *boy*, *v* in *veil*, *th* in *then*, *g* in *George*.

In the production of voiceless sounds, the vocal folds are not set in vibration, but the sound is produced through modification of the column of air by the various organs of speech, teeth, tongue, and lips, after it has passed through the rift of the glottis without moving the vocal folds. Examples of voiceless consonants are *p* in *pay*, *t* in *tin*, *k(c)* in *king, can, f* in *leaf, s(c)* in *sauce*. By placing the finger on the Adam's apple one can with a little practice, easily feel the vibration of the voice box in the production of voiced sounds, and can thus distinguish sounds which are voiced from those which are not, thus confirming the testimony of the ears.

In attempting to classify sounds as to whether they are voiceless or voiced, one must be careful to distinguish between the sound of just the consonant and the name which we give to the letter of the alphabet which usually represents that consonant. The name of the letter *t*, for example, consists of the voiceless consonant *t* followed by a vowel which is the same as the vowel in *tea, he, see*. The name of the letter *s* consists of the vowel of *bet, let, met*, followed by the voiceless consonant *s*. In forming or pronouncing consonants for the purpose of observing or classifying them, always distinguish between the consonant and any accompanying vowel.

4 ▨ Vowels and Consonants

When the passages through the mouth and through the nose are left open, so that the air passing through the larynx and there setting the vocal folds in vibration may continue without further obstruction through these passages to the outer air, a vowel sound is produced. The passage is widest open in pronouncing such vowels as *a* in *father* or *o* in *loss*. It is variously modified in pronouncing the other vowels, but at no time is it completely closed. It comes nearest to being so in pronouncing the vowel *ee* in *seen, keen*, etc. It should be noticed that vowels can be lengthened indefinitely in pronunciation, the only limit being the amount of breath one has at one's disposal.

When the column of air from the lungs, as it approaches the outer air is (a) completely stopped, or (b) permitted to escape

91

only through a fairly narrow aperture, producing friction rather than resonance, the sound produced is a consonant.

In the first case, when the column of air is completely stopped and then suddenly released, the consonant produced is called a stop or plosive, both names being descriptive of the formation of these sounds. Examples of stop or plosive consonants are *p, t, k, b, d, g*.

In the second instance, when the column of air is only partly stopped in its escape to the outer air and can in effect go on as long as the breath holds out, the consonant so produced is called a continuant. Continuants are of various kinds, depending upon the nature of the interference with the breath stream caused by different parts of the speech organs. 1. When the breath stream is hindered by the various articulators in such a fashion that a noticeable friction-like quality ensues, the sounds are called fricatives, as, for example, *v* in *vat, s* (*z*) in *lose, maze, th* in *father*, all voiced; and *f* in *fat, s* in *say, th* in *thin, sh* in *mesh*, all voiceless. 2. What appears to be a combination of a stop and a fricative, or considered in another fashion, a slow-opening stop, is called an affricate. English has but two of these: *ch* in *cheese* and *j* (*g*) in *join, gem*. 3. The nasal sounds are frictionless continuants, in which the mouth passage is obstructed and the breath stream passes through the nose; the examples for English are *m, n*, and *ng* as in *ring*. 4. Classified separately as a lateral continuant is the sound *l*, so-called because the breath stream is forced over the sides of the tongue.

Finally there is a class of consonants, neither stop nor continuant, in which the articulating organs shift from a fixed starting point to the position required by the next sound. Examples are *y* as in *yet, w* as in *wet, r* as in *race*.

5 ⊠ Classification of Consonants

Besides the classification of consonants as voiced and voiceless, oral and nasal, stop, continuant, or affricate, consonants are further classified and named according to the part of the mouth passage which is chiefly concerned in their production. Considered from this point of view, the English consonants fall into the following categories:

1. BILABIAL OR LIP CONSONANTS. These include the stops *p* and *b* and the nasal continuant *m*, in all of which both lips are instrumental in forming the sound.

2. LABIODENTALS OR LIP-TEETH CONSONANTS. In making the sounds *f* and *v* the breath stream escapes between the upper front teeth and the lower lip.

3. INTERDENTAL CONSONANTS. These are represented in English by the sounds of *th* in *thin* and *then* respectively. The breath stream escapes through an aperture formed by the tip of the tongue protruding slightly between the teeth.

4. ALVEOLAR CONSONANTS. Examples are *t*, *d*, *s*, *z*, *l*, and *n*. They take their name from the Latin *alveolus*, 'small hollow,' which came to be applied to the gum ridge, just back of the upper front teeth, the point where the tongue makes contact in forming them. They are sometimes incorrectly classified as dental consonants, on the supposition that in forming them, the tongue is placed against the upper front teeth. This is not the case in the normal English articulation of these sounds. The French *t* and *d* are real dentals, the tongue being pressed firmly against the upper teeth in producing them.

5. ALVEOLO-PALATAL CONSONANTS. These include the fricatives *sh* in *sheen*, *z* (sometimes spelled *s*) in *azure*, *pleasure*, and the affricates *ch* as in *chin* and *dg* as in *ridge*. The point of contact or near contact with the tongue is an area which extends from the alveolar ridge to the hard palate.

6. PALATAL AND VELAR CONSONANTS. The palate is the name for the hard portion of the roof of the mouth. The soft part of the roof of the mouth, back of the palate, is called the *velum*, from the Latin for 'veil.' Included in this group are the stops *k* and *g* and the nasal *ng* as in *sing*. Note carefully the point of contact for the initial sounds of *keen* and *geese* and the final sound of *sing* contrasted with the point of contact for *cold*, *gold*, and *song*. The first three are palatals; the second three are velars.

Certain of the consonant sounds must be considered somewhat outside of the classes which have just been defined. The glides have already been described as deriving their characteristic qualities by shifting from a fixed starting point to whatever position is required to produce the following sound. Thus, in forming *w* the lips are rounded and the tongue is high in the back part of the mouth at the beginning of the sound. As the transition is made to the following vowel, the lips open and the tongue assumes a position that is lower and somewhat more forced. The sound of *y* in words like *yet* or *you* begins with the tongue high and concentrated in the front of the mouth. In proceeding to the following sound, the tongue drops if the following sound is a front vowel and retracts if a back vowel follows. Initial *r* as in *rat, roll* is also a glide. At the beginning of the sound the tongue is in a retroflex position, curved upward with the tip close to the palate. As the sound continues, the tongue straightens out, assuming the position required for the following vowel. Thus, *w* is a lip glide; *y* and initial *r* are tongue glides.

In producing the sound of *h* in *have, hate, hole*, the jaw, tongue, and lips assume the position required for the following vowel; the distinctive quality of the consonant comes as a result of a breath impulse through the open vocal folds. The sound of *wh*, which might be written more accurately *hw* begins with an impulse of the breath with the lips and tongue in a position for *w*. As the sound proceeds, the breath impulse subsides, but not before the lip glide begins.

In fully describing or classifying a consonant, there are three things to be noticed: first, whether it is voiced or voiceless; second, the manner of articulation, that is whether it is a stop, continuant, affricate, or glide; third, what part or parts of the mouth passage is chiefly involved in its formation, The table on p. 102 is designed to identify the English consonants from these three points of view.

6 ◨ Classification of Vowels

The vowels lend themselves somewhat less easily to description and classification than the consonants because their particular quality is determined by the shape of the oral cavity serving as a resonance chamber, whereas the consonants derive their characteristic features by the modification of the breath stream at a particular point, which may be specifically stated. In forming the resonance chamber the positions and movements of the organs of voice are less easily observed than they are in the production of consonants. Moreover, it is evident that three of the criteria which have been recognized for the description and classification of consonants are not likely to be helpful in dealing with the vowels, since all of the vowels are voiced, they are all continuants, and in English at least, they are all oral.

In general, however, the shape and nature of the resonance chamber may be described in terms of three factors: the height of the jaw, the position of the tongue, and the configuration of the lips. If the vowels of the three words *keep*, *cape*, and *cap* are pronounced in that order, it will be seen that the jaw drops slightly as the sequence progresses. The same is true of the series *coop*, *cope*, *cop*. This suggests height as an initial criterion, and in terms of the two series which have just been given, we find it convenient to speak of high, mid, and low vowels. The vowels of *keep* and *coop* are high; those of *cape* and *cope* are mid; those of *cap* and *cop* are low.

If one next compares the position of the tongue in pronouncing *keep* and *coop*, he will notice that it is concentrated or bunched toward the front of the mouth in pronouncing the first, and that the bunching or concentration is toward the back for the second. The same is true for the pair of low vowels *cap* and *cop*. In a series such as *cape*, *cup*, *cope* there are three areas of concentration, one at the front for *cape*, one at the back for *cope*, and a more or less central position for *cup*. Just as we speak of *high*, *mid*, and *low* in terms of height, so we recognize *front*, *central*, and *back* as categories of tongue position. Thus the vowel of *coop* would be classified as a high back vowel; that of *cap* as a low front vowel.

A comparison of the configuration of the lips in pronouncing *keep* and *coop* will show that whereas the lips are spread in the first instance, they are rounded in the second. This is also true of *cape* and *cup* as contrasted with the lip configuration for *cope*. Thus we speak of rounded and unrounded vowels. We can now classify the

95

vowel of *keep* as high front unround; that of *cope* as mid back round. In English only certain of the back vowels are rounded; the front vowels are consistently unround. In French and German, however, there are rounded as well as unround front vowels: note the sounds of *lune* in French and *grün* in German.

Although the foregoing classification takes us a long way toward a workable description of the vowels of English, it does not offer a complete solution. The vowels of *beet* and *bit*, for example, are both high, front, and unround; those of *bait* and *bet* are both mid, front, and unround; those of *food* and *foot* are both high, back, and round. We still need a consistent method of distinguishing between such pairs. This is to be found in the condition of the tongue muscles. In *beet*, *bait*, and *food* the tongue muscles are tense; the tension can be felt by placing the fingers behind the chin, underneath the jaw. In *bit*, *bet*, and *foot* they are lax. We now have a fourth criterion. The vowel of *bit* is accordingly classified as high front unround lax; that of *food* as high back round tense. The diagram on p. 102 will help to identify the English vowels in terms of these characteristics.

A final distinction which should be observed is that between simple vowels and diphthongs. As its name indicates, a simple vowel consists of only one vowel sound; a diphthong is a double sound which begins with one vowel quality and shades off at the end into another. The vowels of *note*, of *fate*, of *food* are all simple, relatively speaking; it is possible at times to hear a slight off-glide at the end. Words like *house* and *now*, on the other hand, begin with the sound of *a* in *father* and end with the sound of *u*, giving the combination *au* (so spelled in German *haus*, *laut*, etc.). The other English diphthongs are the vowel of *try*, *buy*, *ride*, composed of $a+i$, equivalent therefore to *ai*; the diphthong $o+i$, that is *oi*, as exemplified in *boil*, *boy*, *coin*; and the combination $i+u$ as it occurs in *few*, *view*, and *beauty*.

It should be noted that simple vowels are sometimes written with two letters, as for example, the simple vowel in *great*, *pair*, *lead*, *pay*, *boat*, *through*, and many others. On the other hand, diphthongs are often written with one letter, as in *ride, try, mule,* etc. One should always observe the sound and not the spelling in determining whether the sound in question is a simple vowel or diphthong.

7 ⬚ Alphabet and Sounds

The symbols or letters of which our alphabet is composed are, it is obvious, quite conventional and arbitrary. There is no inherent reason why the symbol T, with its variant forms t and $\mathcal{T}$, or the symbol D, with its other forms d and $\mathcal{D}$, should stand each for its own sound. As far as the appropriateness of the symbols to the sounds goes, they might be interchanged without loss. Originally alphabetic symbols may have had some peculiar appropriateness to the sounds which they represented, either as a sort of "visible speech," indicating the position of one or another of the vocal organs by the shape of the symbol, or as picture writing, like the hieroglyphics of the Egyptians, indicating objects which bore definite relations to the various sounds. The English alphabet, however, has long since passed out of any such stage of development. It is now a set of intrinsically meaningless symbols to which specific values have become arbitrarily attached.

It is also obvious that the number of distinctive sounds in the English language is greater than the number of symbols available for representing them. At a conservative estimate, English has at least forty clearly distinguishable sounds; the number of symbols in the alphabet is twenty-six. Since the language has not at its command a sufficient number of characters to represent all its sounds, it is driven to use the same symbol for different sounds, as, for example, the vowel *a* in the words *hat, hate, father, any, ball, about.* The conventional symbols of the alphabet, it is thus seen, may vary as to their significance within certain pretty wide limits.

If we turn now to the sounds of the language themselves, we shall find them in many ways very imperfectly and inconsistently represented. Thus we may have a simple sound represented by

97

two symbols, as the vowel *oa* of *road*, or the consonant *th* of *thing*. Or the same sound may be represented by several different symbols or groups of symbols, as, for example, the sound of *s* (*c*) in *race* and *erase*; or of *k* in *call, king, quell, shock, box*; or the vowel sound which appears in the words *late, pay, great, fail, veil, they, fete*. Or the same group of letters may represent such various values as *ough* in *bough, through, thought, cough, hiccough, enough*. Letters are frequently used, also, without any value: the so-called silent letters, like the *e* of *ride*, the *c* of *scissors*, the *k* of *knife*, the *s* of *island, aisle*, the *w* of *write*, the *g* of *foreign, sovereign*.

In the light of facts such as these, we can understand what people mean when they say that, "English is not a phonetic language." On its face, the statement is nonsensical. Every language that is spoken, that is to say every living language, is phonetic. It conveys meaning through the medium of a system of sounds. What such a statement is intended to convey is the fact that the writing system of English represents the sounds of the language in an imperfect and inconsistent manner.

A wholly consistent writing system would be one in which every sound had its appropriate symbol, and no symbol had more than its single value. Needless to say, neither English nor any other language ever in practical use has had a writing system which met these requirements. Writing systems vary in the degree of consistency and completeness with which they represent the sounds of their language. The earlier periods of English were much closer to the ideal than is the current form of the language.

Of the modern European languages, Italian and Spanish are closest to the ideal of consistency. German and French are somewhere between Italian and Spanish on the one hand and English on the other. But even the writing systems of Italian and Spanish are not wholly consistent, and in fact all that can be said of the existing languages is that their writing systems cover a wide range of consistency.

We must remember, however, that for the practical uses to which language is usually put, the carrying of a complete and exact system of sound representation would be an unnecessary burden. It is not important that every minute difference of sound should have its own particular symbol, since the language would be made no more intelligible thereby. Practical utility, however, demands that a writing system distinguish phonemes, that is differences in sound values which convey differences in meaning. Without question it is a grave defect that in English the gap between the written or printed symbols and the distinctive sounds of the language is as great as it is. Indeed the values of the letters of our ordinary alphabet are so various and uncertain that it becomes necessary to settle beforehand upon some scheme of sound representation before it is possible to discuss matters which have to do with sound changes, pronunciation, and spelling.

8 ◢ A Phonetic Alphabet

The purposes for which a phonetic alphabet may be devised are various. The advanced student of phonetics may devise some scheme whereby the minutest shades of difference in the quality, duration, tone, and stress of sounds can be indicated. Such a system would be almost phonographic in its exactness. Or the phonetic reformer may invent a "practical" alphabet, designed to take the place of our present alphabet in daily printing and writing. The ideal of the phonetic specialist is beyond our present purpose. The vain hope of the spelling reformer we may set aside as belonging to the group of those visionary projects, the realization of which is questionable at best.

The modest needs of the everyday student of language demand also some system of phonetic representation, one that is simple and intelligible and at the same time capable of recording the essential characteristics of English sounds. The alphabet presented here is for this purpose. Basically, it is a slightly modified form of the International Phonetic Alphabet, and is intended merely as an aid in the discussion of pronunciation, of spelling, and of sounds in general. This alphabet makes use, as far as possible, of the ordinary letters of our English alphabet. It avoids diacritical marks. No distinctive sound has more than one symbol, and no symbol has more than one value. There are thirty-five symbols, thirteen for the simple vowels and twenty-three for the consonants. In a number of instances, symbols are combined. Four such combinations are used to indicate diphthongs, three in connection with the consonants. A list of the symbols and appropriate key words follows:

SYMBOL	KEY-WORDS	TRANSCRIPTION
ɑ	far, odd, father	fɑr, ɑd, fɑðər
æ	fat	fæt
e	fate	fet
ɛ	felt	fɛlt
i	feet	fit
ɪ	fit	fɪt
ɔ	fought, ford	fɔt, fɔrd
o	foam	fom
u	food	fud
ʊ	foot	fʊt
ʌ	fun	fʌn
ɝ	fur, fern	fɝ, fɝn
ə	afoot	əfʊt
ɑɪ	fight	fɑɪt
ɑʊ	foul	fɑʊl
ɔɪ	foil	fɔɪl
ɪu	few	fɪu
b	bait	bet
d	date	det
f	fate	fet
g	gate	get
h	hate	het
j	yet	jɛt
k	cane	ken
l	late	let
m	mate	met

SYMBOL	KEY-WORDS	TRANSCRIPTION
n	net	nɛt
ŋ	sing	sɪŋ
p	pet	pɛt
r	rate	ret
s	set	sɛt
ʃ	shut	ʃʌt
θ	thing, myth	θɪŋ, mɪθ
ð	then, lathe	ðɛn, leð
v	vat	væt
w	wait	wet
z	zeal, says	zil, sɛz
ʒ	vision	vɪʒən
ʧ	check	ʧɛk
ʤ	jet, gem	ʤɛt, ʤɛm
hw	whale	hwel

The use of most of these symbols is self-explanatory, over half being exactly as one would most readily infer from their use in the conventional Modern English alphabet. For the others, however, a few words of explanation are needed.

In the first place, it should be noted that the symbols **a, e, i, o,** and **u** have what is known as their continental values, that is the values which they have in all the European languages except English, and which in the earlier periods of English they also had in that language. The vowel **a** has, therefore, the value of the vowel in *father*, **e** that of the vowel of *fate*, **i** that of the vowel of *feet*, **o** that of *foam*, and **u** that of *food*. Although these are popularly, that is to say nontechnically, spoken of as "long" vowels, in contrast to the vowels of *fat, felt, fit, odd*, and *foot*, which are called "short," the difference between the two members of each of the corresponding pairs is not one of duration, to which the terms *long* and *short* might be properly applied, but rather one of quality.

When it is necessary or desirable to show the duration of a sound, for example in contrasting the vowel length of *field* with that in *feet*, a colon is placed after the vowel symbol to indicate

CLASSIFICATION OF ENGLISH CONSONANTS

	Bilabial	Labio-dental	Inter-dental	Alveolar	Alveolo-palatal	Palatal/Velar
STOPS	p b			t d		k g
CONTINUANTS						
Fricatives		f v	θ ð	s z	ʃ ʒ	
Affricates					ʧ ʤ	
Nasals	m			n		ŋ
Laterals				l		

Voiceless consonants appear at the left of each column; voiced consonants to the right. Glides are not listed since they have no fixed point of articulation, nor is the [h] sound. Sounds in the column farthest to the right are either palatal *or* velar, depending on the nature of the following sound.

CLASSIFICATION OF ENGLISH VOWELS

length: [fiːld]. The same symbol is used at times to indicate the double impulse of air or the lengthened hold in consonants, as might occur in *penknife* [pɛnːaɪf] or *bookcase* [bʊkːes]. From the point of view of production, these are lengthened rather than doubled consonants.

Some phonetic transcriptions indicate the vowels of *fay* and *foe* as diphthongs [eɪ, oʊ] rather than as simple vowels. This is

102

largely a question of degree. Actually, very few of the English vowels, as most speakers ordinarily pronounce them, are pure; in most instances there is a second element or off-glide which is a bit higher than the principal vowel. In some varieties of American English, a word such as *cat* may be heard as [kæᴵt]. For the sake of simplicity, the simple vowel transcription is employed here.

The symbol ə is used only in unstressed situations, chiefly in the lightly stressed syllables of polysyllabic words (*accommodate* [əkˈɑməˈˈdet]) or in words which have light sentence stress: *The man sees a boy and a dog.* [ðə mæn siz ə bɔɪ ən ə dɔg]. The symbols ʌ and ɝ are used in stressed situations only: *above* [əbʌv], *Bertha* [bɝθə]. In words like the two in the preceding sentence, it is not necessary to employ stress marks since the symbols themselves indicate the stress placement. In a word such as *accommodate,* transcribed above, or *aristocrat* [əˈrɪstəˈˈkræt] stress marks must be used to indicate the placement of the primary as opposed to the secondary stress. Note that the stress marks precede the syllable to which they apply. Observe also that different derivatives of the same root may shift stress: *aristocrat* [əˈrɪstəˈˈkræt]; *aristocracy* [ˈˈærəsˈtɑkrəsi].

The unstressed final sound usually spelled with a *y* presents a problem. With some speakers, the sound seems to be close to [i]; with others it sounds more like [ɪ]; thus *candy* might be transcribed either as [kændi] or [kændɪ]. In some parts of the country *candid* and *candied* are homophones, both pronounced [kændɪd]; in others they are differentiated.

The symbol **j** represents the consonantal sound of *y*, as it does in the alphabets of several Germanic languages. The symbol **ŋ** represents the velar nasal continuant, as in *hang, thin, long.* It is a simple sound, although it is written in our conventional spelling with the two letters *ng*. In a word like *finger,* however, we have the velar nasal followed by the voiced velar stop; it should therefore be transcribed as [fɪŋgər]. Compare also the pronunciations of *long* and *longer,* and contrast the value of *ng* in *singer* and *finger.* [lɔŋ, lɔŋgər, sɪŋər, fɪŋgər].

103

The continuant usually represented by *sh* in the regular alphabet has again to have a unit symbol, ʃ. The symbols θ and ð represent respectively the voiceless interdental continuant, as in *thin, thick, thing, thought*, etc., and the voiced interdental continuant, as in *thee, those, their*, etc. The symbol ʒ is the voiced equivalent of ʃ.

The sound usually spelled *ch* presents a problem. It bears some similarity to the sound [t] followed by [ʃ], though they are by no means identical. Yet an important aim in designing a phonetic alphabet is to keep the number of different symbols as small as possible. For this, among other reasons, the combination tʃ is used here for the ordinary value of *ch*, and similarly dʒ represents the voiced counterpart, as in *edge*. The same question arises in connection with the sound usually spelled *wh*, and the combination **hw** is used for it.

For the purpose of further study of the alphabet and practice in using it, a part of Lincoln's Gettysburg Address is here given with its phonetic transcription:

Four score and seven years ago our fathers brought forth on this continent a new nation, conceived in liberty and dedicated to the proposition that all men are created equal. Now we are engaged in a great civil war, testing whether that nation, or any other nation, so conceived and so dedicated, can long endure. We are met on a great battle-field of that war. We have come to dedicate a portion of that field as a final resting place for those who here gave their lives that that nation might live. It is altogether fitting and proper that we should do this.

fɔr skɔr ənd sɛvən jirz əgo aur faðərz brɔt fɔrθ an ðɪs
kantənənt ə nɪu neʃən, kənsivd ɪn lɪbərti ənd ˈdɛdɪˈketəd tə ðə
ˈprapəˈzɪʃən ðət ɔl mɛn ər krietəd ikwəl. nau wi ər ɪngedʒd ɪn ə
gret sɪvəl wɔr, tɛstɪŋ hwɛðər ðæt neʃən, ər ɛni ʌðər neʃən, so
kənsivd ənd so ˈdɛdɪˈketəd, kən lɔŋ ɪndɪur. wi ar mɛt an ə gret
bætlfild əv ðæt wɔr. wi həv kʌm tə ˈdɛdɪˈket ə pɔrʃən əv ðæt fild
æz ə faɪnəl rɛstɪŋ ples fər ðoz hu hir gev ðɛr laɪvz ðət ðæt neʃən
maɪt lɪv. ɪt əz ˈɔltəˈgɛðər fɪtɪŋ ənd prapər ðət wi ʃud du ðɪs.

To one unfamiliar with it, a phonetic transcription such as the above seems baffling at first and somewhat comic as well. In this connection let us recall that much of the humor of dialect stories and poems consists in an attempted phonetic or partially phonetic transcription of actual speech. The humorous effect is due largely to the novelty of the new forms, which intrinsically are no funnier than the symbols of the regular alphabet.

9 ⊠ Sound Changes

Sounds are the least stable element in language. The words themselves, the order of the words, the written or printed forms, all these, though they are subject to constant change, are relatively fixed and permanent as compared with sounds. Sounds, the most sensitive part of language, respond delicately to the slightest and most evanescent influences. It is likely that if the speech of an individual were recorded on tape or disk, it would be found that no phrase or sentence ever exactly repeated itself. We may compare the sound-material of the language to a restless, ever-fluctuating ocean, always the same in its essentials, but never two moments the same in the forms assumed by the elements of which it is composed. Day by day, minute by minute, shiftings of our sounds are taking place. Although most of these are too minute to attract attention at the time, in the course of years, of a generation or two, they result in the substitution of altogether new sounds for the old ones. Just as the light of day at two successive moments appears to be the same, but is not, since it is by the accumulation of momentary changes that the great result of day and night is obtained, so our speech, which at a given moment we think we hold firmly in our grasp, is constantly slipping away and assuming new forms.

So far as human observation goes, it is difficult to see that anything is gained by the constant series of changes which are affecting the phonetic side of the language. If a process of beneficent evolution, or the contrary, has been at work in the vast majority

105

of the changes in English sound, it is difficult to assess. The principles of development are difficult to formulate. In this respect, the behavior of sounds through the centuries differs from that of the inflections and vocabulary of the language. The changes in the English inflectional system have resulted in at least a greater surface simplicity; the development of the vocabulary has made the language richer and more variously expressive. But sound changes appear to have taken place largely because it is the nature of sound to be impermanent and variable.

Many of the changes which take place in language sounds are so light and of such momentary importance that they never demand consideration. It is not essential to intelligibility that the sounds of language should always conform to what we may regard as the perfect types of the sounds. We allow a considerable latitude in the speech of individuals, for we understand when words are only approximately correctly pronounced. There is, therefore, a large area of permissible variation in the sounds of speech.

When a sound change, however, is persistent to the degree that it affects the language in general, or the speech of a particular community, it then becomes matter worthy of observation, and, as far as is possible, of scientific generalization. Generalizations of this sort based upon the observation of sound changes which have proceeded in a regular fashion, have been called "phonetic laws" in the past. The tendency today is to conceive of them rather as historical events. They merely state what has taken place; they are not capable of verification through repetition, nor do they have a predictive value. Their principal similarity to scientific law lies in the assumption of universal applicability, and in the insistence that exceptions to the general rule must be accounted for.

The sounds of a language reflect habit and custom, and any discussion of the phonological aspects of language must necessarily take into consideration why and how general habits and customs are formed. Imitation is undoubtedly the most powerful single factor in the determination of change or the preservation of stability. This applies not only to sounds but to all other aspects of language.

106

This imitation may be conscious or unconscious, though it is usually the latter. Children, for example, imitate the sounds and the words which they habitually hear, without giving any thought to the matter. It is chiefly the adults, who have learned to observe their speech and to reason about it, who become aware of the changes that are taking place. But even among adults, the conscious attitude of mind towards language is relatively rare. They also usually form their habits in language by an unconscious adaptation to the familiar use about them. It is obvious that no discredit attaches to imitation of the kind we are describing. Everyone must be imitative to a very large extent in his use of speech, because speech is a common social possession and not the exclusive property of any one individual. There could be no worse kind of speech than one which was altogether original, altogether different from the speech of others, because such speech would be unintelligible.

Many sound changes are due in their origins to organic causes, such as the modification of the physical organs of sound production. Thus it is a general and obvious principle that a syllable which bears a heavy stress is likely to be pronounced more sharply and distinctly than it would be if it bore only a light stress. Or the rapidity with which one speaks will usually be observed to affect very markedly the clearness and distinctness of the sounds. Changes which are due to such natural tendencies as these affect the people altogether; they tend to become general, therefore, without imitation, because the same natural law operates upon all equally. It will be necessary now to examine the changes in sounds more fully from these two points of view, the imitative and the organic tendencies towards change in the sounds of speech.

10 ✐ Imitative Sound Changes

It is only when we look back over the history of English sounds and observe them in a long perspective that we can see the results of imitative sound changes on a large scale. When we compare the system of sounds used in Old English with that used in Modern English, we see that there has been an almost complete displacement. This is especially true of the vowels, which are always much less stable than the consonants. On the whole our Modern English consonants differ but little from their use fifteen hundred years ago. The vowels, however, have undergone great changes. Words which in Old English, for example, had the vowel [ɑ:], by the Middle English period had changed this vowel to [ɔ:], and Modern English has gone a step further and changed the Middle English [ɔ:] into [o]. Thus Old English *stān* [stɑ:n] became Middle English *stoon* [stɔ:n] and Modern English *stone* [ston]. Following the same phonetic development, Old English *bān* [bɑ:n] became Middle English *boon* [bɔ:n], Modern English *bone* [bon]; Old English *bāt* [bɑ:t] became Middle English *boot* [bɔ:t], Modern English *boat* [bot]. Other instances of the same development are the following:

OLD ENGLISH		MIDDLE ENGLISH		MODERN ENGLISH	
gān	[gɑ:n]	*goon*	[gɔ:n]	*go*	[go]
wrāt	[wrɑ:t][1]	*wroot*	[rɔ:t]	*wrote*	[rot]
fām	[fɑ:m]	*foom*	[fɔ:m]	*foam*	[fom]
blāwan	[blɑ:wan]	*blowen*	[blɔ:wən]	*blow*	[blo]
pāpa	[pɑ:pa]	*pope*	[pɔ:pə]	*pope*	[pop]
wā	[wɑ:]	*woo*	[wɔ:]	*woe*	[wo]

Other vowels have changed just as completely. Thus Old English [o:], omitting the transition stages, has become regularly [u] in Modern English, as illustrated by the following examples:

OLD ENGLISH		MODERN ENGLISH	
mōd	[mo:d]	*mood*	[mud]
mōna	[mo:na]	*moon*	[mun]
cōl	[ko:l]	*cool*	[kul]
dōn	[do:n]	*do*	[du]
fōda	[fo:da]	*food*	[fud]
tōþ	[to:θ]	*tooth*	[tuθ]

[1] The *w* in *wr*, as well as the *h* in *hl*, *hr*, were all pronounced in the Old English period.

Continuing with the long vowels, Old English [e:] has become the Modern English [i]; Old English [i:] has become the Modern English diphthong [aɪ]; and Old English [u:] has become the Modern English diphthong [aʊ]. These three groups of changes are illustrated by the following words:

OLD ENGLISH		MODERN ENGLISH	
cēn	[ke:n]	*keen*	[kin]
tēþ	[te:θ]	*teeth*	[tiθ]
mēd	[me:d]	*meed*	[mid]
slēpan	[sle:pɑn]	*sleep*	[slip]
pīpe	[pi:pɛ]	*pipe*	[pɑɪp]
wīd	[wi:d]	*wide*	[wɑɪd]
īs	[i:s]	*ice*	[ɑɪs]
rīdan	[ri:dɑn]	*ride*	[rɑɪd]
hūs	[hu:s]	*house*	[hɑʊs]
mūþ	[mu:θ]	*mouth*	[mɑʊθ]
brū	[bru:]	*brow*	[brɑʊ]
scrūd	[ʃru:d]	*shroud*	[ʃrɑʊd]

If we extend our examination to the other vowels and diphthongs, short and long, of the Old English period, we find that nearly every one of them has shifted from its original form, that the original form has become lost, and that through imitation a new form has become general and regular. Just who it was who started each specific change, and for what reason, it is impossible to say. It is not probable that at any period one could put his hand on a definite individual, or group of individuals, and say that this person or that was responsible for a specific change. The changes advanced undoubtedly by minute degrees, and the man of the Old English or the Middle English period was at no time conscious that his speech was changing to such an extent that a few hundred years later it would seem to his descendants almost entirely a different language from their own.

There is no reason to believe that our own speech today is much more stable than was that of the Old English period.

109

Unconsciously to ourselves we are being drifted here and there
on those currents of speech-sounds which our descendants two
or three hundred years hence will be able to trace through their
curves and meanderings, and thus to formulate and generalize
into phonetic statements, as now we formulate the changes in the
speech of our Old English ancestors. In some few instances, however, we can trace changes and tendencies in our contemporary
speech, and these deserve a few words of special consideration.

Before passing on to the consideration of contemporary imitative sound changes, it may be interesting to examine a passage of
Old English and the same passage in Middle English in their
respective phonetic forms, and to compare these earlier sounds of
the language with those of Modern English. For this purpose we
may choose a passage from the New Testament, giving it first in
an Old English version, made before the year 1000, accompanied
by a literal translation and a phonetic transcription, and then
the same passage in Wycliffe's version, made in the last quarter
of the fourteenth century. The Old English version is as follows:

Ðā hī æt hām wǣron, he
ācsode hī: "Hwæt smēade gē
be wege?"

θɑ: hi: æt hɑ:m wæ:rɔn he:
a:ksɔdɛ hi: hwæt smæ:ədɛ je:
bɛ wɛjɛ

Ond hī suwodon. Witodlīce
hī on wege smēadon hwylc
hyra yldost wǣre.

ɔnd hi: suwɔdɔn wɪtɔdli:tʃɛ
hi: ɔn wɛjɛ smæ:ədɔn hwɪltʃ
hɪrɑ ɪldɔst wæ:rɛ

þā hē sæt, hē clypode hī
twelfe ond sǣde him: "Gif
ēower hwylc wyle bēon fyrmest,
bēo sē ēaðmōdust ond
ēower ealra þēn."

θɑ: he: sæt he: klɪpɔdɛ hi:
twɛlvɛ ɔnd sæ:dɛ hɪm jɪf
e:owɛr hwɪltʃ wɪlɛ be:ɔn fɪrmɛst
be:o se: æ:əðmo:dust ɔnd
e:owɛr æəlrɑ θe:n

þā nām hē ānne cnapan
ond gesette on hyra middele. þā
hē hine beclypte, hē sǣde him:

θɑ: nɑ:m he: ɑ:nnɛ knɑpɑn
ɔnd jɛsɛttɛ ɔn hɪrɑ mɪddɛlɛ θɑ:
he: hɪnɛ bɛklɪptɛ he: sæ:dɛ hɪm

"Swā hwylc swā ānne of þus
gerādum cnapum on mīnum
naman onfēhð, sē onfēhð mē.

swɑ: hwɪltʃ swɑ: ɑ:nnɛ ɔf θus
jɛrɑ:dum knɑpum ɔn mi:num
nɑ:mɑn ɔnfe:hθ se: ɔnfe:hθ me:

And sē þe mē onfēhð, hē ne
onfēhð me, ac þone þe mē
sende."[2]—MARK IX, 33–37.

and se: θɛ me: ɔnfe:hθ he: nɛ
ɔnfe:hθ me: ak θɔnɛ θɛ me:
sɛndɛ

The same passage from the Wycliffe Bible follows:

And whanne thei weren in the
hous, he axide hem: "What
tretiden ye in the weie?"

ɑnd hwɑnə θæɪ wæ:rən ɪn θə
hu:s he: ɑksɪd hɛm hwɑt
træ:tɪdən je: ɪn θə wæɪə

And thei weren stille. For thei
disputiden among hem in the
weie, who of hem schulde be
grettest.

ɑnd θæɪ wæ:rən stɪlə fɔr θæɪ
dɪsprutɪdən əmɔŋg hɛm ɪn θə
wæɪə hwɔ: ɔf hɛm ʃuldə be:
gretəst

And he sat, and clepide the
twelue, and seide to hem: "If
ony man wole be the firste among
you, he schal be the laste of alle,
and the mynster of alle.

ɑnd he: sɑt ɑnd kle:pɪdə θə
twelvə ɑnd sæɪdə to: hɛm ɪf
ɔ:nɪ mɑn wɔlə be: θə fɪrst əmɔŋg
ju: he: ʃɑl be: θə lɑst ɔf ɑlə
ɑnd θə mɪnɪstər ɔf ɑlə

And he took a child, and sette
hym in the myddil of hem. And
whanne he hadde biclippid hym,
he seide to hem:

ɑnd he: to:k ə ʧi:ld ɑnd sɛtə
hɪm ɪn θə mɪdɪl ɔf hɛm ɑnd
hwɑn he: hɑd bɪklɪpɪd hɪm
he: sæɪdə to: hɛm

Who euer resseyueth oon of such
children in my name, he
resseyueth me. And who euer
resseyueth me, he resseyueth not
me aloone, but hym that sente
me.[3]

hwɔ: ɛvər rɪsæɪvəθ ɔ:n ɔf suʧ
ʧɪldrən ɪn mi: nɑ:m he:
rɪsæɪvəθ me: ɑnd hwɔ: ɛvər
rɪsæɪvəθ me: he: rɪsæɪvəθ nɔt
me: əlɔ:nə but hɪm θɑt sɛntə
me:

[2] From Skeat, *The Holy Gospels in Anglo-Saxon, Northumbrian and Old Mercian Versions*, Cambridge, 1871–1887. Literally translated this goes as follows: "When they at home were, he asked them: 'What considered ye along the way?' And they were silent (suwodon). Verily they on the way considered which of them eldest (i.e., most honorable) was. When he sat, he called them twelve and said to them: 'If of you any will be foremost, be he humblest and of you all servant.' Then he took a boy and set him (the pronoun is not expressed) in their midst. When he embraced him, he said to them: 'Whosoever one of such boys (of þus gerādum cnapum) in my name receives, he receives me. And he who receives me, he receives not me, but him who sent me.'"

[3] From *The New Testament in English according to the Version by John Wycliffe* about A.D. 1380 *and revised by John Purvey* about A.D. 1388. Ed. Forshall and Madden (Oxford, 1879).

111

It is of interest to add the same passage in the King James version:

33 And being in the houfe, he afked them, What was it that yee difputed among your felues by the way.
34 But they held their peace, For by the way they had difputed among themfelues who fhould be the greateft.
35 And he fate downe, and called the twelue and faith unto them, If any man defire to be firft, the fame fhall be laft of all, and feruant of all.
36 And he tooke a child, and fet him in the midft of them; & when he had taken him in his arms, he faid unto them,
37 Whofoeuer fhall receiue one of fuch children in my Name, receiueth me; and whofoeuer fhall receiue me, receiueth not me, but him that fent me.[4]

Finally a current modernization, though not so important for evidence of change in pronunciation, is indicative of the pronounced alteration in verb structures and sentence structure which has occurred.

And when he was indoors, he asked them, "What were you arguing about on the way?" They were silent because on the way they had been discussing who was the greatest. He sat down, called the Twelve, and said to them, "If anyone wants to be first, he must make himself last of all and servant of all." Then he took a child, set him in front of them, and put his arms around him. "Whoever receives one of these children in my name," he said, "receives me; and whoever receives me, receives not me but the One who sent me."[5]

11 ◙ Contemporary Imitative Sound Changes

One of the frequently discussed instances of contemporary sound change is that which centers about the pronunciation of cer-

[4] *The Holy Bible*, London, 1611. 1st ed. of the King James Version. The pronunciation is approximately the same as that of Modern English. Notice the large number of silent letters as compared with the Middle English and the Old English pronunciation.

[5] From *The New English Bible*, *New Testament*. © The Delegates of the Oxford University Press and The Syndics of the Cambridge University Press 1961. Reprinted by permission.

tain words containing the vowel [æ] or [ɑ]. Without attempting to follow the history of these sounds through the whole course of their development, we shall merely point out the fact that they have been constantly changing, that the word *path* was pronounced [pæθ] by one generation, [pɑθ] by another, and [paθ] [6] by still another. Generally, the feeling which determined the use of one sound or the other seems to have been that the particular sound chosen was more "refined" than the others; and it is a curious fact that each of the three sounds has at different times been elevated to this position of eminence. Thus in the first quarter of the nineteenth century, in London the pronunciation of the vowel of words like *path, past, ask, glass, bath, dance*, etc., as [æ], like the vowel of *hat, cat*, etc., lengthened, was regarded as elegant, and, of course, by those to whom it was strange, as affected. This is well illustrated by Leigh Hunt's description of a night watchman, who was affecting the speech of his betters. "Of varieties among watchmen," says Hunt, [7] "we remember several. One was a dandy watchman who used to ply at the top of Oxford Street, next the park. He had a mincing way with it, pronouncing the *a* in the word *past* as it is in *hat*, making a little preparatory hem before he spoke, and then bringing out his '*past ten*' in a style of genteel indifference."

A few years later, the elegant pronunciation of this sound in this country became established as [ɑ], that is, the broad sound of *a* in *father*. This was undoubtedly due, in the main, to the influence of the speech of New England, particularly Boston, which, owing to its literary position during the lifetime of Longfellow, Emerson, Hawthorne, Lowell, and the other great figures of the first flowering period of American literature, was often regarded as the seat of culture in America. From Boston, where it was a normal and usual pronunciation, the broad sound [ɑ] passed over by imitation to the speech of other communities.

---

[6] The symbol [a] represents a low central unround vowel intermediate in quality between [æ] and [ɑ]. It is the sound frequently heard in the coastal New England area in words like *car* and *park*.

[7] "Walks Home by Night." *The Companion*, Feb. 6, 1828.

Thus Richard Grant White,[8] a native of New York and the arbiter of taste in his day, went so far as to say that "The full, free, unconscious utterance of the broad *ah* sound of *a* is the surest indication, in speech, of social culture which began at the cradle."

To a certain extent the educated American public seemed to agree with this astonishing dictum. Conscientious speakers, if they did not have it naturally, tried to cultivate this broad *ah* sound which was to be the test of social culture. It was, and still is to some slight extent, taught in schools as the only correct and elegant pronunciation. But the public was not prepared to go the whole way. Instead of the full, broad [ɑ] as in *father*, there was in some quarters a tendency to compromise on a vowel between the [æ] of *hat* and the [ɑ] of *father*, resulting in the vowel which we have symbolized as [a].

For a period, this vowel which has been well described as a "refined transition" between [æ] and [ɑ] tended to become current in certain communities in the United States, chiefly in the East, in words like *path, past, glass, master, dance, glance, plant, answer*, etc., and was to some degree imitated by speakers in communities in which the natural and native pronunciation of the vowel in these words had been [æ]. Just what the future holds in store with respect to the pronunciation of this group of words is difficult to say. Without question an overwhelming majority of speakers of English in America employ the [æ] sound. Undeniably, in the minds of many, the [ɑ] pronunciation still retains some of the prestige which was claimed for it by Richard Grant White. Whether the vowel [ɑ] will ever become natural and general all over the country, or whether the [æ] will regain the prestige it held at the beginning of the nineteenth century can be foretold only by someone who knows how to predict the whims and vagaries of fashion.

The question is often asked, Which of the pronunciations is

[8] *Words and Their Uses*, New York, 1899, Chapter III, p. 50.

the "correct" one, [pæθ], [paθ], or [pɑθ]? It is probably more to the point to observe that the variation among these sounds is highly restricted, occurring chiefly when the vowel in question is followed by [f], [θ], [s] (all voiceless fricatives), or [n]: *calf, path, past, dance.* It does not occur before stops; *cap, cab, hat, lad, back, lag* have [æ] in virtually all varieties of English. Similarly, [æ] is regular before [m] and [ŋ]: *ham, hang.* It has been estimated that of the common English words which have the [æ] sound generally in most parts of the United States, only one-fourth show a tendency to admit [ɑ] as a variant pronunciation. This tends to put the matter in a proper perspective; we are dealing with no more than a definitely limited instance of sound change.

Moreover, if the preceding discussion has been followed and understood, it will be apparent that it is not necessary to choose from among the three pronunciations, that one is not correct to the exclusion of the others, but that all may be equally correct. A phonetic rule or statement, it will be remembered, was defined as a generalization based on observation of the actual use of the language, apart from any notion of a lawgiver who establishes this or that as the law of language. Now if we observe the actual use or custom of the language, we shall see that some people or some communities say [pæθ] and others say [pɑθ], and further that the question of good English or bad English, that is, of correctness, does not enter here, unless we assume arbitrarily that one must be right and the other must be wrong. The question, however, is not one of right and wrong, but merely of two differing customs. In cases of this sort one's own individual preference and taste must decide. There is some question, however, whether it is worthwhile, or even desirable, to attempt to change one's natural pronunciation of a somewhat arbitrarily limited class of words, since it is quite unlikely that consistency of performance will be attained.

Words of another class in which there is a considerable amount of variation are those with the so-called short *o* sound: *fog, hog, cob, cod, stop, not, rock, watch, swallow, quality.* In Standard British

English these regularly have a rounded vowel, [ɔ], and this is the case in some parts of the United States. Elsewhere in this country the words are pronounced with the unrounded [ɑ] vowel. Some speakers, however, may pronounce *fog* and *hog* with a rounded vowel, but *stop, not,* and *rock* with the unrounded variant. Others may make a distinction between [watʃ] noun and [wɔtʃ] verb.

The matter is complicated even more by the fact that many who pronounce [ɔ] in these words will pronounce the vowels of *foreign, orange,* and *forehead* as [ɑ], but *sorrow* and *tomorrow* with [ɔ]. Similarly, those who use [ɑ] in *fog, hog, stop, not,* and *rock* will have a rounded vowel in *foreign, orange,* and *forehead,* but no rounding in *sorrow* and *tomorrow.* In short, just as with the variation between [æ] and [ɑ], we are confronted by a situation far more complex than appears on the surface, but nevertheless one which shows clear evidence of a kind of patterning and one which is capable of description.

Still another group of words may be cited in illustration, words like *roof, root, soot, hoof, hoop, coop,* and others. By some speakers these words are pronounced with the vowel [u], that which they employ in *mood, tool, moon, goose,* and *food.* Accordingly, the phonetic transcription for them would be [ruf, rut, sut, huf, hup, kup]. Other speakers pronounce them with the lower and laxer variety of the high back rounded vowel, the sound which they use in *put, foot, good, hood, stood.* On the basis of this pronunciation they would be transcribed as [rʊf, rʊt, sʊt, hʊf, hʊp, kʊp]. What the final outcome will be in the case of this pair of sounds, [u] and [ʊ], depends on the extent to which imitation will take place.

Perhaps in time all words containing the *oo*-vowel may acquire the [u] pronunciation, *put, foot, good, stood* becoming general as [put, fut, gud, stud], a pronunciation which is now common in Scotland. On the other hand, they may settle on the pronunciation [ʊ], *soot, hoof, root, mood, goose* thus becoming [sʊt, hʊf, rʊt, mʊd, gʊs]. Or the tendency toward imitation may not be strong enough to bring about uniformity of usage, in which case we shall continue as we are at present, some speakers using one sound and some speakers the other.

This will be the most likely state of affairs so long as the different sounds are felt to be equally correct, that is, so long as they are all used by speakers with some claim to education and refinement, If, however for some reason or other, the pronunciation [fɑg] or the pronunciation [rʊf] should come to be regarded as less elegant than [fɔg] and [ruf], just as at one time there was a strong tendency to regard the pronunciation [pɑθ] as more elegant than the pronunciation [pæθ], the likelihood is that [fɑg] and [rʊf] would be given up entirely in favor of [fɔg] and [ruf].

A group of words which at present show a tendency towards sound change, but in which the process meets with some restraining opposition, is that consisting of words like *tube, duke, due, new,* and others. Many speakers pronounce these words with the sound of [u], giving thus [tub, duk, du, nu], like *true, fruit, rule, rude*—after [r] the sound is always [u], not [ɪu], that is [tru, frut, rul, rud]. The [u] pronunciation is more generally heard in words of more than one syllable, as *assume, induce, produce, dutiful,* etc., than it is in monosyllables. Yet both in monosyllables and in polysyllables [u] may be frequently observed, even in the speech of persons who think they always pronounce the [ɪu] sound, as [trub, drʊk, dɪu, nɪu, prodɪus], etc.

There is, among people who attach much importance to traditional and dogmatic rules, a strong feeling that the [u] pronunciation in [tub, duk], etc., is wrong or even vulgar. The only right pronunciation, they say, is [trub, drʊk], etc. But is [tub] incorrect? If it is a widely occurring pronunciation, as our observation attests, then it must be one of the customs of the language. But if it is a custom of the language, it has the same kind of authority as [trub], which itself becomes "correct" only by being a custom of speech. Neither has any other authority than that which it acquires through the habits or customs of those who speak the language.

117

The question of choice is again the question of which group of speakers, that is, which habit or custom, one wishes to follow. If one observes that the pronunciation [tub] is the habitual, customary, and unaffected speech of his linguistic community, one need have no hesitation in following it. If, on the other hand, according to his observation, [tub] is a pronunciation which is characteristic of the uneducated speaker and is heard only from such speakers, his choice is equally easy to make. The difficulty and the duty, in both instances, is to make sure that the observations upon which one's judgments are based are accurate and not prejudiced, and are sufficiently extensive to justify a generalization. Above all they should be derived not from linguistic folklore, but from direct observation of actual practice or from reliable and scientifically conducted surveys.

A few further stray instances of contemporary sound changes may be cited as illustrative of the kind of questions which continually arise for decision. Among old-fashionioned people one used to hear the pronunciation of the word *deaf* as [dif], the usual conventional pronunciation now being [dɛf]. The pronunciation [dif], however, is historically justifiable, the vowel having the same origin as the vowel in *sheaf* [ʃif], *cheap* [tʃip], and *bereave* [bɪriv]. Formerly [dif] was in good current use among educated as well as uneducated speakers. Through some whim or fashion of the moment, which now has been forgotten, the pronunciation [dɛf] managed to creep in, was generally imitated, and became the general, and in that sense the correct, pronunciation. The pronunciation [dif] persisted for some time as a survival in the speech of old-fashioned people, and since the less educated are often slower in accepting innovations than the educated, it persisted also in their speech.

There was also at one time a tendency to discriminate between the use of *rise* as a verb and as a noun. In the former case the word was pronounced [rɑɪz], in the latter, [rɑɪs]. This followed the pattern of words like *use*, as noun [jus] and as verb [juz]; *device* [dɪvɑɪs], *devise* [dɪvɑɪz]. The pronunciation [rɑɪs], however, never became general; it was employed chiefly by more or less conscious and affected users of the language.

The same is true of the two pronunciations of *either* and *neither* as [iðər, niðər] and [aɪðər, naɪðər]. In all communities in America the pronunciation [iðər, niðər] is by far the more general and usual, the second pronunciation often being less natural. The question of correctness and choice between the two is again to be decided entirely by one's preference. One who wishes his customs of speech to be normal and inconspicuous will generally choose to say [iðər, niðər]. One who prefers a slight mannerism of speech, who affects differences of speech that will distinguish him from others, is at liberty to choose to say [aɪðər, naɪðər].

The situation is somewhat similar in the instance of the two pronunciations of *tomato* as [təmeto] and [təmɑto]. Both pronunciations are in good natural use in different sections of the country, though the pronunciation [təmeto] is by far the more common. The second pronunciation [təmɑto], becomes an affectation only when it is assumed by persons whose normal pronunciation is [təmeto] for the sake of distinguishing their speech from that of their environment. It is clear that it would be a much more reasonable and admirable endeavor for a speaker to strive to adapt his speech always to the use of his environment than to search out usages in speech that will set him off and distinguish him as different from his environment.

12 ⌂ Dialect

When, through the process of sound change, the speech of a certain community acquires characteristics peculiar to that community, which thus distinguish the speech of the community from that of the country at large, or from other sections of the country, we have a dialect. Dialect characteristics may affect both the popular and the cultivated speech, although they are almost always much more strongly marked in the speech of the common daily intercourse of the people than they are in the speech of more careful and conscious speakers. Many communities have their local popular dialects, as, for example, the Hoosier dialect of Indiana, so skillfully used by James Whitcomb Riley in his poems; the New England dialect, used by James Russell Lowell in the *Biglow Papers*; the Virginia dialect, made familiar to all of recent years through many a story of Southern life.

We may speak also of dialect not from a geographical point of view, but from the point of view of language mixture. When persons whose native tongue is different from English settle in an English community, they are likely to develop a distinctive type of English, which consists of a mixture of their own native tongue with English. The result is a speech which is neither standard English nor a foreign language, but a sort of mixed popular dialect of English. Many people believe that certain features of American Negro speech may be explained on the basis of the African languages spoken by the slaves when they were brought to this country. Pennsylvania German actually preserves so much of the vocabulary, pronunciation, and structure of Rhenish Westphalian speech of the German settlers that it might better to be called a dialect of German than of English. In certain regions which have been largely settled by Scandinavians, in Minnesota, Iowa, and other places, there has also grown up a mixed popular Scandinavian and English dialect. The Irish brogue, or dialect, is familiar to all; and in cities in which there is a large Jewish population, a Jewish dialect with marked individual characteristics has grown up.

None of these dialects, however, either of the local or mixed kind, tend to spread beyond their own respective communities. When they are used in literature, it is for the purpose of giving local color to a situation, or, in character studies, for the purpose of making the speech of the character harmonize with his surroundings. The use of dialect for local color is found as far back as Chaucer, and is of course very common in later fiction, poetry, and comedy. The value of comic dialect characters on the stage has long been known, and they can be found as far back as Shakespeare's Welshman, Scotchman, and Irishman in *Henry V*. The comic effect in all such instances arises from the violent contrast between what is regarded as the standard and correct speech and the speech of the dialect character, Welshman, Frenchman, village philosopher, or whoever he may be.

The line marking the separation of the popular and local dialect from the standard speech of cultivated persons is not, however, a sharp one. The ascent from the popular to the standard speech is gradual, and since every speaker is necessarily a native of some local community, his speech, especially his daily colloquial speech, is almost sure to bear some traces of its local origin. Just to what extent one is willing to allow these native and local characteristics of speech to remain must be left to individual choice. Most educated persons choose to divest their speech of its local characteristics and to speak a language which is approximately standard. What one shall regard as approximately standard must again depend, in the end, on individual observation; but on this question we shall have more to say later.

13 ▨ Organic Sound Changes

In the preceding paragraphs we have been speaking of certain changes in the pronunciation of English sounds which become general, or tend to become so, through the process of imitation. Besides these changes we must consider a second group in which the changes are dependent less upon the law of imitation than upon purely natural and physical causes. These we may group under the general head of organic changes. The underlying explanation of all these changes of this second kind is to be found in the fact that our speech rests upon varying and entirely different planes of utterance. Sometimes we speak very slowly and distinctly, at others we speak rapidly and with less attention to the form of each individual word. Certain words or groups of words we stress, while others are spoken with a less degree of energy. In general, the principle holds that the amount of energy we put forth in the operation of the organs of speech is in inverse ratio to the obviousness of the idea to be expressed.

In speaking a conventional formula, as, for example, the greeting *How do you do?* we enunciate the words very indistinctly. We do not say [hɑʊ du ju du] but perhaps [hɑʊ də du] or [hɑʊ du] or even, the dialect writers tell us, *Howdy?* It is not only in the speech of the ignorant and uneducated that such relaxed pronunciations find a place, but in the speech of everybody. Some little practice in self-observation is often required, however, before a speaker realizes the actual phonetic character of his language.

We are likely to have some theoretical notion of an ideal perfect pronunciation—the conviction perhaps that we speak as we write—so firmly fixed in our minds that we think we say what we think we ought to say, whereas what we actually say is something quite different. The question whether or not it is right to permit ourselves to use these relaxed pronunciations we shall consider later. In the meantime we should observe that the principle has always been in operation, and that it has deeply affected both the written and spoken form of our language. A few historical illustrations will make this point clear.

In Milton's *Paradise Lost*, in a passage in which the poet is speaking of Dagon, the fish-god, there occurs the curious-looking word *grunsel*:

> In his own temple, on the grunsel-edge,
> Where he fell flat and shamed his worshipers.[9]

The meaning of this word would be hard to guess from Milton's form. But when we know that it is simply worn down from a compound *ground + sill*, the analogy of *windowsill*, *doorsill* gives us a ready clue to its meaning, even though a compound *groundsill* is no longer in current use.

Milton's *grunsel* is only one of many words with a similar

---

[9] Book I, ll. 460–461.

history. Our formula at parting, for example, which we now spell *Good-by* or *Good-bye*, and pronounce, with the stress on the second syllable, [gəd'baɪ], or even without any vowel in the first syllable, [gd'baɪ], was originally the whole phrase *God be with you*. This, however, was entirely too long for a conventional formula, and, its literal sense being lost, it gradually came to be pronounced in an obscured and indistinct way. From the very start it became *God be wi' ye*. This further contracted into *God bwye*, a form which appears in the dialogue of the comedies of the eighteenth century. Having gone so far, the original meaning of the phrase became altogether lost; the first syllable was mistaken for our word *good* and the second for our word *by*, and we reach thus our modern form *good-by*.

Many words of the language have become obscured in form in the same way. Our Modern English word *lord* is derived from the Old English compound *hlāf-weard*, the first element of which is English *loaf* (of bread), the second *ward* (i.e., guardian), the whole word meaning originally the guardian of the loaf, or supplies in general. This word was, of course, originally a descriptive epithet for protector or leader of the people. In time, however, the elements of the word ceased to be appreciated separately, and since the word stood for a single idea, which was not analyzed into the two notions of *bread* and *guardian*, it came to be pronounced as a simple word. From *hlāf-weard* it became *hlāford*, then, with the loss of the *h*, which was general in all words in the initial position followed by another consonant, *lauerd* and, finally, *lord*.

By a similar process, Modern English *woman* has been derived from Old English *wīf-man*, the second element being the generic name for human beings, and the first element *wīf-*, the indication of sex. The word having become fixed in the language consciousness of the people as the conventional symbol for the idea woman, it was no longer felt to be necessary to analyze it into its descriptive parts, and it thus contracted into the form *woman*. A like change has made Modern English *stirrup* out of Old English *stīg-rāp*, which literally meant *mounting-rope*, from *stīg-*, meaning "to mount" (cf. German *steigen*, and Modern English *stile*, from Old English *stīg-ol*), and *rāp*, English *rope*. Modern English *nostril* is derived from the Old English compound *nos-*, 'nose' + *ðyril*, 'hole,' the original compound meaning thus 'nose-hole.' The word *window* is derived from the two elements *wind*, and *ēage*, 'eye,' the whole meaning 'wind-eye,' 'the eye or hole by which the wind enters the house.' The word *punish* appears also in the obscured form *punch*, the relation in meaning being obvious.

Many further illustrations might be cited of what were originally careless, or better, relaxed, pronunciations, making their way into the written as well as spoken language. For the present, however, it will suffice to point out a few instances in which these relaxed pronunciations have made their way into recognized use in changing the written language to accord with the pronunciation. Thus we write the compound of *sheep* + *herd*, *shepherd*, but we pronounce it *shepperd* [ʃepərd]. The nautical terms *leeward* and *boatswain* are pronounced *luard* [luərd] and *bosen* [bosən]. The adverb and preposition compound *towards* is pronounced *tords* [tɔrdz], although other compounds with -*wards*, as, for example, *forwards* and *backwards*, are pronounced approximately as they are spelled. Other illustrations are *wristband*, pronounced [rɪzbənd], *cupboard*, pronounced [kʌbərd], *forehead*, pronounced [fɔrəd].

A similar development has taken place in many place names and family names. Thus the name Salisbury is phonetically Solsbery [sɔlzbəri]. The name of one of the colleges of the University of Oxford is *Magdalen*, which is pronounced Maudlin, and which is etymologically precisely the same word as the English adjective *maudlin*. The name Gloucester, originally from Old English *Glēawan-ceaster*, is phonetically Gloster; Leicester is pronounced Lester; and Cirencester, a town in southern England, is sometimes pronounced Sister. The discrepancy between the spelling and the pronunciation is much more marked in place names in England than it is in any other English-speaking country. It is so great, indeed, that it offers fair justification for the old story of the traveler, who on his return from a visit to England insisted that the English name Cholmondeley (pronounced Chumly) was spelled Marjoribanks (pronounced Marchbanks).

In all obscured words of the kind that we have been discussing, the same principle is involved. The words were originally spoken distinctly and in full. As time went on, however, and words came to be very familiar to all persons, it was felt to be unnecessary to give them their full value. They were intelligible in an abbreviated and "telescoped" form, and following a natural tendency towards economy, they came to be used only in this abbreviated form.

If we turn now to our contemporary speech we shall find that the same principle holds good. When we speak rapidly or speak even in an ordinary conversational and colloquial tone, we have an entirely different kind of utterance from that which we have when we speak carefully and formally. In the latter cases, each word is given a sharp and clear enunciation. In the former cases the words are run together more; only one or two important words in a group are stressed, the rest being pronounced more or less indistinctly and vaguely.

But when a word which in other instances ordinarily has no stress, for some reason, usually that of emphasis or antithesis, is given a stress, then it becomes clear and distinct, and usually has a different phonetic form from that which it has when in unstressed position. Thus the sentence *I saw your sister yesterday* would normally be pronounced [ə sɔ jər sɪstər jɛstɔrdi]. The sentence *I didn't see your sister, but he saw mine*, in which we have two pairs of antithetic and consequently emphatic words, *I* and *he*, *your* and *mine*, would be pronounced [aɪ dɪdnt si jur sɪstər bət hi sɔ maɪn].

This difference in the phonetic form of words is sometimes recorded in the spelling. The preposition *of*, for example, usually pronounced [əv], or simple [ə], as in the phrase *time of day* [taɪm ə de], or *four o' clock* from *four of clock*, is actually the unstressed form of which the adverb *off* is the stressed. Likewise

125

the prepositional *to*, pronounced [tə], as in *I'm going to town* [aɪm goɪŋ tə taun], is the unstressed form corresponding to the adverbial stressed form *too* [tu].

To illustrate this relaxed or natural form of speech a few connected sentences may be quoted, first in the conventional spelling, then in the actual phonetic form of the author's colloquial speech. The sentences are as follows:

What's the French for " I don't understand " ? I want to let this French-man know I can't understand what he's saying. It's rather odd, I can talk French myself, but I can't understand it when it's spoken. You should tell them not to speak so fast. I don't believe they can speak slow; they are too excitable.

In ordinary conversation the phonetic form of these sentences would be as follows:

[hwats ðə frɛntʃ fər ə dont ʌndərstænd ə wantəlɛt ðɪs frɛntʃ-
mən no ə kænt ʌnderstænd hwat iz seɪŋ ɪts ræðər ad ə kən
tɔk frɛntʃ məsɛlf bət ə kænt ʌndərstænd ɪt wɛn ɪts spokən ju
ʃəd tɛl əm nat tə spik sə fæst ə dont bəliv ðe kæn spik slo
ðɛr tu ɪksaɪtəbəl.]¹⁰

Perhaps not all speakers would use exactly the forms which have been put down in this phonetic transcription as representing, as nearly as possible, the use of the present writer. We must allow for variations among individuals, some persons not only following different customs, but also by nature speaking more slowly and distinctly than others. Thus the phrase, *I can talk French myself* might, in the pronunciation of some speakers, take a fuller form of the pronouns than those given above, being pronounced [aɪ kən tɔk frɛntʃ maɪsɛlf]. But the more obscure forms of the pronoun will certainly be heard in the pronunciation of the majority of speakers.

Another point should be noticed which our phonetic transcrip-

¹⁰ Adapted from *Report of a Joint Committee*, etc., p. 42.

tion does not take into account, and that is the matter of binding, or *liaison*, to borrow a term from French. Our custom of separating the words of connected discourse by spacing is purely conventional. It has grown up largely in modern times since the invention of printing. The manuscripts of the earlier periods, in Old English, for example, do not usually separate the individual words, but run them together in a straight ahead, running or cursive, style of writing.

This method of writing, though it would seem strange and inconvenient to us now, is indeed more in accord with our actual manner of speaking than our present printed and written use. For in speaking we do not normally pronounce individual words, but rather phrases or breath groups, the pauses coming where they are demanded by the logical sense and not before and after each word. A phonetic transcription of the first two sentences of the preceding passage, taking account of this liaison or binding of words into breath groups, would therefore be as follows:

[hwɑtsðəfrɛntʃ   fərədontʌndərstænd   əwɑntəlɛt
ðɪsfrɛntʃmənno   əkæntʌndərstænd   hwɑtizseŋ]

Perhaps the most interesting and important question which arises from the observation of these facts is, What shall be our attitude towards these relaxed pronunciations? Shall we try to get rid of them as careless, lazy, and inelegant? Is there an ideal form of the language towards which we should strive and in which such pronunciations shall find no place? One not infrequently meets with speakers who are possessed of this conviction. In theory, at least, they believe that the article *the* should always be pronounced [ði]; the preposition *of* should be [ɑv] or [ɔv]; the verb *can* always [kæn], never [kən], and so with all other words. They tell us that every word should be separated sharply from its neighbors, that there should be no liaison of word with word. They would have us pronounce the phrase *a good deal* as [e gʊd dil] instead of [əgʊdil]; *at all* as [æt ɔl] instead of [ətɔl].

If the word *suggest* has two *g*'s in the spelling, they would have us pronounce two, [sʌgdʒɛst] instead of the normal and natural [sədʒɛst]. In such words as *nature* and *educate*, they would have us pronounce the words as [netjur] and [ɛdjuket] instead of [netʃər] and [ɛdʒəket]. Needless to say, this "prunes and prisms" sort of pronunciation is both absurd and impossible. The attempt to carry it out would result in what we should rightly say was a language affected, unnatural, and un-English.

The fact is that such theorists have an entirely false conception of the nature of language, of the authority of the printed or written word, and of the source of what shall be regarded as standard and correct. They forget that the written and printed form of language comes after the spoken form, that it is merely a mechanical invention devised to recall and suggest the real and living language, which is the spoken language. They forget also that the mechanical device of printing and writing can only imperfectly and inadequately represent the sounds of speech, and that speech, to use the figure again which we have already used, like the waves of the ocean, is constantly changing and assuming a multitude of new forms, whereas printing and writing tend to become more and more fixed, conventional, and unchanging. To make speech conform to the printed and written forms of language is very much as though one should try to make the trees of a forest grow in conformity to an artist's picture of them. Both speech and trees have a life of their own which is free and independent of man's attempts to reduce them to a descriptive formula.

The standards of correct speech must be found, therefore, not in the printed or written form of language, but in the normal, natural conversation of daily life. It might seem that, having elevated the natural speech to this place of dignity, we have justified as right and correct all pronunciations of the colloquial and uncultivated speech which have followed the laws of natural development. It would follow that if we may say [tɔrdz] for *towards*, we may just as correctly say [fɔrərdz] for *forwards* and [bækərdz] for *backwards*. It is true that in some areas the popular pronunciation for *forwards* and *backwards*, and a host of other words, has followed exactly the same principles that have resulted in the standard pronunciation of *towards* and words of like kind. It is not true that we are at equal liberty to choose either in our pronunciation.

To repeat the statement of a preceding paragraph, one that cannot be too clearly held in mind, phonetic observations, as well as all other statements about language, acquire their validity because they sum up or generalize the custom or usage with respect to a body of similar phenomena. They are not laws because they express the mandate of some person or authority empowered to declare what shall be done, but they are accurate statements because they report what actually is done.

There is no individual or autocratic power in language, but all work together voluntarily in groups. The popular or uncultured speech has its rules just as truly as has the standard or correct speech. Consciously or unconsciously every speaker follows the customs of his own special group; for him these are the rules of his language. It has already been sufficiently demonstrated that these rules are not fixed once and for all, but are constantly adapting themselves to each other and changing.

What a speaker of today is chiefly concerned to know is what the rules of his own present day speech, of his own group, shall be. To determine this there is only one means, and that is observation. He must turn and examine the speech, the living speech, of those persons with whom he is thrown in contact, with such added help as he may get from books and dictionaries in extending the field of his observation. In case of a doubtful or divided pronunciation, he must determine what group of speakers he will unite himself with—that is, the customs of what speakers he will imitate or follow. He will observe that at present the practice of the popular speech is to pronounce *forwards* as [fɔrərdz], and, extending his observation, he will perceive that it is not the custom of cultivated speech so to pronounce the word. The choice of the group with which he will unite himself then lies in his own hands, and, other things being equal, will usually be in favor of the cultivated speech.

It is obvious from what has been said that no pronunciation is absolutely and inherently right and another wrong. Although the standard *towards* [tɔrdz] and the popular *forwards* [fɔrərdz] follow the same natural law and linguistically are on the same level, in the one case the result has been accepted by the group of speakers to which the cultivated and educated person wishes to belong, in the other it has not. In so far, therefore, the one is "correct" and the other is "incorrect." It needs, however, only the acceptance of the popular form into general use to make it as correct as the other.

Historically it has, of course, often happened that there has been a shifting back and forth of popular and standard forms. Thus, the word *sound* appears without the final *d* in Chaucer:

> Soun is noght but air y-broken.[11]

This is the correct form, historically, since the word is derived from Latin *sonum*, the *d* being gratuitously added in later times. Thus, the Elizabethan poet and translator Stanyhurst, commenting on the length of certain syllables in English meter, says: "Yeet *sowning* in English must bee long, and much more yf yt were *sounding*, as thee ignorant generaly, but falslye dooe wryte."[12] Yet the same writer drops a final *d* in the word *rind* from Old English *rinde*, spelling it *ryne*: "Not onlye by gnibling vpon thee outward ryne of a supposed historie."[13] As it happens the forms of these words which later custom has settled upon are *sound* and *rind*, but they might just as well have been *soun* and *rine*. In further illustration of the shifting of the *nd* sound, the word *lawn* may be cited. In Middle English, for example in Chaucer, this word is always *launde*, with a final *d*. Later English has dropped the *d*, as Stanyhurst wanted to do with *rind*.

---

[11] *House of Fame*, l. 765.   [12] In Gregory Smith, *Elizabethan Critical Essays*, I, 142.

[13] *Ibid.*, p. 136. His spelling *gnibling* he apparently derives by analogy to *gnaw*.

It is obvious, then, that the burden of responsibility in making a choice between two divergent pronunciations rests on the individual. Every person has not only the liberty of choice, but the necessity of choice. When a question of pronunciation comes up, each must decide for himself the form he will choose to use. If he attempts to put off the responsibility on another, say on a dictionary or the opinion of some one whose advice is sought, he is merely removing the appearance of responsibility, for in these instances he must decide for himself the value of the sources of information which he seeks and which he is willing to imitate or follow.

Plainly, also, if the responsibility rests with the individual, the penalty also falls upon him. If any speaker of the language pronounces *radiator* as [rædɪetər] or *mischievous* as [mɪsˈʧivɪəs] because the field of his observation and experience has not made him acquainted with the standard pronunciation of these words, he must accordingly bear the odium of being classed with speakers of non-standard English. He pays the penalty of his unawareness, and so does every one else who uses forms of language which he would not use if his sensitiveness to, and observation of, language had been keener and broader. Each must decide for himself what customs of what group he wishes to follow. Each must decide for himself, also, what innovations he can risk. If he choose unwisely, if he follow a false standard of refinement and cultivation, he must bear the consequences until experience and observation shall so far widen his horizon as to enable him to follow the practice of the group of which he really wishes to consider himself a part.

14 ⍁ The Standard of Pronunciation

The question of a standard pronunciation has been to a large extent answered in the discussion of the preceding paragraphs. By the term standard of pronunciation, one usually means a fixed norm, an established and accepted form of the language, which serves as the model upon which all speakers shall fashion their speech. This model is elevated to the position of the standard speech, all deviations from it being regarded as incorrect. A grave difficulty, however, confronts the student, and this is the difficulty of determining whether there actually is a standard of English pronunciation which shall serve as the pattern and model for all English-speaking people, and if so, where it is to be found.

In the first place, we may safely say that there is no ideal and perfect inherent form of the language, towards which all speakers should strive as towards an ultimate goal. There is no objective system of language outside of the minds and experiences of the people who use and speak the language. In seeking for a standard of pronunciation, consequently, men must look to themselves and their own use, not to some extra-human and ideal system towards which they shall dutifully strive. Any standard which is chosen must be made up from the actual spoken use of some group of speakers, because it is only in actual spoken use that language really exists.

In the attempt to fix upon some body of spoken use as the standard language, the question may be approached from two points of view, first, the geographical, and, second, the social or educational point of view. In attempting to establish a geographical standard of spoken use, the speech of some one region or community comes to be regarded as the model for all other communities. In other words, one dialect is chosen as the standard to which all other dialects shall conform.

In some countries this principle is recognized in actual practice. The standard French dialect is the dialect of Paris; the standard Italian dialect is the dialect of Florence, or rather of Tuscany, the province in which Florence is situated; and the standard Spanish dialect is the Castilian, the dialect of Madrid. These dialects are standard for their respective countries, however, because the people of these various countries have voluntarily accepted them as their standard, not because Parisian French or Tuscan

Italian or Castilian Spanish have any inherent right to the exclusion of other dialects. It simply so happens that the people of these various countries, in the development of their civilization, have come to look upon certain communities as the center of their national life and culture.

Turning to the English-speaking countries, however, we find an entirely different state of affairs. No one community is now accepted as affording the model of speech to which all others must conform. Theoretically we might say that London, as the capital of the native home of the English language, ought to be regarded as the home of the standard language. As an actual fact, however, the speech of London is not so regarded, not even by all the people of the United Kingdom. The English-speaking people throughout the world do not look upon London as affording the ideal speech which it is their duty to imitate and follow.

Indeed, so different is the manner of speech of Englishmen from that of Americans that the former has often been used in America as the mark of a comedy character on the stage—just as in England "the American accent" is similarly used as a laughter-provoking device. Of course the stage Englishman and American are usually exaggerations, but the normal speech of the two countries is sufficiently divergent to be easily perceived, and too divergent to allow one to stand as a model for the other. "No American speaker or writer ever thinks it needful to adopt the British form of his own language, any more than a British speaker or writer thinks it needful to adopt the American form." [14]

Practically it would be impossible for British English to serve as the model for American English, or American English for British English. Standards of speech, particularly of pronunciation, reflect not only the cultural and social history of the country but the class structure and the educational organization and practices as well. Despite the many similarities and relationships between the two peoples, and although direct communication

---

[14] Freeman, *Some Impressions of the United States*, p. 56.

between them has increased markedly, these basic social factors are still distinctly different.

Coming nearer home, neither do we find in our own country any city, Washington, for example, or any region, which can lay claim for the place of distinction which the French accord to Paris and the Italians to Florence. The speech of Chicago does not feel itself under any compulsion to adapt itself to that of Boston, or that of Boston to that of Chicago. The speech of New York cannot impose itself upon that of New Orleans, or that of San Francisco upon that of St. Louis. In short, we do not acknowledge that the speech of any one community has compelling power over that of any other. We have no acknowledged seat or center of national life and culture, and consequently we do not elevate to the position of a standard the speech of any city or state.

Failing a local geographical standard, the next position would be that the standard speech is not the speech of any one community but the speech of the country as a whole. In answer to this the obvious query comes, Is there a common general speech of the country as a whole? Does the average Bostonian speak like the average Chicagoan? Most certainly not. He does not, not only because he does not want to, but because he could not if he would. The citizen of one community does not know how the citizens of another speak, because it is only by a long-continued residence in a strange community that a visitor can acquire a wide and exact knowledge of its manner of speech. All we can say is that some comparatively few widely traveled and cosmopolitan speakers have acquired a manner of speech which is general enough not to betray the immediate locality of its origin, though it must always have characteristics individual enough to class it broadly as Eastern or Southern or a rather more general type.

With the vast majority of speakers the local characteristics are even more marked. The local characteristics of one community may extend over a wider area than those of another, the dialect

134

Enter Nerriſſa.

Dʋ. Came you from Padua from *Bellario*?

Ner. From both.

My Lord *Bellario* greets your Grace.

 Baſ. Why doſt thou whet thy knife ſo earneſtly?

 Iew. To cut the forfeiture from that bankrout there.

 Gra. Not on thy ſoale : but on thy ſoule harſh Iew

Thou mak'ſt thy knife keene : but no mettall can,

No, not the hangmans Axe beare halfe the keenneſſe

Of thy ſharpe enuy. Can no prayers pierce thee?

 Iew. No, none that thou haſt wit enough to make.

 Gra. O be thou damn'd, inexecrable dogge,

And for thy life let iuſtice be accuſ'd:

Thou almoſt mak'ſt me wauer in my faith;

To hold opinion with *Pythagoras*,

That ſoules of Animals infuſe themſelues

Into the trunkes of men. Thy curriſh ſpirit

Gouern'd a Wolfe, who hang'd for humane ſlaughter,

Euen from the gallowes did his fell ſoule fleet;

And whil'ſt thou layeſt in thy vnhallowed dam,

Infus'd it ſelfe in thee : For thy deſires

Are Woluiſh, bloody, ſteru'd, and rauenous:

 Iew. Till thou canſt raile the ſeale from off my bond

Thou but offend'ſt thy Lungs to ſpeake ſo loud:

Repaire thy wit good youth, or it will fall

To endleſſe ruine. I ſtand heere for Law.

 Du. This Letter from *Bellario* doth commend

A yong and Learned Doctor in our Court;

Where is he?

 Ner. He attendeth heere hard by

To know your anſwer, whether you'l admit him.

 Du. With all my heart. Some three or four of you

Go giue him curteous conduct to this place,

Meane time the Court ſhall heare *Bellarioes* Letter.

The First Folio of Shakespeare

Merchant of Venice, IV. i. 119–151

(For description, see Appendix, p. 289)

characteristics of tidewater Virginia, for example, covering a more limited territory than those of the northern tier of states in the Middle West. Each nevertheless, has its local metes and bounds, and for its section they are distinctive.

We have already remarked that the speech of large cities especially tends to become markedly local and dialectal. Thus to one observant of such matters, the speech of Boston or Philadelphia is soon perceived to be noticeably different from that of their near neighbor, New York. Theoretically one might say that it is the duty of the speakers of each community to strive for a common and universal speech; that, if the Bostonian will not speak like the Chicagoan or the Chicagoan like the Bostonian, then they should come together on some middle ground. Each region thus yielding some of its individual characteristics, we should arrive at a compromise among the various local speeches which would be a universal, cosmopolitan speech.

The obvious obstacle in the way of this theory is that the behavior of language is not based on theory, but arises from actual use. When the Bostonian and Chicagoan are thrown so intimately together, when intercourse between them is so frequent and long-continued that they become practically one in their habits and customs, then, and not till then, will they speak a single speech. Then they will develop a new dialect comprehensive enough in its limits to include both Chicago and Boston. A standard speech cannot be imposed dogmatically, it cannot even be chosen voluntarily. It must grow, as all other customs grow in language, gradually and naturally. And until some such change takes place in the country as a whole, until from a group of more or less clearly defined communities, it becomes one great homogeneous community, so long we shall have local differences of speech and so long will the theory of a universal standard speech remain a vain and empty dream.

Besides the local or geographical aspect of the question, the matter of the standard speech may be approached from a second point of view, the social or educational. We have already pointed out that the speech of different social groups or classes differs widely. The popular speech is different from that of the educated person, and the colloquial and everyday speech of the latter is different from his careful and formal speech. The question of choice between the popular speech and the speech of educated and cultivated people presents little difficulty. Perhaps every one will agree without question that the speech of the uninformed and uninstructed has no claim to be regarded as the standard speech, and that, on the contrary, the speech of the cultivated portion of society has every claim to be so regarded.

The difficulty comes not in making the choice, but in preparing the way for the choice, in determining just who are the cultivated and educated speakers whom we are willing to regard as affording the models or laws of the correct or standard speech. The difficulty of defining education, culture, and refinement is one that has often been felt. They are qualities that may be readily perceived when they are exemplified in individuals, but often defy precise description and analysis. Perhaps the main source of the difficulty lies in the fact that the qualities mentioned are largely matters of opinion, that no person is absolutely educated or refined or cultured. One whom I might regard as an educated and refined person, another, with higher or at least different standards, might regard as uneducated, as crude and vulgar, or vice versa. Everything depends upon the point of view, the predilections, the background, the customary habits and ways of thinking of the person who acts as judge and critic.

The bearing of this upon the question of the standard of correct speech is direct. What shall I regard as an appropriate model? Where shall I place the line between that which is to be approved and that which is to be condemned and rejected? To these questions there is no general answer. Each person must put the questions to himself and must answer them for himself. He must judge and choose according to his own light and according to his own opportunities of experience and observation. It is the end of education to enable one to make right decisions in

137

such matters, and the whole process of education cannot be stated in a word. It is obviously necessary to make these decisions not only with respect to a few great figures or authorities, not only with respect to public speakers, for example, whom one hears only at rare intervals, but also with respect to one's daily associates and the hourly customs and habits of familiar life. The decisions of the latter kind are naturally the more important ones, but at the same time the ones concerning which it is least possible to give a general guiding rule. Here again individual judgment is the only way we have of deciding who the good speakers are among those whom we meet. We are naturally inclined to regard our own judgment in such matters as universal and final, but this is an assumption that is likely to be questioned as soon as we try to impose our standards and decisions upon others.

The authority of dictionaries and other printed works rests upon somewhat the same basis as that of persons. Dictionaries and other guidebooks are the work of finite human beings, and though, in general, the compilers of them are men of exceptional weight and authority because of their greater information and extent of observation, they are nevertheless fallible and limited in their experience. Consequently, when the statement of a dictionary differs from one's own observation, the sensible thing to do, *after one has made sure that the observation is true*, is to disregard the dictionary altogether and to follow the example of actual use. Moreover, from the nature of the case, dictionaries are bound to become antiquated. Before one gives much weight to the decision of a dictionary, one should make sure that the dictionary is a record of contemporary use. Early editions of Webster's dictionary,[15] for example, record the pronunciation [dif] for *deaf*, as well as many other uses that are no longer current or have become quite dialectal. But even the more contemporary dictionaries are not always a certain guide. In the great proportion of instances they, of course, are, since the problem of choosing

[15] The later editions are known as Webster's *International Dictionary* and Webster's *New International Dictionary*.

from among variant pronunciations arises only infrequently. One should exercise considerable caution, therefore, before one differs from the *Oxford English Dictionary*, Webster's *New International* or the *Random House Dictionary*, and all the more caution when these various dictionaries agree.

Furthermore, over the past thirty or forty years, dictionaries in the United States have made considerable advances in the accuracy with which they record current pronunciation. This is another reason for their differing from each other much less than they used to. In the original edition of this book, the author was able to point out marked deviations in one dictionary or another from what was even then current usage. Examples included *peremptory* with stress on the first syllable, *octopus* and *inquiry* with the stress on the second, *vizor* with its first vowel that of *bit*. Even as late as 1934, the earliest printings of the second edition of Webster's *New International Dictionary* failed to record all the current pronunciations of *altimeter*, *caries*, and *dour*, and frequently omitted variant pronunciations of high incidence in the southern part of the United States. There is no question, however, that the careful observation and systematic surveys of current usage which formed the basis of such specialized dictionaries as Daniel Jones's *Pronouncing Dictionary of the English Language* and Knott and Kenyon's *Pronouncing Dictionary of American English* had a beneficial influence on the treatment of pronunciation in the general dictionaries. Still, occasions may occur in which reputable use is at variance with the united opinion of even the best dictionaries.

Despite this improvement in the reporting of pronunciation, unfortunately the pronunciations given in the generally excellent dictionaries now available to the public are often misused and misinterpreted. This stems primarily from two causes: an inability to interpret correctly the devices employed by the dictionary for indicating the quality of sounds, and a failure to understand the degree of approval given to variant pronunciations. These will be considered in turn.

139

In general there are two types of schemes for representing sounds graphically. One is to assign to each symbol employed a particular configuration of the organs of articulation. This is the principle behind the phonetic alphabet. For example, in the phonetic alphabet employed in this book, the symbol [ɑ] represents a low back *unrounded* vowel; the symbol [ɔ] represents a low back *rounded* vowel. Thus, in the discussion of the variant pronunciations of such words as *cod, fog, not*, and *stop*, earlier in this chapter, it was necessary to transcribe each of them twice, once with the symbol for the rounded vowel and once with the symbol for the unrounded vowel. In connection with words of the *calf, path, pass* type, three transcriptions were employed.

In short, although a phonetic alphabet is precise, it is by no means economical. In a finely graded alphabet, as many as five or six transcriptions might be necessary to represent all the variant pronunciations a word might have throughout the English-speaking world. This would require more space than dictionaries are generally willing to devote to pronunciation; space is at a premium in most dictionaries. It would also require more editing and proofreading time, thus resulting in added expense.

The primary factor, however, which has militated against the use of a phonetic alphabet in American dictionaries is that the American public doesn't like it. Dictionary users seem to be confused by the Latin or continental values for the ordinary vowel letters and distracted by the unconventional shape and appearance of some of the other characters. Over the past half-century the only phonetic symbol which has gained general acceptance has been the schwa—ə—now used by most dictionaries for the neutral vowel of unstressed syllables, the *a* of *about*, the *u* of *circus*. For the most part, the dictionary-buying public prefers respelling with the conventional letters of the alphabet, modified when necessary by such diacritical marks as the macron, the breve, the circumflex. This is what the American dictionary publishers have continued to supply.

What the public often fails to understand in connection with such a system of diacritically modified alphabetic characters is that they tend to represent a class of sounds rather than the particular configuration of the vocal organs which produces a specific sound. For example, most American dictionaries will represent the vowel of the *fog, cot, stop, not*, group of words by the character ŏ. Some of the better dictionaries, in discussing the value of this character in the preface, will explain that it represents a variety of pronunciations, ranging all the way from [ɑ] to a raised and fairly rounded [ɔ]. Unfortunately, many dictionaries are not so specific. Thus, for some speakers of the language, the ŏ character merely duplicates the symbol ä, which they already employ for the vowel of such words as *father* and *calm*.

The principal objection, however, to the diacritical respellings is that those who consult dictionaries rarely take the trouble to find out precisely what the symbols are intended to represent. They fail to read the prefaces, depending instead upon the running key, which usually appears at the bottom of the page or the inside of the cover. These running keys merely give a particular word in which the sound occurs. For example, *odd* may be used as the key word for the ŏ character. But many speakers of the language pronounce this word with an *ah*-like sound, whereas others normally employ an *aw* type of sound. Consequently, the pronunciation key will be interpreted differently by these two groups. Moreover, as we have already seen, even with the same speaker, pronunciations within the short *o* class of words may vary according to the kind of consonant which follows, so essentially the dictionary has given them very little help.

It is true that symbols representing a phonemic class of words can be defended on the ground of economy. They eliminate the necessity of indicating many alternative pronunciations. Unfortunately the dictionary editors have not yet solved the problem of conveying a proper understanding of the symbols, either to the public at large or to teachers in the schools, whose responsibility it is to train their pupils in the use of the dictionary. For the present we are at something of an impasse.

141

The fiction that the first pronunciation in a dictionary carries a high degree of preference is another major bar to a precise understanding of the information that it conveys. There is every reason to believe that most dictionary editors make a conscientious attempt to survey current usage with respect to pronunciation. But the scale on which they are able to make such a survey is so limited that it would be unrealistic to attach any marked significance to the resulting measures of frequency of one pronunciation as over against another. There is no assurance, for example, that one survey of two or three hundred speakers might not show a slight majority in favor of *róbust*, whereas a second survey of two or three hundred equally cultivated speakers would show a similar majority in favor of *robust'*, with the stress on the second syllable. Yet the dictionary editor must place one of these pronunciations ahead of the other, and all he can do is to set down first the one for which he has the most evidence, slight as the majority may be.

Most dictionary prefaces have been less than candid about the real weight of such evidence and have tended to ascribe a much greater degree of authority or preference for their first pronunciations than the facts actually warrant. It is only rarely that an editor has displayed the courage of Clarence L. Barnhart, who says flatly in his preface to the *American College Dictionary* that *any* pronunciation recorded in that dictionary may be used without hesitation, and that it is not worth the effort to change from one dictionary pronunciation to another.

15 ⊠ Spelling Reform

The consideration of the question of spelling reform rightly finds a place in a discussion of English sounds, for the reason that English spelling is merely an outward and visible means of representing the sounds of the language. The language itself existed in all its essentials centuries before it was reduced to a written or a printed form, just as today the rare illiterate person who knows nothing about reading or writing is neverthe-less possessed of the power of language. Spelling or writing is, therefore, nothing more than an attempt to reduce to a fixed and permanent formula what was already preexistent in the imper-manent use of the spoken language.

It has already been pointed out, that whatever the immediate descriptive or pictorial character of written language may have been in its origin, it has now completely lost its pictorial value and is merely a set of conventional and arbitrary signs, the significances of which have to be learned and held in mind by a pure act of memory. In this respect the written language does not differ materially from the spoken language.

In the latter, as a result of many successive ages of custom and use, we have settled upon certain sounds and sequences of sounds as conveying certain ideas. The value and meaning of these sounds and groups of sounds have to be learned anew by every individual who acquires command of the language. Children, through a long period of trial and error, learn how to make the sounds and to comprehend what ideas the sounds stand for. No child has the command of language inherently and by nature, but only as he learns it by imitating the speech of others. In the same way, through a long process of development, we have come to settle upon certain written symbols and groups of symbols as standing for certain sounds and groups of sounds. Every child now learns to make this arbitrary connection between the symbol and the sound, just as before he had learned to make a connection between the various sounds and the respective ideas which they were used to designate. Now, having settled upon a conventional set of visible written symbols to stand for audible spoken sounds, the question of reform in our system of visible written symbols arises when an endeavor is made to improve or to make more consistent our system of symbols. Spelling reform, indeed, is only a name for this endeavor when it becomes conscious.

More or less unconscious spelling reform has been going on ever since the beginning of written language, because from the very beginning written language has been changing in order to adapt its system to the changes in the spoken language. When, for example, in the Middle English period, the initial consonant in such Old English words as *hring*, *hlēapan*, and *hrōf* ceased to be pronounced, and the words consequently were spelled *ring*, *leap*, and *roof*, that was as much a spelling reform as any that can be advocated nowadays. It is safe to say that every change in spelling has taken place because some one thought the change a necessary or advisable improvement in the system of spelling. The motive underlying the change may not always have been wise or well considered, but it is certain that changes have never taken place in a completely haphazard and causeless way.

The question is sometimes asked, Why is it necessary for us to think about the matter of spelling at all? Since our system of spelling is an arbitrary and conventional one, does it matter much what conventions we use? Why should we set to work consciously to alter or improve that which, when all is said, is certainly capable of performing, and for many generations has performed, the service for which it is intended? Or it is urged that if any changes are to be made, we should leave them to the next generation or the third or the fourth, or to whatever generation feels compelled to make them.

To all these queries and objections the answer is that we are under no necessity of considering the question of spelling reform. No matter how complicated or inconsistent or imperfect our system of written speech may be, if we wish to do so, we can make it serve. Englishmen have not lived and spoken and written all these generations without evolving a writing system which is to some degree adequate to the purposes for which it was devised. The question, therefore, of the improvement of English spelling is not one of necessity; it is one of desire and inclination.

If the present English spelling affords a fairly serviceable medium of written expression, it does so because it has been an object of thought and consideration to many generations of English-speaking peoples. Spelling is a human institution, and

144

like all human institutions, it has had its crude beginnings, it has grown as a result of the effort of individuals, and it has improved by rectifying its errors and by correcting its imperfections. That English spelling has now reached a state of ultimate perfection, that it is incapable of further improvement, is of course utter nonsense, and the idea may be dismissed out of hand.

Anyone who is even slightly familiar with the writing systems of such languages as Italian, Spanish, German, and Turkish cannot escape the conclusion that in terms of consistency and ease of learning, they are vastly superior to ours. Hours of school time are spent in teaching every English-speaking child how to spell and, in American schools at least, the results leave something to be desired. Over the past two or three generations a number of men of influence in the English-speaking world had firm convictions about the absolute necessity of spelling reform. Theodore Roosevelt employed many simplified spellings in his own writings. Andrew Carnegie generously supported a spelling reform movement. In his will, George Bernard Shaw sought to subsidize the development of an improved alphabet and frequently levelled the shafts of his satire at our present one. It has often been said that the greatest present obstacle to a wider use of English throughout the world is its unsatisfactory spelling system.

It stands to reason, therefore, that the question of spelling reform is one deserving of careful consideration and of a fair and reasonable answer. Our danger of error is no greater, perhaps is less great, than it has been in any preceding period. Equable judgment and sound scholarship should be as well able to care for the language of the future as they ever were in the past.

Just in what respect the accepted spelling may be improved and simplified must be determined by a separate discussion of individual instances. As in the case of the changes in sounds discussed in preceding paragraphs, the final acceptance of these changed or improved or reformed spellings must rest upon the individuals who use the written and printed form of the language.

It should be remembered that the chief obstacle in the path

145

of improved spelling is a result of exactly the same cause which has made change and improvement desirable. Spelling was at first free to adapt itself to the spoken forms of words. The simple and natural rule of spelling was to write as you speak. Consistency in the spelling of an individual and general uniformity among all writers were not regarded as necessary, or even as virtues towards which one should strive.

In Old English, for example, not only will the same word be spelled differently by different writers, but even the same writer does not always use the same spelling. This freedom in the treatment of spelling persists down through the time of Chaucer, even down through Shakespeare and later. One need only turn to an early quarto or folio edition of one of Shakespeare's plays, an edition in which the spelling has not been normalized and modernized, to see that the rules of Elizabethan spelling were much less uniform and consistent than they are in Modern English.

To find in our time an attitude towards spelling parallel to that of Shakespeare's, we must turn to the use of those whom we should now call the imperfectly educated, those who spell very much as they speak or as they feel inclined. The reason why the spelling of Shakespeare and of the contemporary imperfectly educated person is on the same plane, is that neither of these has acknowledged, or in fact is aware of, the ideal, current in our culture, of a consistent and uniform system of spelling. This is an invention of comparatively modern times, and it is only in modern times that it has been made a requirement and a test of the conventionally educated person.

The causes which have operated to bring about this change of attitude towards spelling are mainly the extension of the reading public and the influence of the dictionaries and spelling books. The influence of printing and of the rules of the printing houses upon English spelling has been very great. In the first place, the printer, with his professional sense of the importance of the mechanical side of his art, always strives for complete consistency and regularity. He makes his margins always the same width, his words are always spaced exactly so far apart, he uses the same kind of type always for the same purpose, and in countless ways he endeavors to make his work as mechanically uniform and regular as possible. Obviously, one of the first things to which he would direct attention would be the question of a uniform spelling. Thus we find with the rise of the great printing houses in England in the eighteenth century the origins of a rigidly uniform system of spelling.

About the same time regularizing tendencies began to show themselves also in the making of dictionaries and spelling books, the purpose of which was to choose from the various spellings and to record what was regarded as the one standard and correct spelling of words. This standard of correct spelling was usually derived from contemporary printed books, and consequently the dictionaries gave little more than the statement of the spelling rules of the printing houses. Among the dictionaries, the most influential was Dr. Johnson's, the first edition of which appeared in 1755. This book purported to give the correct spelling of all words, and it and other later dictionaries after its model have had great influence in spreading the belief that words have only one permissible and correct spelling, and that the one recorded by themselves.

Despite the amount of language that comes over the air waves and is taken in through the ear, the written language still assails us on every side: books, magazines, newspapers, advertisements in every form, an ever-increasing amount of mail. Because of this the printed word has come to seem almost more real than the spoken word. The former certainly is more obvious, more tangible, one might say, and more permanent. It leaves a more definite and lasting impression on the memory than the spoken word.

The result of these influences, of that of the printing houses, of the dictionaries and rule books for spelling, and of printed literature in general, has been to raise the printed word to a position of undeserved importance. It tends more and more to detach itself from the spoken word and to become an independent and conventional symbol for the former. Spelling thus becomes a thing apart, a system with its own rules and regulations that have no relation to anything else. We thus have spelling for spelling's sake, instead of the natural state of affairs, which is spelling for speaking's sake.

Recognizing the danger of being tyrannized over by an unyielding system of conventional spelling, we have the relief in our own hands. We should remember that whatever authority the dictionary maker and the printer have, they have it because the voluntary assent of the people grants it to them. Neither dictionary maker nor printer is a lawgiver who has power to legislate finally as to what spellings shall be and what shall not be. They are individuals, as are all other users of the language, and they acquire their authority just as other individuals do, that is, by the willingness of others to follow and imitate them.

Granting this, the way of the spelling simplifier or improver is clear. He may choose to follow the spelling of the dictionaries and the printers when he sees no good reason for deviating from it. But when he chooses to deviate from it, he has as great right, and if his judgment is sound, as good authority for doing so, as the dictionary has for preventing him.

The most radical scheme of spelling reform is that which is proposed by the advocates of a phonetic alphabet. They point out to us that spelling, or the visible form of language in general is intended merely as a representation of spoken language, and that as such it should be used with systematic consistency and exactness. They show that, on the contrary, our present spelling in some instances uses letters which are not pronounced at all, as the final *e* in *late*, the *ue* of *tongue*, the *l* of *walk*. In others, we use the same letter with different values, as the *c* in *cent* and *call*; the *a* in *hat, hate, hall*. In still others, different letters will have the same value, as *s* and *c* in *sent, scent*, and *cent*; *a* and *-ey* in *hate* and *they*; *e* and *ee* in *he* and *see*. In short, they point out what is certainly true, that our present spelling, for one reason and another, has become a very imperfect and inconsistent means of representing our present sounds.

As a corrective of all these evils, the phonetic reformers propose that an entirely new alphabet be invented, one in which each sound has its own symbol and in which no symbol has more than one value, that this new alphabet replace the old traditional alphabet, and then that every word be written in this new set of symbols as it is pronounced. Anglic, a reformed alphabet devised by the Swedish scholar R. E. Zachrisson, is one example of this approach to the problem.

On the surface the arguments for this kind of reform seem to be persuasive. It would result in a logical and systematic equivalence between sound and symbol, the ideal relationship which should exist between the spoken and written word. Upon closer examination, however, the reasons adduced in favor of such a system break down, and one can only conclude that short of a complete upheaval in the English-speaking world, such a reform could never be put into operation.

To begin with, we have already seen that the pronunciation of some two hundred and sixty million native speakers of English is far from uniform. This poses a dilemma. Either a phonetically-based system must take a single mode or standard of pronunciation as its model or it must give up the idea of uniformity. Most Americans pronounce *calf* with the vowel of *hat*. Many speakers of British English pronounce *calf* with the vowel of *father*. If the spelling of *calf* is to be the same throughout the English speech community, it will inevitably fail to represent the pronunciation of a considerable segment of it. If it is to represent pronunciation accurately, it will not be uniform.

If our language were in the hands of some autocratic power who by an imperial edict was able to declare that this or that shall henceforth be the law of the language, there might be some hope for the phonetic reformer. But the English language is not in the hands of an individual, or even in the hands of a group of individuals. It is the most democratic of all the institutions of a

149

democratic people. What the people do and what the people will determine the nature of the language.

Experience has shown that the will of the people is inalterably opposed to any such wholesale and violent overturning of their traditional language as the phonetic reform supposes. Our present system of spelling has come to be as it is slowly and gradually. It has its roots deeply fixed in the past. It is the form in which an ancient and dignified literature is recorded. Imperfect as it is, it is a part of our heritage of national and social tradition. The attempt, therefore, to replace the accepted spelling by a system of entirely new manufacture is not only impossible, but it does violence to a sentiment of respect and a feeling for the language which has long existed. It is not by such revolutionary methods that the spelling of the future is to be made better than the spelling of today. Now, as ever in language, changes must take place slowly and gradually. They must come because they meet with the approval of the general body of the users of the language, not because they seem good to some maker of systems and theories.

A compromise phonetic reform is that which would endeavor to get along with our present alphabet, but would so reconstruct the spelling of words that they would be spelled systematically in the phonetic way as far as is possible with the traditional alphabet. Thus the words *doe* and *dough*, being pronounced alike would be spelled alike, both perhaps *do*, by analogy to *so*. The same spelling could not of course answer for *doe* and *dough* and also for the verb *do*; the latter would therefore have to be changed, say to *doo*, to conform to the spelling *too, school, food*, etc. If, however, *oo* were settled upon as having the value of the vowel in *do*, then the word *rule* would have to be spelled *rool* (like *spool*), *through* would be spelled *throo, who* would become *whoo, fruit* would become *froot* (like *root*), and so on through a countless number of similar changes.

Again, although many of these changes would doubtless conduce to simplicity and regularity, the same objection holds against

150

carrying out a systematic and comprehensive scheme of spelling reform along these lines as against one based on the use of a phonetic alphabet. The changes necessitated are too numerous, and the violence done to the natural conservative feeling for the language is too great. The work of reform must proceed more slowly. Noah Webster, the first great American lexicographer, discovered this when, in the first edition of his *American Dictionary of the English Language*, he attempted to establish an extensive program of spelling reform along these lines. The reaction was violently unfavorable and, in subsequent editions, he was forced to retreat from his position.

A third comprehensive and systematic scheme of spelling reform, which is the exact opposite of that proposed by the phonetic reformers, is the one which, recognizing the difficulty of making English spelling conform to English pronunciation, seizes the other horn of the dilemma, and proposes that English pronunciation be made to conform to English spelling. The advocates of this theory, if there are any serious enough in its defense to be called its advocates, point out that we now have an approximately fixed and rigid system of spelling, and that it seems to be easier for us to make our spelling fixed and permanent and standard than our pronunciation. Why not, therefore, make spelling the standard of pronunciation, and instead of trying to write as we speak, speak as we write?

This ingenious proposal has one main obstacle in its way, an obstacle which, as we have had occasion to remark, lies in the way of many another proposal for the reform of language. That is, the English language does not grow and adapt itself to the far-reaching plans of theorists, but develops as it lives and is utilized in the everyday intercourse of life.

The history of English pronunciation has shown that in a comparatively very small number of words, the written form has reacted upon the spoken form and altered its pronunciation to conform to the spelling; thus, our word *perfect* [pɜfɪkt] is originally a learned spelling, based on the Latin *perfectum*, for the word which

151

was spelled *parfit* in Chaucer and which was pronounced as it was written. The learned spelling, however, not only crowded out the spelling *parfit*, but even, in time, made the pronunciation *parfit* conform to the spelling *perfect*. On the other hand, the word *debt*, which Chaucer spelled and pronounced *det*, because it is ultimately derived from Latin *debeo, debitum*, was given a *b* by the Renaissance spelling reformers. This *b*, though we have retained it in our spelling, *debt*, has never succeeded in making its way into the pronunciation as has the *c* in *perfect*. Other examples might be cited, but the instances in which pronunciation has adapted itself to the spelling of words are so few that they show the futility of the endeavor to make the principle of speaking as you write one of general application.

But if the theories for the reconstruction of English spelling which have just been discussed must be pronounced as impossible and visionary, it does not follow that nothing can be done for the English spelling of the present and of the future. We may refuse our support to radical and revolutionary movements without passing to the other extreme of ultra-conservatism. There is a middle ground between the complete reform of English spelling and unquestioning acquiescence in and acceptance of that which we have; and instead of attempting the thorough reconstruction of our spelling, we may more safely and with greater hope of success strive for the improvement and simplification of our present system.

Any changes which are made must be duly assessed. They must be tested by the principles which have governed the growth of the language in the past. It is only by the study of these historical principles that we can arrive at safe rules of guidance. Each change or each group of changes, therefore, offers a special problem which demands special consideration. Only a few of the more important can be discussed here.

A large number, perhaps the majority, of instances in which the question of spelling arises, come under the general head of choice between two spellings, both of which already are in current use. The determination of the choice rests of course upon the circumstances of each case, but a good rule of general application is, of two spellings choose the simpler. Other things being equal, that is always the simpler and the preferable of two spellings which is the shorter, or which is in conformity with the more general phonetic practice of the language. When one has the choice between a familiar English spelling and a strange or unusual spelling, the preference should be for the former. Thus there is little justification for spelling *gaol* when we have the form *jail*, or for the spelling *plough* when we have *plow*.

In making simplifications in spelling, however, it should be remembered that it is not necessary, or indeed possible, to be thoroughly consistent. We may decide to omit certain silent letters, but it does not follow that we should omit all silent letters. We may omit the *u* in *mould* without omitting it in *mourn*, thus spelling that word like the noun *morn*. The only safe guiding rule is to simplify spelling when there are advantages to be gained and no counterbalancing losses.

By observing the efforts to simplify and regularize English spelling over the past century and a half, we can arrive at some idea of what is possible at the present moment and in the near future, and what is likely to be doomed to failure. In the first place, we must recognize that certain attempts at simplification of spelling have made more headway in the United States than in Great Britain. This is due largely to the influence of Noah Webster who, as has been pointed out, embarked on a more ambitious program than he succeeded in establishing. Nevertheless, Americans are indebted to him for the following deviations from British practice:

1. The spellings *center, meter, miter, theater,* etc., with -*er* instead of -*re*, following the pattern of *father, winter, manner*.

2. The spellings *honor, ardor, fervor, color, savior,* etc., with -*or* in place of -*our*, following the pattern of *tailor, horror, pallor*.

3. The spelling -*ize* for the verbal suffix in such derivative

formations as *criticize, legalize, penalize*. However, the attempt to extend the spelling to non-derivative forms like *surprise, comprise* was not successful.

4. The omission of final *-e* in *ax, adz, develop,* and more recently to a few derivatives ending with *-in(e)* such as *glycerin*.

5. The omission of medial *-e-* in *judgment, acknowledgment, abridgment*.

6. The simplification of double consonants in such words as *fagot, wagon, woolen* in place of *faggot, waggon, woollen*.

More recently in the United States the following practices have also been adopted:

1. The simplification of the doubled consonant and the omission of the final *-e* in words like *program, epaulet, omelet, cigaret*.

2. The abandonment of the dieresis in such words as *encyclopedia, medieval, esthetic, archeology*.

3. The omission of final *-ue* in words like *prolog, catalog, decalog*.

Two influences have operated to retard or restrain what might otherwise seem to be justifiable attempts at spelling simplification. One of these may be termed the etymological principle. This has been felt with particular force in the learned sector of the vocabulary, where attempts to respell words of Greek derivation have met with strong resistance. Phonetically considered, the initial *rh-* of words such as *rhetoric, rhinoceros, rhomboid* have no more justification than the etymological *hr-* of words like *ring* and *raven*, but the spelling in the first group lingers on, just as does the *pn* of *pneumonia*, the *ps* of *psychology*, and the *ph* of a host of words, including *phonetic, photograph, phosphate, sulphur*, etc. The attempt to substitute *f* for *ph* in the latter group of words has met with only indifferent success.

Nor can we proceed too fast and too furiously with any spelling changes that seem to do great violence to the visual images to which we have become accustomed. For all their adherence to tradition on some points, the British have been somewhat more successful in substituting a final -*t* for -*ed* in the past tenses of verbs like *cross, crush, clip, mix,* in which the verb stem ends in a voiceless consonant, and even in such irregular formations as *learnt* and *spelt,* though even in Britain their adoption has not been universal by any means.

The spellings with -*gh* constitute a particular case in point. The sound represented by the *gh* spelling, a voiceless velar fricative like the German *ch* disappeared from the language about five hundred years ago. Sometimes it became [f], as in *laugh, enough,* and *trough;* elsewhere it merged with the preceding vowel, as in *though* and *thorough, taught, thought, and drought.*

After an interval of five hundred years we still employ the *gh* spelling in most of the words which once had it. We have come to adopt *plow* almost universally. *Tho, thru,* and *thoro* have had a measure of acceptance and are recognized as variant forms by most dictionaries. *Nite* for *night, rite* for *right* occur in such non-literary uses as advertisements and trade names but scarcely elsewhere. *Laff* and *enuf* are relegated chiefly to the comic strips.

The conclusion to be drawn from this is that change in spelling is likely to be piecemeal rather than sweeping in character. The Anglo-Saxon temperament, even when modified by an American willingness to innovate, has clearly indicated its reluctance to embark on a program of radical change with respect to spelling, or even to consider the problem officially at regular intervals, as is the practice in the Netherlands. Certain changes will come about over the years, but unless some unforeseen development occurs, these will not extend beyond the limits that our historical survey has indicated. Yet we need not conclude on a wholly negative note. In spelling, as in all other developments in language, our best recourse is to trust to frank, open, and enlightened discussion and to have the courage to go forward with what, on the basis of it seems most likely to be of permanent and general value.

6

ENGLISH WORDS

1 ⬚ The Study of Words

The study of words is in many respects the most approachable side of the study of language. This is true partly because the word is, in a way, an independent fact of language, and is thus much more readily appreciated than are sounds or inflections. Besides, the word has very immediate connections with thought. A history of the words of a language is almost a complete history of the thought and the civilization of the people who speak that language. The study of words is also of very great importance in the practical affairs of everyday life. One of the most valuable accomplishments a person can have is the ability to express himself clearly and forcibly in language, and to do this he must know how to use words, must know their significances, their connotations, and their possibilities. Of course no one supposes that mere information about words, however wide that information may be, will make a good writer or speaker; it is the just combination of thought with its appropriate words that is the result to be attained, and it is the proper purpose of the study of words to provide the unclothed thought with its fitting garb of expression.

156

All words have established themselves in the language in one of two ways, first, either by original creation, that is, the actual formation of new words or the new adaptation of old ones, this latter process being as much creation as the formation of new words outright; or second, by borrowing from other languages. These two methods of building up the vocabulary of the English language will now be considered in detail.

2 ✐ Word Creation

The question which probably rises first in the mind of the student of vocabulary is, What is the ultimate origin of the native words of the language with which we are so familiar? Did some primitive language creator fashion all words at one fixed time, and have we continued to use this original stock since then without adding our creations to it? Or does the creation of words still continue as an active process? To these questions the first answer is that by far the greater number of words are inherited from countless generations of speakers of the language who have preceded us. Our native words are therefore mainly a traditional inheritance just as our other common social possessions, as, for example, the organization of the family or the state, are traditional inheritances. They go back so far that their first origin is prehistoric and can be considered and explained only with the aid of theory.

The earliest and most primitive theoretical stage of language about which it is fruitful to reflect is the period of root-creation. To understand this stage of language we may examine the parallel to it in the language of children when they are first learning to speak. To a child such a word as *ball* may mean anything which has one of the characteristics of a ball, for example, that of roundness. Thus he may call an apple "ball," or a stone, or the moon, or anything round. To him the word *ball* expresses the root-idea of anything with the quality of roundness. In very primitive stages of human development we may suppose a state of affairs similar to that in the language of the child. Language consisted of a more or less limited number of generalized word-forms, or root-words, of wide application, but of corresponding indefiniteness of meaning.

The first thing which primitive speakers would naturally tend to do, would be to make these root-words more specific in their values so that language could be more exact. There would thus begin a development and specialization in the use of words which has continued to the present day, and which will continue so long as the language is a living, spoken and written medium of expression.

These later developments in specialization did not often take the direction of the creation of new roots. This is a power which probably became restricted in very early periods of the development of language, and which is now almost completely lost in English, being exemplified only in the invention of words the mere sound of which is descriptive of the objects they name. Examples of such "echoic words," as they have been called, are *boom, fizz, simmer, pop, snicker, sizzle, whir, whiz*, etc. More usually, however, specialization in vocabulary has come about in historic times not through the creation of new roots, but by means of the adaptation and development of old material. Such adaptations are still to be regarded as creations in language, since it is by an internal development of its own resources that the language increases its power and variety. This remains today a frequent method of growth in language, and some of the more important of these changes, which may be grouped under the general head of differentiation in vocabulary, will now be considered.

3 ⊠ Differentiation by Gradation

As a means of differentiating the meaning of words, gradation is no longer an active principle in English, although the workings of it in earlier periods are still to be observed in many Modern English words. The way in which words are differentiated in meaning by gradation may be best described by means of an illustration. We have, for example, the verb *drive*, with its principal parts *drive, drove, driven*. The form *drive* may also be a noun, as in the phrase *a long drive*. Also *drove* appears as a noun in *a drove of cattle*, as do the first three letters of *driven* in *a drift of snow*. We have, therefore, in these words a sort of root-form of word for the general idea of driving, which might be expressed by merely the consonant framework of it as *dr-v* or *dr-f*. To differentiate this generalized root-meaning, the language places different vowels in this consonant frame, in this instance the vowels [ɑɪ, o, ɪ].

Gradation is most readily observed in Modern English in the tense formation of the irregular or strong verbs, as *sing, sang, sung*, to which add also the noun *song*; *ride, rode, ridden*, to which add the nouns *raid* and *road*; *rise, rose, risen*; *bear, bore, borne*, to which add the noun *bier*, that upon which a body is borne, and *bairn*, one who is born in the natural sense, and the nouns *birth* and *burden*. Many of the words of the language are thus held together in such gradation groups, all of the words of the respective groups having the same general meaning but each being a specific application of that meaning.

Not all words, however, are members of gradation groups, some of the oldest and most familiar words in the language, such as *house, stone, water*, etc., apparently standing quite separate and independent. Words of this sort are, therefore, the only recognizable surviving representatives of the original root-words.

4 ⬛ Differentiation by Composition

The method of word formation or differentiation by composition is one that has existed from very early times and is still actively employed in the English language. It consists not in changing the root-form of the word, but in adding something to it, in placing side by side two previously independent elements, which then fuse into a single meaning, different from the

159

meaning of either element taken singly. The most obvious kind of composition is that in which we have the juxtaposition of two words each of which, taken separately, has a definite and clear meaning. We may call this the composition of full-words, the various kinds of full-words still compounded in English being as follows:

1. Noun + noun compounds, as in *typewriter, doorsill, sawhorse, window frame, pleasure trip, newsletter, airstrip, network, Disneyland, shotgun, silvertip* (the grizzly bear), etc. In all these instances we have two ideas loosely approximated, to form a new idea, the specific value of the new idea being intrusted to the inference of the speaker or hearer. This method of composition approaches the use of the adjective before the noun, but differs from it, as can be seen by comparing *a gold ring* and *a goldmine*; or the sentences "This cane has a silver tip" and "This bear is a silvertip."

2. Adjective + noun compounds, as in *blackbird, blackberry, Broadway, highway, bluegrass, hotbed, busybody, dark horse, quickstep, sweetbread*, etc.

3. Noun + adjective compounds, as in *penny-wise, pound-foolish, watertight, grass green, man-shaped, purse-proud, stone-cold*; cf. *King Richard III*, ACT I, Sc. 2, l. 5: "Poor *key-cold* figure of a holy king."

4. Adverb + verb compounds, forming nouns, as in *downfall, downpour, output, upstart, upshot, offshoot, undertow*, etc.

5. Verb + adverb compounds, forming nouns, as in *go-by, comedown, breakup, cutoff, walkover, dugout*, etc.

6. Adjective or adverb + adjective or adverb, as in *blue-green, ever-young, evergreen, long-winded, worldly-wise, outright*.

7. Adverb + verb compounds, forming verbs, as in *upgrade, outrun, overdo, underrate, gainsay, withstand*, etc.

8. Preposition compounds, as in *into, because, beside, alongside, unto, until*, etc.

9. Particle compounds, as in *nevertheless, although, altogether, notwithstanding, always*, etc.

10. Verb stem (originally imperative) + noun, expressing the object of the action of the verb idea, as in *breakwater*, *breakfast*, *driveway*, *standpoint*, *scapegrace*, *scarecrow*, *turnkey*, *carryall*, *viewpoint*, etc.

11. Phrase compounds, groups of words which through long custom have come to be written together, as in *father-in-law*, *man-of-war*, *tradesman* (originally *trade's man*, a man of trade), *goodnight* (from *I wish you a good night*), *hand-to-mouth*, etc.

It is often very difficult to tell whether a compound should be written solid (*textbook*), with a hyphen or hyphens (*will-of-the-wisp*), or as separate words (*fire insurance*). The usage of good writers, of dictionaries, and the printing houses differs widely in this respect. If any current trend is discernible at all, it is toward the gradual lessening of the use of the hyphen, except for combinations of more than two elements (*hand-to-mouth*). Combinations of words which would bring vowels together at the point of juncture are seldom written solid, for example *life insurance*, *fire escape*, but even here *firearm* constitutes a notable exception.

This suggests, moreover, that there is often no essential difference between words which are written as compounds and other words which are never so written, as, for example, *out of* and *into* in the sentence, "He fell out of the frying pan into the fire." So words like *notwithstanding*, *nevertheless*, etc., are written together, whereas the approximately equivalent words, *on the contrary*, *in spite of*, etc., are never so written. The question is one which often has to be left to the arbitrary decision of usage.

5 ◼ Obscure Components

Attention has already been called to the fact (pp. 122 ff.) that one element of a compound word may become obscured in pronunciation, and thus lose its significance. As a result of this tendency we now have a great many words in English which were formerly compounds of full-words, and which were felt as such, but which now no longer show the elements of which they are composed. Examples are *window*, from Old English *wind + ēage*, 'wind-eye'; *nostril*, from Old English *nos + þȳrel*, 'nose-hole'; *starboard*, from Old English *stēor + bord*, 'steer-board,' the board (cf. sea-board), or side of a boat, from which the steering is done; *hussy*, from Old English *hūs + wīf*, 'house-wife'; *woman*, from Old English *wīf + man*; *gossip*, from Old English *god + sib*, literally 'god-friend,' used first of the sponsors at baptism, then of any familiar friend of the family, then by natural transition to its present meaning of gossip; *stirrup*, from Old English *stīg + rāp*, 'mounting-rope'; *dipsey* (as in dipsey chantey), from *deep + sea*; *brimstone*, from *brin* (by metathesis from 'burn,' cf. Germ. brennen) *+ stone*, 'burn-stone'; *barn*, from Old English *ber + ærn*, *ber*, 'barley,' *ærn*, 'building,' the whole word meaning, therefore, 'building in which barley was kept'; *orchard*, from Old English *ort + geard*, literally 'garden yard,' the first element being probably the same as Latin *hortus*.

In a word like *cupboard* the compound has become obscured in pronunciation, although the spelling still keeps clear the elements of which it is composed. In many instances popular etymology has endeavored to make full compounds out of words which were of quite different etymological origin. Thus the word *hiccough*, pronounced *hickup*, seems really to be derived from a form *hicket*, the first syllable *hick-* being allied to the form *hack-*, as in "a hacking cough," and the syllable *-et* being merely a diminutive suffix. The spelling *hiccough* arose apparently because the word was thought to have something to do with the word *cough*. Other familiar instances of similar popular etymologies are *sparrowgrass* from *asparagus*; *ash-falt* from *asphalt*; *causeway* from the French word *chaussée*, meaning a high-road; *crayfish*, or popularly *crawfish*, from Old French *crevice*, Modern French *écrevisse*. The word *hackneyed*, as in "*a hackneyed phrase*," meaning something worn down from constant usage, derived from the Old French *haquenée*, 'an ambling horse or mare,' then by extension,

any horse put out to public hire, and by still further extension, anything overworked, was sometimes etymologized into
hack-kneed. In all these instances more or less unfamiliar words
are explained in terms of other words, the forms of which at
least are more familiar, although their connection in meaning
with the original word is often quite remote.

6 ▨ Compositional Elements

Besides the composition of full-words, English makes
frequent use of certain word-forms which, taken separately,
do not have any clear and full meaning, but which are used only
as prefixes and suffixes to make more specific the meaning of other
words. These compositional elements, as they may be called,
may possibly all have been full-words at some remote period,
but if so this full meaning of most of them has been lost more
completely than it has in the case of the obscure compounds mentioned in the preceding section. The method by which compositional elements are used to differentiate the meaning of words
is too familiar to need extended illustration. The element *-dom*,
for example, forms compounds like *kingdom, wisdom, freedom,*
etc.; *-hood* forms the compounds *knighthood, childhood, manhood,*
priesthood, etc.; *-ship* appears in *friendship, kinship, worship, fellow-*
ship, etc.; *-er* is very common as a suffix in nouns of agency, as
in *baker, writer, singer, driver, speaker, abstainer*, etc. Examples of
prefixes are *a-* in *arise, alight*; *be-* in *bedeck, berate, bespeak*, etc.

It is to be noted that the free use of compositional elements
to form new words has been very much restricted by traditional
usage. With the suffix *-th* we can form the noun *youth* from *young,*
truth from *true, mirth* from *mer(ry), wealth* from *weal, health* from
heal; but we cannot form *gloomth* from *gloom*, or *wrongth* from
wrong, or *illth* from *ill*, although jocularly we sometimes form
coolth from *cool* as a parallel to *warmth* from *warm*.

Moreover, certain compositional elements tend to take on a very
specific value, not of course to the extent of becoming full-words,

although they acquire the power of changing the root-word in a very definite way. Thus the prefix *be-* has acquired to a considerable extent the power of giving a derogatory or slightly contemptuous sense to the word with which it is compounded, as in *bepraise, befog, bedeck, bedizen, bedevil, belabor, bedaub, besmear, bemire, befuddle, becalm, bedraggle, bemuse.* This value of *be-* is illustrated in the following stanza of Kipling's *Cruisers*:

> As our mother, the Frigate, *bepainted* and fine,
> Made play for her bully, the Ship of the Line;
> So we, her bold daughters by iron and fire,
> Accost and destroy to our master's desire.

So also the suffix *-ard*, when it is limited to persons, is often used in a derogatory sense, as in *coward, sluggard, niggard, wizard, dullard, dastard, bastard, dotard, drunkard,* beside which we have only a few nouns, such as *blizzard, gizzard, custard, mustard,* etc., of various etymological origins.

The suffix *-ish* also has an interesting history. In the earlier periods of the language it was used to form adjectives of quality without particular connotation, as in *Englisc,* 'English,' *folcisc,* 'folkish' (i.e., to use the modern Latin equivalent word, 'popular'); and Chaucer (*Troilus and Criseyde*, v, l. 1813) even speaks of "hevenish melodye." Later the suffix came to be applied to adjectives in order to indicate a slight degree of the quality named by the adjective, as *bluish, brackish, sweetish,* etc., and then, perhaps through such words as *boyish, girlish,* to give a somewhat contemptuous or scornful turn to the word, as in *womanish, mannish, childish,* as compared with *womanly, manly, childlike,* and in other adjectives like *bookish, heathenish,* etc.[1] In Chaucer, however, the suffixes *-ly* and *-ish* had not yet been differentiated. This is shown by his phrase, "heavenish melody," with which

---

[1] It is interesting to note that a parallel development has taken place in the case of the same ending, *-isch*, in German, as in words like *diebisch, närrisch,* etc. See Brugmann, *The Nature and Origin of the Noun Genders*, pp. 28–30.

compare his use of *fiendly* where we should now have to say *fiendish*:

That man hath a feendly herte.—*Book of the Duchess*, 593.

Inflectional elements are often closely related to compositional elements, and, as has already been pointed out,[2] some of them may have been independent full-words which have become very much obscured in the course of time.

7 ◻ Differentiation by Metaphor

This method of differentiating the meanings of words consists in changing a word from one order of thought to another without changing its form. This may be done in various ways, as follows:

1. A concrete term may be changed from one concrete sense to another, as, for example, the word *crane*, originally the name of the bird, becomes also the name for the hoisting machine, the most notable thing about both cranes being their long legs. The word *horse*, first the name of the animal, may mean also a piece of gymnasium apparatus, or a rack for hanging objects on, as a clotheshorse. The noun *key* from its first literal sense passes to numerous metaphorical senses, as, for example, its use to designate a book which gives answers to problems contained in another book; or we may speak of an important fact as "the key to the mystery." Primarily the word *chest* meant only a box, usually a box in which valuables were kept; but about the sixteenth century it came to be used also of the framework of the breast which encloses the heart, a figurative use which is exemplified in various conscious metaphors before it settles down into the literal meaning. Thus we have the following couplet in Shakespeare's *Richard II*, ACT I, Sc. 1, ll. 180–181:

> "A jewel in a ten-times barr'd-up chest,
> Is a bold spirit in a loyal breast."

[2] See above, pp. 49–51.

165

Shakespeare's contemporary, Sir John Davies, elaborates the same figure in the following stanza of his *Nosce Te Ipsum* with a fullness of detail which to a modern writer would be quite impossible now that the word *chest* has acquired literal and commonplace meanings:

> "O ignorant poor man! what dost thou beare
> Lockt up within the casket of thy brest?
> What jewels, and what riches hast thou there!
> What heavenly treasure in so weake a chest!"[3]

This feeling for the figurative use of *chest* may be further illustrated by the use of *box* in a similar way in the following passage from a seventeenth century writer: "I had yours lately by a safe hand, wherein I find you open to me all the Boxes of your Breast."[4]

The parts of the human body are used very frequently with this transferred metaphorical value. Thus *head* may be used of the head of a nail, screw, or pin; of a head of lettuce; the front of an automobile or locomotive, as illustrated by *headlight*; and of many other similar objects. We also speak of the *leg* of a table or chair; the *foot* of a mountain; the *hand* of a watch or dial; the *eye* of a needle; the *nose* of a boat or ship; the *ear*, meaning handle, of a bottle, as in Cowper's *John Gilpin's Ride*, "Each bottle had a curling ear";[5] the *mouth* of a vessel or a river; the *beard* of a head of wheat or barley; the *teeth* of a saw; the *tongue* of a wagon; the *cheek* of a peach; the *arm* of a lever; the *bosom* of the earth. There are many other instances, literally too numerous to mention.

2. A concrete word may be changed from a physical sense to an intellectual or spiritual sense, as the adjective *burning* in "a burning desire," or *cold* in "a cold disposition," or *heavy* in "a heavy heart." The word *sad* had originally a physical meaning

---

[3] Davies, *Nosce Te Ipsum*, ed. Grosart, I, 114.

[4] Howell, *Familiar Letters*, ed. Jacobs, II, 378.

[5] The word *ear*, in "ear of corn," is etymologically a different word, though now it is usually thought of as being a metaphorical use of the name of part of the body.

which persisted into the present century in a few uses, like *sadiron*, or as descriptive of heavy, soggy cake or bread.

The adjective *sullen* has a somewhat similar history. It is derived ultimately from a Late Latin *solanus*, through the French meaning 'single, solitary.' Thus Chaucer in his *Parlement of Foules* (1. 607) has the cuckoo say that if he can have his mate, the other birds may be *sullen*, or in Chaucer's spelling, *soleyn*, all their lives. This meaning persists fairly late, as may be seen from its use by Defoe (*Essay on Projects*, London, 1697, p. 244): "But there is a direct Signification of Words, or a Cadence in Expression, which we call speaking Sense; this, like Truth, is *sullen* and the same, ever was and will be so, in what manner and in what Language soever 't is express'd." From single or solitary in the physical sense to the meaning aloof, *sullen*, in the spiritual or mental sense, is an easy transition.

3. An intellectual word, on the other hand, may be used to designate a concrete person or object, as the word *wit*, in its intellectual sense meaning brilliance or ingenuity, in its concrete sense, as in the sentence "He is a great wit," meaning "a witty man." So *trust* in its intellectual sense is the name of an abstract quality, in its concrete sense it is the name of a group of men organized for certain purposes of business. Dialectally, also, the abstract noun *misery* takes a concrete sense in sentences like "I've got a misery in my back"; compare also the use of *pain* as both abstract and concrete.

4. Words appropriate to living beings may be transferred to inanimate objects. This process is frequently exemplified in poetry, where Ruskin has given it the name "pathetic fallacy." Thus Coleridge in *The Ancient Mariner* speaks of "the *silly* buckets," and Ruskin quotes such lines as "the *cruel, crawling* foam."[6] In addition we have such common phrases as "a *dumb*

---

[6] *Modern Painters*, Part IV, Chapter XII: "The foam is not cruel, neither does it crawl. The state of mind which attributes to it these characters of a living creature is one in which the reason is unhinged by grief. All violent feelings have the same effect. They produce in us a falseness in all our impressions of external things, which I would generally characterize as the 'Pathetic Fallacy.'"

waiter," "a *blind* alley," "a *crying* need," etc. These are, or were originally, very strong metaphors and had the effect of personifying the objects to which they are applied. They differ thus from the examples given under (1), such as the "*leg* of a chair," which is a perfectly matter-of-fact use of the word *leg*.

5. Words appropriate to one group of sense perceptions may be extended in their use by applying them to a different group, as when we speak of "a *loud* color," or "a *sweet* voice," "a *dull* sound," "a *bright* melody," etc.

8 ▨ Differentiation by Functional Change

One of the most interesting of the ways in which our vocabulary is given variety in use is by the passage of a word from one part of speech to another. Modern English is especially free in its use of this kind of differentiation, or specialization in words, as is shown by the following illustrations:[7]

1. Adjectives become nouns, as in "the *good*, the *true*, and the *beautiful*"; "so much to the *good*"; "he has gone to the *bad*"; "he was ordered to the *front*"; "a *nickel*"=a five-cent piece; "a *pug*"=a pug dog; "the *young* of the eagle"; "the village *green*"; "a *square*"=a city block or square; "the *blues*"; "the pine *barrens*." This happens frequently in the case of proper adjectives, which lose their adjective value and become pure nouns, as *china*, from "China ware"; *calico*, from "Calicut cloth"; *bantam*, from "Bantam fowl."

2. Nouns become adjectives, as in "a *New York* bank," "a

---

[7] Note how closely some words in Modern English, because of the various functional and figurative values which they may have, have come to approach the use of root-words in their ability to express a large group of related ideas. The word *head*, for example, may be a noun naming the part of the body; or the beginning of anything, as the head of a list, or page, or river or lake; or anything shaped somewhat like a head, as a head of cabbage, the head of a drum, the head of a nail or screw, etc. It may also be a verb, as in the sentence, "He heads the list," or "This lettuce heads early," i.e., makes a head. It may further be an adjective, as in "the head waters of the rivers," "the head clerk," "the head (cf. *chief*, from Latin *caput* through French *chef*) difficulty," etc.

168

beefsteak dinner," "a *home* leave," "a *stone* house," "a *railway* official," "a *city* superintendent," "an *afternoon* program," etc.[8]

3. Verbs become nouns, as in "a *brand* of goods," from the act of branding; "a *drive* of logs"; "the *help*" (i.e., the servants); "to give one a *lift*"; "a *find*"; "a *kill*"; "a *combine*."

4. Nouns become verbs, as in "to *house* the poor"; "to *carpet* a room"; "to *stone* a cat"; "to *bridge* a stream"; "to *board* a ship or train."

5. Pronouns become nouns, as in "In the south only the *shes* with young and the fat he-bears retire for the sleep." (T. Roosevelt, *Hunting the Grisly*, p. 54.)

6. Adverbs become verbs, as in "He *downed* his opponent in the first round"; "Then he *offs* with his hat."

7. Adverbs become nouns, as "*Now* is the accepted time"; "A noise was heard from *without*"; "I have just come from *there*."

8. Adjectives become verbs, as in "The house *fronts* the street"; "Acid *sours* milk"; "Who will *brown* the toast?" "He *backed* the horse," etc.

9. Prepositions become adjectives, as in "a *through* train"; "the *under* dog"; "*by* product." In *bystander, byword*, etc., the preposition has been united to another word forming a close compound. The word *by-laws* is sometimes mistakenly supposed to be made up of the preposition *by* + the noun *law*, the compound having the sense of secondary or minor law. In origin, however, the element *by* in *by-law* is a Scandinavian word meaning 'town,' as it appears in place-names like *Whitby, Derby*, etc. The original meaning of the compound was therefore 'town law,' and this, in distinction to the general or national law, readily passed over into the derived modern meaning of secondary or minor law.

10. Adverbs become adjectives, as in "the *off* horse"; "the *then* Bishop of Lichfield" (Newman, *Apologia*, p. 31); "waiting

---

[8] Some of these examples are essentially the same as the noun + noun compounds described above, differing chiefly in that the primary stress is on the second member. The first members are sometimes called noun adjuncts.

for the *down* mail to Falmouth" (ibid., p. 32); "*outer* darkness"; "over rocks and *down* timber" (T. Roosevelt, *Hunting the Grisly*, p. 59).

11. Verbs usually intransitive become transitive, as in "Cornell will *row* Wisconsin"; "to *walk* a horse"; "to *walk* the streets"; "to *jump* a fence."

12. Verbs usually transitive become intransitive, as in "I don't *sing*, but I'm fond of *playing*."

To some slight extent we also have differentiation by stress in Modern English. Thus we have the verbs *object'*, *compound'*, *contract'*, *present'*, etc., with the corresponding nouns *ob'ject*, *com'-pound*, *con'tract*, *pres'ent*, etc.

9 ◪ Slang

Any consideration of creation in language, or the differentiation in the meanings of words, must necessarily take up the question of slang. There is an initial difficulty, however, in that it is extremely hard to give a satisfactory definition of slang. The matter is very largely one of individual feeling. What is regarded as slang by one person is regarded as perfectly correct, colorless English by another. Thus the phrases *on the wrong tack*, *at dead center*, *to play the market*, etc., may be regarded by one speaker merely as good vigorous colloquial English, whereas an over-cautious speaker may reject them as "slangy," that is to say lacking in propriety.

So also the phrase "out of sight" acquired a certain slang use which for a time was widely current; but certainly no one would think that Lowell meant to use the phrase with this value in the following lines from the *Vision of Sir Launfal*:

> He sculptured every summer delight
> In his halls and chambers out of sight.

A similar illustration is to be found in the use of *fire* in the sense of discharge or expel, as in "to fire a person out of a room."

Exactly the same occurs in Shakespeare, without any of the connotation of slang, in the following lines, the thought of which is the presence of two spirits, one good and one evil, in man's heart:

> Yet this shall I ne'er know, but live in doubt,
> Till my bad angel fire my good one out.
>
> *Sonnets*, CXLIV.

Indeed the feeling for slang is on the whole of rather modern origin. In Shakespeare's day and earlier the language was free to be as expressive as it could and in any way in which it could. Slang can arise only when certain things are not permitted, for there is always the flavor of forbidden fruit in slang. In reading early authors, consequently, one is frequently struck by forms of expression which would have been slang if the conventions of the time had been more rigid. Thus Chaucer (*Parlement of Foules*, l. 595) says: *There been mo sterres, god wot, than a paire*, "There are more stars, God knows, than a pair," which is a fairly close parallel to "There's more than one pebble on the beach." In the *Digby Plays* (p. 14, l. 338) occurs the expression, *thou to make me a knight, that were on the newe*, which structurally, at least, cannot fail to remind one of such current phrases as "on the make" and "on the town."

An Elizabethan critic, Richard Carew, wrote a little treatise on the excellency of the English tongue, about the year 1595, in which he illustrates the richness of the English language by showing in how many different ways we can get rid of a person; his list is as follows, and it is interesting to see how many of his phrases would now fall under the general condemnation as slang: "neither cann any tongue (as I am perswaded) deliuer a matter with more varietye then ours, both plainely and by prouerbes and Metaphors; for example, when wee would be rid of one, wee vse to saye *Bee going, trudge, pack, be faring, hence, awaye, shifte*, and by circumlocution, *rather your roome then your companye, Letts see your backe, com againe when I bid you, when you are called, sent for, intreated, willed, desiered, inuited, spare vs your place, another in your steede, a shipp of salte for you, saue your credite, you are next the doore, the doore is open for you, theres noe bodye holdes you, no bodie teares your sleeue,* etc." [9]

The term slang is sometimes used in a very loose sense to include all those characteristics of language that one disapproves of which do not come under the head of bad grammar or of vulgar and improper speech. Such a definition of slang, however, is decidedly too wide. For there is a certain group of words with very clearly defined characteristics which everybody feels as having something in common, a spirit or tone, to which we should limit the term slang. To fall in this group a word must possess certain elements of novelty and originality in its use, it must be of a somewhat quaint, picturesque, playful, or humorous color, and above all it must have patness, freshness, and timeliness in its applications. Slang words, however, are always more readily felt than described, and the best way to consider them is, perhaps, to take up the various types of words which fall in the class.

1. COUNTER WORDS. By counter words are meant such words as are chosen by common social understanding to do service for a great variety of uses. These words become a sort of blank counter for certain ideas to which we do not then give exact and definite expression. The invention of such words is a social convenience. It is not always necessary to state precisely what we mean, and it is therefore often convenient to have an accepted conventional word to take the place of a specific word.

Though it can scarcely be considered as slang any longer, *nice* offers an excellent illustration of a counter word. From the fourteenth to the nineteenth centuries it had a host of specific meanings, ranging from 'ignorant,' 'foolish,' to 'finely discriminating.' Then it came to be generally applied as a term of approval: a walk, a day, a place, a dinner, a person can all be *nice*—if the speaker has nothing more specific to say about them.

---

[9] In Gregory Smith, *Elizabethan Critical Essays*, II, 292.

Similarly the word *awful*, the earlier meaning of which is still discernible, began to serve as a general term of disfavor, equally applicable to walks, days, places, dinners, persons, or almost anything else imaginable.

Counter words because of their constant use became weakened in value, indeed almost colorless in meaning, with the result that they indicate no more than a general attitude of mind of the speaker as favorable or unfavorable to the objects spoken of. Owing to this tendency, old worn-out counter words are at times replaced by new ones. Looking back over only a few years, one can recall numbers of counter words, or phrases, which sprang up and were used for a time and then dropped completely out. *Swell, keen, cool,* and *sharp* come to mind as terms of general approval; *fierce, vile,* and *lousy* as terms of condemnation.

If we examine the literature of earlier periods we shall find that each had its own counter words. Thus in the eighteenth century the counter word used in commendatory senses was the word *elegant*. It was used in all the ways in which *nice* is now used, and in certain directions its use was more extensive, as in such phrases as "the elegant author of the Essay on Man," "An elegant essay, novel, or poem," etc. It has persisted to the present time, mainly in the phrase, "An elegant time."

In the Elizabethan period the favorite counter word, equivalent to *nice* and *elegant*, was *fair*. Such a play as Shakespeare's *Love's Labour's Lost*, which is very contemporary in its diction, is full of illustrations; note especially the beginning of scene one in Act Four. The variety of its use may perhaps be better illustrated by the following passage in prose, taken from one of the works of a contemporary of Shakespeare:

"There is now building in Amiens a very *faire* Nunnery for the same Carmelite Nunnes which do now live in another Nunnery that is more obscure and less delightful for their contemplation. They remove shortly from that wherein they now live to that which is now building, because it is a more private and solitary place for their meditation, and the service of God. Unto this new Nunnery there belongeth a *faire* garden full of fine spacious walkes, beset with sundry pleasant trees. I was at the monastery of the Capucins, in whose church there were two *faire* altars, with many pictures of Christ and Saint Francis. They have a *faire* garden belonging to their Monastery, neare to which they have a Cloister, wherein are hanged many religious pictures, emblemes, and posies tending to mortification.

"At Saint Germans Church there is a wondrous rich altar, very abundantly decked with precious ornaments, especially a gilt Tabernacle. This is the *fairest* Altar by many degrees that I saw in all the City.

"The towne house which is very neare to the gate as you come into the city from Pickeney is very *fair*, being three stories high, and built with bricke, having goodly armes in it.

"The *fairest* cage of birds that I saw in al France, was at the signe of the Ave Maria in Amiens, the workmanship whereof was very curious with gilt wyres.

"A little on this side Paris, even at the towns end, there is the *fayrest* Gallowes that ever I saw, built upon a little hillock called Mount Falcon, which consisteth of fourteene *fair* pillars of free-stone: this gallowes was made in the time of the Guisian Massacre, to hang the Admiral of France Chatillion, who was a Protestant, Anno Dom. 1572."[10]

The question of the attitude which we shall assume towards the use of these counter words is of considerable interest and importance. It is sometimes said that we should avoid using such words of generalized meaning, that to do so impoverishes thought, and that we should always strive to use definite and specific words. But suppose the idea we want to express is not definite and specific, but vague and general? Suppose we meet a person casually and in friendly salutation remark that it is a nice day? Does not the word *nice* express there all that it is necessary to express? It shows that we have in general kindly feelings towards the weather and nobody cares particularly whether it is because of the warmness or coolness or wetness or dryness of it. In short,

---

[10] Coryat's *Crudities*, reprinted from the edition of 1611, London, 1776, Vol. I, p. 19. The concluding paragraph is on p. 26.

there are many occasions when we need to express indefinite and conventional ideas or feelings, and for this purpose we need indefinite and conventional words.

There is, therefore, a proper time for the use of counter words, and then no other words would take their place. When the mind has occasion to use definite and specific words to express its thought it will look about and find these words; but the person who never uses any other than colorless, indefinite, and general words does so because the character of his thought is always colorless, commonplace, and vague. The corrective, therefore, of a too vague and general use of words is not merely to discontinue the use of the offending words, but to have something really definite to say.

2. SLANG AS PICTURESQUE METAPHOR. This is probably the source of the largest number of slang words. They originate from a striking and novel metaphor which is almost always of a ridiculous, or at least humorous, color, because of a grotesque contrast between the literal and the figurative meanings of the word. Thus some years ago slang took the two nouns *peach* and *honey*, and used them in all manner of commendatory senses; anything admirable or excellent could be spoken of as a *honey* or a *peach*. A person who expresses an opinion differing from one's own may be said *to be off his base*, a metaphor apparently taken from baseball. Or one whose mental operations are peculiar is described as *cracked*, or *off his nut*, both derived from the metaphor of the head as a nut.

The word *kick* was first used in a slang, metaphorical sense 'to oppose' or 'to object.' Then it came to be used as a noun plural to signify an exhilarating experience. One does something "for kicks." The metaphorical use of *fire*, probably from the figure of firing a gun, has already been mentioned; with it may be compared the similar use of *bounce*. The word *pull* passed in slang from its literal meaning to the metaphorical one of influence. The verb *to chisel* and the derived noun form *chiseler*, both acquired the meaning of dishonesty in financial transactions.

175

In the same general group belong the words *graft*, *grafter*, which literally apply to the grafting of something extraneous to an original stock, as a twig on a branch, but metaphorically to the person who gets more than the legitimate income from his position. In a trial held early in the century a motion to dismiss a slander suit was made on the ground that *grafter* was not a recognized word of the language. The judge wisely overruled the motion, and if he had not, the report goes on to say, "what legal redress would a man have when called a *muckraker* or a *mollycoddle*, both of which words are of much later vogue than *grafter*?"

Illustrations of these metaphorical slang creations might be increased indefinitely. Each day in each community the number is added to. Most of such inventions have a very short existence; they take the popular fancy for a time, are excessively used, and then are crowded out by some new novelty. It should be observed, however, that this method of word creation by the invention of slang through metaphor is a natural linguistic process that has gone on for a long time, that to it the language owes much of its effectiveness and expressiveness, and that as a natural helpful linguistic process, our attitude towards it should not be too scornful.

It needed only the acceptance of usage, for example, to make a good, expressive word of the originally slang word *pull*. In many other instances words which were originally striking and picturesque metaphors have been accepted into conventional good use, as, for example, the word *sulky*, the name of a vehicle, first used because the vehicle being one-seated suggested the idea of selfishness and sulkiness. If slang words do not now make their way into good use so freely as they did formerly, the reason may well be that our standards and conventions in language have become more fixed. We are inclined to estimate language not immediately from the point of view of its power and value in the expression of thought and feeling, as was the tendency in Shakespeare's day, but from the point of view of its agreement or disagreement with the preceding traditional use of the language.

Among those who live in our urban centers and who have had little formal education, however, such a thing as the idea of slang does not exist. To another person their speech may be very slangy, because it is contrary to the customs and traditions which he accepts as established and correct. But to the boy or man on the street all language is used merely for the sake of expression; to him that is its only purpose and justification, and he consequently feels free to adopt and change as much as he pleases. In other words, language is more likely to be a natural, growing, developing medium of communication among the untrained and unconventional than it is among the educated and conventional.

3. SLANG AS CANT PHRASEOLOGY. Every profession, or every group of people engaged in the same activity, tends to develop a vocabulary peculiar to itself, which we may call a class, or technical, or cant vocabulary. It is the professional or occupational jargon of the respective groups of people. Thus the stock markets have invented a great number of professional words and phrases, such as *bull* and *bear*; one is *long* on a certain stock when one is well provided with it, and *short* on it when one is inadequately provided; a person who engages in speculation is *playing the market*. Among those who have developed a fairly extensive group jargon are the college students. The student *flunks* an examination when he fails; *aces* it when he does extremely well. When he studies, he *hits the books*. A course which requires little exertion to pass is a *snap*, a *pipe*, a *gut*, depending upon the particular campus.

Still other groups which make frequent use of cant terms are sportsmen of various kinds, the racetrack, the kennel, the baseball and football field, for example, each having its own special vocabulary. Shoe salesmen, structural steel workers, circus and carnival employees all have their occupational terms, and perhaps more than any other, the floating population of crooks and tramps. With the recent concern over drug addiction, the public has become aware of *pot* for marijuana, *snow* for cocaine crystals,

177

as well as such expressions as *to take a trip* and to have *a monkey on one's back*.

It should be noted that the cant vocabulary of one group is largely unintelligible to another group, the terminology of the stock market having meaning chiefly for brokers and investors. It is obvious that the jargon of a profession or of any group of people may cease to have slang value to the people who habitually use it, becoming to them merely the literal names for the activities of their occupation and thus a part of their technical vocabulary. Words of this sort do not often pass beyond the limits of their group and into general use.

4. SLANG AS PICTURESQUE SOUND. Often a slang word does not apparently have any clear logical meaning, but comes into use merely because its sound is amusing or suggestive of some idea. Such a word was *skidoo*, heard everywhere shortly after the turn of the century, a later equivalent of an older *skedaddle*. Similar words are *yack*, meaning to 'talk or chatter,' *goon*, 'a ruffian,' *burp*, 'to belch' or 'a belch,' *zap*, 'to strike,' *chump*, 'a stupid person.' In this class might be included such clipped forms as *stupe* for stupid, *mag* for magazine, *pix* for pictures, *pop* for popular, as in *pop art, pop tune*. Many slang words seem to be suggested by the high-sounding Latin vocabulary, such as *bogus, frambunctious, slantendicular, catawampus, bamboozle, cahoots, spizzerinktum*. Occasionally an actual Latin phrase, for example, *non compos mentis*, or simply *non compos*, is used as a slang expression by persons who know nothing of the origin of the phrase.

10 ◙ Attitude towards Slang

Since slang is not an abnormal or diseased growth in language, but arises in the language just as other words arise, there is no reason why such words in themselves should be condemned. Intrinsically they are not bad, but rather good, in so far as they show activity of mind and a desire to be vigorously expressive on the part of the speaker. But since from the circumstances of their development and use, slang words carry with them a certain individual color, flavor, or tone, whatever we may wish to call it, that gives them a marked distinctive value, the use of them should be determined by their appropriateness to the mood or thought which we wish to express. Perhaps we should make a distinction between speaking and writing, allowing ourselves somewhat more liberty in speaking than in writing, in neither instance, however, completely suppressing the creative instinct in language.

In answer to the frequent charge that "Slang is vulgar," we may say that slang in itself is no more vulgar than other words of the language, that there is nothing inherently vulgar in a slang word. A word is vulgar only when the idea which it expresses or connotes is vulgar, and this is true of other words as well as slang. But that slang words often carry with them by suggestion or connotation ideas or shades of thought that may fairly be called vulgar, or at least undignified, cannot be denied. The reason for this is that the slang words often come from the language of a grade or of classes of society the activities of which as a whole are looked upon as vulgar or undignified. The very term itself once referred principally to thieves' jargon. On the other hand certain words may carry with them exactly the opposite connotation when they are the cant terms current among people who are regarded, or who regard themselves, as leaders in matters of fashion and conventional manners, as was the case in the England of the Regency period.

A second statement that "Slang limits vocabulary" might be accepted if it were true that vocabulary limits thought. But the true statement is that vocabulary is the expression, the measure of thought, and its extent and character is determined by the extent and variety of thought itself. To say that slang limits vocabulary is literally to say that vocabulary limits vocabulary. That loose and lazy thinkers are inclined to use one word to express many shades of thought is true not only in the use of slang words, but of many other words of the language. It may

179

be said in general, however, that the continual use of slang, since much of its effect depends upon a kind of temporary conventional smartness, is a fair indication of a shallow mind. The slang habit cheapens by excessive use an activity of language which is needed, but which, to produce its proper effect should be employed only when it is needed.

Slang is nearly always conscious in its origin and in its use. It is almost always more expressive than the situation demands. It is indeed a kind of hyperesthesia in the use of language. It differs thus from idiom, which is normally expressive. *To laugh in your sleeve* is idiom because it arises out of a natural situation; it is a metaphor derived from the picture of one raising his sleeve to his face to hide a smile, a metaphor which arose naturally enough in early periods when sleeves were long and flowing. On the contrary, *to talk through your hat* is slang, not only because it was once new, but also because it is grotesque exaggeration.

11 ✑ Word Borrowing in English

The background and the basis of the English vocabulary is of course Teutonic or Germanic, by inheritance, just as its inflectional and general grammatical systems are. From the earliest historical times, however, this Teutonic base has been enriched by the borrowing of words from other languages, sometimes more rapidly and abundantly than at others, dependent upon the extent to which the English, or their Anglian, Jutish, and Saxon ancestors, were brought into contact with other peoples.

The first historic borrowings which we can clearly trace are borrowings from Latin while the Angles, Jutes, and Saxons were still resident on the Continent. Words of this sort are the common possession of a number of Germanic languages. Examples are *wine*, from Old English *wīn*, Latin *vinum*; *monger* (as in fishmonger), Old English *mangere*, Latin *mango*, 'to buy or sell'; *pound*, Old English *pund*, Latin *pondo*; *wall*, Old English *weall*, Latin *vallum*;

street, Old English *strǣt*, Latin *strata* (*via*); and a few others. Not many words were taken over from the Latin at this early period, those that were borrowed being chiefly commercial terms, like *monger*, *pound*, etc., and military terms like *wall* and *street*, the Roman streets or roads being built primarily to facilitate the passage of troops from one part of the Empire to another.

12 ▨ Celtic Borrowing

After the migration to England of those Continental tribes which later constituted the Anglo-Saxon people, the language and the people with which they were first brought into contact and from which we should expect them to borrow words were the native Celtic language and the Celts. The relation of the Celts to the Anglo-Saxons was that of a subdued race to its conquerors,[11] and we should hardly expect, therefore, that the Anglo-Saxons would borrow very abundantly from the Celts. The tendency would be in the other direction, for the Celts, the weaker and less influential people, to give up their language for Old English. The Anglo-Saxon would feel neither necessity nor inclination to borrow from the Celt. And in fact, so far as we are able to judge now from the Celtic words used in the literature of the earlier periods that has been preserved, the influence of the Celts upon the Anglo-Saxons was very slight.

Scholars have been able to find less than a score of words in the English language before the eleventh century which can be said with any degree of probability to have been derived from the Celtic. Some of these, for example the word *drȳ* in Old English, meaning 'magician,' and cognate with the first syllable of *druid*, have disappeared from later English. Others, for example *mattock*, which it was formerly supposed were borrowed from Celtic, have been shown to be Celtic borrowings from English.

[11] Cf. Old English *wielen*, 'slave-woman,' the feminine form of the name *Wealh*, 'Welsh,' literally 'foreign,' the term which the Anglo-Saxons applied to the subdued peoples.

The words which we can be reasonably certain were borrowed by Old English from Celtic and which are still found in Modern English are very few in number; among them the following are the most probable: *brock* (badger); *down* (a hill); *slough* (a muddy pond).

To find any extensive influence of Celtic on English we must turn to the proper names of the language, such as the names of rivers, mountains, districts, etc., many of which naturally retained their original Celtic names. This is especially true of regions like Devonshire and Cornwall which for a long time resisted the attacks of the Anglo-Saxons and thus remained largely Celtic after the rest of southern and eastern England had been completely Teutonized.

It should be remembered, also, in estimating the Celtic element in English, that the small number of early Celtic words in English has been increased, though not to any considerable extent, by later borrowings from Irish, as, for example, *brogue, galore, shamrock, shillelagh, spalpeen, Tory*, etc.; from Scotch, in such words as *clan, glen, kail, pibroch, plaid, slogan, whiskey*, etc.; and from Welsh in *coracle, cromlech, flannel*, and a few others. But the entire number of Celtic words in English is surprisingly small.

13 ✎ Latin Borrowing of the First Period

After the settlement of the Anglo-Saxons in England and the establishment of their supremacy over the Celts, the first great event, important for the development of their civilization and language, was the introduction of Christianity and of Roman civilization, by means of the Augustinian mission in the last decade of the sixth century. The Anglo-Saxons were thus brought into direct contact with a civilization that was superior to theirs, culturally in this instance, rather than politically. By the same principle which accounts for the slight influence of Celtic upon Old English, we should expect a strong influence of Latin upon Old English.

There is abundant evidence to show that the influence of Latin was profound. The Roman missionaries were not only preachers, they were also teachers. One of their first projects was the establishment of schools in which Anglo-Saxon children were to be educated for the priesthood. The teachers in these schools were at first naturally Romans, or at least not Anglo-Saxons, but in the course of comparatively a short time persons of pure Anglo-Saxon birth attained distinction as teachers and scholars. Of these we may mention two, Aldhelm, born about 650 and dying in 709, a pupil of the school at Canterbury, who was the author of a number of Latin treatises which are still extant; and Alcuin, who lived from about 735 to 804, a pupil of the cathedral school established at York. Alcuin has been described as "the most learned man of his age,"[12] and when Charlemagne wished to establish schools at his own court, he invited Alcuin to become master of them, a post which he held from 782 to 790. Latin learning was also cultivated by other Anglo-Saxons, as, for example, the Venerable Bede (c. 673–735), the author of the *Ecclesiastical History of the English People* (*Historia Ecclesiastica gentis Anglorum*); King Alfred (849–901), who translated many Latin works into English; and Ælfric (c. 955–1020), author of many treatises both in Latin and in English.

A natural result of this familiarity with Latin was the incorporation of a considerable number of Latin words into the English vocabulary. It has been estimated that before the year 1050 nearly four hundred words are found in extant Old English literature.[13] As we should expect, many of these words are of ecclesiastical character, the new religion and its organization naturally bringing with it many of its own words. Words of this sort which appear in the Old English period and have persisted in use today are *bishop*, Lat. *episcopus*; *apostle*, Lat. *apostolus*; *alms*, Lat. *eleemosyna* (which in turn is of Greek origin); *creed*,

[12] See Sandys, *History of Classical Scholarship*, Vol. i, p. 460.

[13] See Serjeantson, *History of Foreign Words in English*.

Lat. *credo*; *candle*, Lat. *candela*; *organ*, Lat. *organum*; *priest*, Lat. *presbyter*.

Another large group is made up of words which might be called scientific or learned words, as, for example, names of plants, as *cedar*, Lat. *cedrus*; *box* (boxtree), Lat. *buxus*; or of mathematical divisions of space and time, as *calends*, Lat. *calendae*; *mile*, Lat. *milia*; *noon*, Lat. *nona* (literally the ninth hour of the day); *meter*, Lat. *metrum*.

The number of words of familiar daily life which passed from the Latin into Old English was relatively small. Most of them had been used in Britain, by Latins, Celts, or both, prior to the withdrawal of the Roman legions. Examples include such words as *trout, port, mount,* and *chester* (Latin *castra*), occurring today chiefly in place names. These words can be distinguished from the earlier layer of Latin words in Germanic by the lack of cognates in the other Germanic languages. Words such as *mile, street,* and *chalk,* all from the pre-Christian group, have descendants in German, Dutch, and Norse as well as English; *trout* occurs only in the latter.

On the whole, however, the influence of Latin upon English in this period was chiefly upon the scholarly language. But even here the influence was by no means revolutionary. A good many of the approximately four hundred words occurring in texts before 1050 are used merely as glosses, or are single occurrences obviously due to the immediate need of a translator to find a word to express some object or idea in his original. Old English, in the main, was very conservative in the matter of borrowing words. Even when it came to the expression of the abstract ideas of Christianity or of philosophy, Anglo-Saxon authors endeavored to get along with their own native stock of words and usually succeeded remarkably well.

For example, in King Alfred's translation of a philosophical work by the Latin writer Boethius, entitled *De Consolatione Philosophiae*, in a typical passage of about 660 words discussing the abstract question of the nature of God, only one Latin word, *englas*, Lat. *angeli*, 'angels,' occurs. There are frequent words, however, of abstract meaning, such as we usually express now by means of words of Latin origin. Examples are *mildheort*, literally 'mild-heart,' where we should now probably say *merciful* or *gracious*, both Latin words through the French; *rūmmōd*, literally '*room-mood*,' our modern *magnanimous*; *gāstlīce*, literally '*ghost-like*,' that is, *spiritual*; *tō-scēad*, an idea which we should now express by *difference* or *discrimination*; *hwīlwendlīc*, literally *while* (i.e., time), *wend* (turn), and the adjective suffix *-līc*, the whole meaning *temporal*.

And so with many other words it could be shown that where Modern English uses a word of Latin origin, Old English uses its own native words. In this respect Old English consequently resembles modern German more nearly than it does Modern English, the present tendency in English being to express new ideas, especially of a somewhat abstract character, by means of words of Latin origin, whereas modern German generally uses native words for this purpose.

14 ▨ Borrowings from Scandinavian

After their settlement in England the Anglo-Saxons came into renewed contact with the Scandinavians of the Continent, the Danes, Northmen or Norse, and Swedes, at the beginning of the Scandinavian invasions towards the close of the eighth century. These invasions, which at first were merely predatory, soon became wars of actual conquest and settlement. By the heroic efforts of Alfred and his successors the Danes were kept out of Wessex for a time, but the other parts of England, especially the northern, soon succumbed to them. With the conquest of Cnut, in 1016, the whole of England passed under Danish control, and a Danish king ruled at the same time both Denmark and England.

The Danish conquerors of England readily amalgamated with the native Anglo-Saxon population. In this instance the

Anglo-Saxon civilization, having passed through several centuries of peaceful development, was the higher one, and the Danes consequently tended to give up their language for the English language. The two languages, however, were much alike, and it is often difficult to tell when a word is pure Old English and when it is of Scandinavian origin. Many words, so far as their form goes, such common words, for example, as *man, wife, father, mother, folk, house*, etc., might as well be of Scandinavian as of Old English origin, because they are the same in both languages.[14]

In some cases, however, ideas or objects of Scandinavian origin have left their impress plainly upon the names which were borrowed to designate them. A number of words were taken over by the Anglo-Saxons which have not persisted in the language, as, for example, words connected with the sea, *barda, cnear, scegð*, different kinds of ships; *lid*, 'a fleet'; *ha*, 'rowlock,' etc. The Scandinavians appear also to have been active legal organizers, and a number of their law terms passed over to Old English, such as the word *law* itself; *by-law* (for the etymology of *by-*, see above, p. 169); *thrall*, 'slave'; the verb *crave*; the second element in *hus-band*; and others.

Other Scandinavian words in English are the nouns *sky, skull, skin, skill, haven*; the adjectives *meek, low, scant, loose, add, wrong, ill, ugly, rotten, happy, seemly*; the verbs *thrive, die, cast, hit, take, call, scare, scrape, bask, drown, ransack, gape*; probably the pronouns *they, their, them*; and the prepositions *fro* (to and fro) and *till*.

These words it will be observed are mostly ordinary words of common daily intercourse, and in this respect they differ widely from the Latin words that were taken over in the Old English period. From the nature of these Scandinavian borrowings we may infer that the Scandinavians and Anglo-Saxons lived together on a plane of equality. Their relation to each other was not that of a learned people to an ignorant, like the Latin to the Anglo-Saxon, or of an aristocratic ruling class to a conquered and

---

[14] See Jespersen, *Growth and Structure of the English Language*, p. 65.

ignoble group of subjects, like the Anglo-Saxons to the Celts. Anglo-Saxons and Scandinavians, moreover, lived together probably without much realization of a difference of nationality. This being the case, we might expect that the number of Anglo-Saxon borrowings from the Scandinavians would be much greater than it is. But the very similarity of the two languages and of the two peoples probably tended to prevent this. The Scandinavians apparently gave up their language without much struggle, and the Anglo-Saxons felt little need of borrowing words from their Teutonic kinsmen, having already an equivalent vocabulary in their own language.

15 ☒ Borrowings from the French in the Middle English Period

The words which English borrowed from other languages, Celtic, Latin, and Scandinavian, before the period of French influence, were comparatively few in number. They were not of sufficient importance to change in any considerable degree the character of the language, or even to add much to its resources. English remained throughout a unilingual tongue, a language made up largely, or almost exclusively, of words of the same linguistic stock.

As a result, however, of the French influence upon English, we have the introduction of a large number of words of French origin, so large a number that they modify the general character and tone of the language. So numerous and important are these French innovations that English changes from a unilingual to a bilingual tongue. The basis of the language remained English, as it always has through all stages of its history, but the accretions to this original English stock were of such a character as to make English sensitive to two language traditions, one Teutonic and the other Romance. This bilingual character of the language of the Middle English period has been transmitted to, and augmented by, later periods of English, so that today our language is made up of two historically clearly distinguishable, though in practice, closely interwoven strands, the Romance or Latin, and the English or Teutonic, strands.

The causes which brought about the introduction of French words into Middle English were partly political, but mainly social. The relations between England and France first became politically significant in the time of Edward the Confessor, who was king of England from 1043 to 1066. Edward had spent the early years of his life in Normandy in France, and there had acquired French sympathies and French tastes. When he became king, these sympathies and tastes were naturally brought over by him to his English court. Moreover, Edward filled high political and ecclesiastical offices in England with Normans, in the face of the disapproval of the English, who finally rose up in rebellion in 1052 and drove these French favorites from the country.

On the death of Edward, the English chose Harold, son of Earl Godwin, a very powerful English nobleman, as their king. But a cousin of Edward's, William, Duke of Normandy, made claim to the English throne on the basis of some promises alleged to have been given him by Edward, and in support of his claims he appeared on English soil with an army at his back, fought and defeated Harold at the famous battle of Hastings, on October 14, 1066. Thus a duke of Normandy became the king of England and the English people.

The effect of the Norman Conquest upon English institutions and life in general was profound and wide-reaching. In the first place, William the Conqueror was a strong and a wise executive. He became the real ruler of the country, he introduced a system of government, and saw to it that it was carried out. The persons to whom offices of trust were assigned were at first naturally his own Norman followers, and the language of the court and the higher official life was of course Norman French.

But secondly, and, so far as the history of the language is concerned, more importantly, the Norman Conquest was significant because it changed England from an insular, self-dependent country to one with interests beyond itself. Through the Norman Conquest England became more fully acquainted with continental customs and habits of life, with French learning and with French literature, than it had been before. What all this meant to England can hardly be overestimated. The French of the eleventh and twelfth centuries were undoubtedly the most highly civilized nation of Europe, and of this civilization the English thus became partakers and sharers.

There is a frequent misapprehension which needs to be corrected, concerning the attitude which William the Conqueror assumed towards the English language. It is often assumed that William's attitude towards English was hostile, that he endeavored to crush it out and to substitute Norman French in its place. The investigations of historians[15] have shown, however, that this was not William's purpose, either with respect to the English language or with respect to the political institutions of the English people. William was too wise a statesman not to make use of everything that would help him, and instead of being hostile to the English language and English customs, the indications are that he rather strove to use them in the effective organization of his kingdom.

English was never, therefore, a forbidden language, though naturally it was regarded for a long time as an ignoble language. The speech of the court and the higher official life was French, and Englishmen who sought favor at court of course learned French. There were thus two strata in the social body, each with its own language. English continued to be spoken uninterruptedly after the Conquest, but it persisted as a popular dialect. French, on the other hand, became the accepted speech of the higher political and social life.

The number of Normans in England, as compared with the number of Englishmen, must always have been small. There were

[15] See especially Freeman, *The Norman Conquest* and A. C. Baugh, *History of the English Language.*

several reasons, however, why these Normans were not immediately absorbed by the more numerous English. In the first place, a civilization which momentarily has the upper hand, though confined to relatively few people, does not readily yield to influences from below. It is conservative and strives to be self-perpetuating.

Second, French culture in England was continually refreshed by communication with the Continent. William was king of England, but also duke of Normandy, and many of his nobles who held possessions also had important relations with France. There was thus a continual passing back and forth of the official society between England and Normandy.

In the meantime, however, those Frenchmen whose possessions and interests were all in England would be compelled in self-defense to learn English. Their workmen and their overseers, the people upon whom all the practical affairs of daily life depended, would be English. As these English would have little opportunity to learn French, however great their inclination, the only thing for the landlords to do was to learn English.

In the year 1204 an event happened which made communication between French and English in England more than ever frequent and necessary. This was the loss of the province of Normandy in the reign of King John, and the consequent loss of their French possessions by the Norman nobles in England. From this time on English continued to gain as the national speech of the country. French remained as the cultivated speech of the higher social classes, but it came to be more and more felt as an accomplishment, an artificial, aristocratic class language, as distinguished from the general, national language of the people. As soon as this had come to pass, French as a spoken language in England was doomed. It might continue to be used as the language of polite conversation, to some extent as the language of literature and scholarship; but the language which does not send its roots down into the actual, everyday life of a people is condemned to sterility and death.

190

French managed to maintain itself as a cultivated language far into the fourteenth century. Robert of Gloucester, writing about 1300, speaks of English as the language of "lowe men," but of French as the language of "heie men," by "high men" probably meaning men of high official rank. The *Cursor Mundi*, a long poem written in the north of England in the first quarter of the fourteenth century, defends English on patriotic grounds as the right language for Englishmen to use.

Ralph Higden, in a Latin historical work called the *Polychronicon*, written near the middle of the century, says that children in school were compelled to leave their own language (showing that English was the *native* language of school children in his day) and to construe their lessons in French, a state of affairs which Higden regards with disfavor. Higden also says that gentlemen's children are taught French from the time that they are rocked in the cradle. The *Polychronicon* was translated into English by John Trevisa about the year 1385. In his translation Trevisa comments on Higden's statement, observing that in his day matters had changed somewhat, that children now studied their lessons in English; whereby, says Trevisa, they have this advantage, that they learn their lessons more quickly, but this disadvantage, that they know no more French than their left heels. In the meantime, in the year 1362, it had been ordered that pleadings in the law courts should be in English and not in French. By the end of the fourteenth century it was for once and all determined that English was to be the language of England.

This final triumph of English is indicated most forcibly by the choice of English for literary purposes by Chaucer. Familiar as he was with French, Chaucer could have written in that language if he had so desired. But his observation had convinced him that French was a decaying and passing language in England, that the real, vital language of the country was English, and that any literature which should express English character and life must be written in the English language. Chaucer, therefore, while his example contributed to raise English in the respect of

191

the people, did not by his single effort make English a language fit for literature. It had become so before Chaucer wrote, and what the poet did was to see his opportunity and use it. In his choice of English we have the final victory of English over French, the language of the people against the language of the higher life, of the court, of polite conversation, and of literature.

16 ⊠ Chronology of French Words in English

When we come to consider the question of the times at which French words were taken over into English, we are met by an interesting condition of affairs. As we have already seen, intimate relations between France and England began in the time of Edward the Confessor, continuing after the Conquest in a much more influential way to the time of the loss of Normandy in 1204. Even after the loss of Normandy, however, French continued to be used in England as a cultivated or polite language, and it was only at the beginning of the fourteenth century that English began to take the place of French, a tendency that became complete at the end of the century. Now it is remarkable that it is not until we come to English works written near the beginning of the fourteenth century that we find French words abundantly used.

In the *Ormulum*, for example, a poem of about ten thousand long lines, written near the year 1200, only twenty-three words of French origin are used.[16] The *Brut* of Layamon, a poem of more than 56,000 short lines, written early in the thirteenth century, contains only 150 words of French origin.[17] The proportion varies slightly with different writers, other works contemporary with the *Ormulum* and the *Brut* showing some a larger and others a smaller relative number of French words. But the number for two centuries after the Conquest is never very large.

[16] A list of them is given by Kluge, *Englische Studien*, xxii, 179 ff.

[17] For a list of them, see Monroe, in *Modern Philology*, iv, 559 ff.

Gradually, however, the use of French words in Middle English texts increases until it reaches its highest point between 1300 and 1400, or more exactly between 1350 and 1400, just the period in which French was losing ground as a national language and English was gaining ground.[18] How is this to be explained? First of all, by the fact that when the higher classes, the speech of which is naturally reflected in the language of the period, took to speaking English, a language for which they had hitherto had more or less contempt, they naturally carried over into English many words from their French. Their English was a sort of Gallicized English, improved and polished, as they probably thought, by being interlarded with French words. The very tendency, therefore, which brought about the elevation of English resulted also in the introduction of numerous French words into English.

Moreover, we need not suppose that the English themselves of the middle and lower classes were averse to borrowing French words in this period. French was recognized as a polite language, the language of culture, education, and travel, especially as the language of literature, and the occasional use of a French word conferred a touch of distinction upon the person who used it, just as within the past century we have had a sort of "society French," such words as *débutante*, *fiancée*, *distingué*, *éclat*, etc., which persons of a somewhat unripe culture were fond of using.

The French which was thus cultivated at the end of the fourteenth century was no longer the old Anglo-Norman French of the original conquerors of England. That had in the course of time grown old-fashioned, though from this Anglo-Norman French are of course derived most French words taken into English before 1350. The new and the fashionable French which was cultivated in the last half of the century was Central French, the dialect of Paris, the chief city of the French, and the dialect also in which the great body of French literature was written. We thus see that the Conquest itself and its immediate political

[18] See A. C. Baugh, *History of the English Language*, p. 214.

results were less influential in bringing about the introduction of French words into English than these later social causes. Indeed the influence of French upon the English vocabulary did not become pronounced until the Conquest had become practically forgotten and the racial distinction between Norman and English obliterated. The real explanation of the influence of French upon English is to be found where the influence of one language upon another is almost always to be found, in the give and take of the members of one social group upon another in the daily concerns of life.

17 ▨ Kinds of Words Borrowed from French

In general, words of all kinds, of all parts of speech, and from all walks of life were taken over into English, both from Anglo-Norman and from Central French, during the Middle English period. As a result of this borrowing, many English words were lost, French words like *mercy, charity, power, soldier, peace*, etc., taking the place of words which in the Old English period were drawn from the Teutonic stock.

It often happened as well that an Old English word was preserved beside a French word of similar content, the Old English word, however, generally taking on a somewhat less dignified meaning than the French word. Examples are: French *chair* beside English *stool*; French *city* beside English *town*; French *labor* beside English *work*. Sir Walter Scott, in *Ivanhoe*, has called attention to pairs of words of this sort, such as French *beef, mutton, veal,* and *pork*, as compared with English *ox, sheep, calf,* and *swine*. He draws the inference that the ox and the other animals, so long as they were only objects of care and expense, were the concern of the humble Saxons, but when they were dressed for the table and were ready to be enjoyed, then they passed into the possession of the Normans and took the French names, such as beef, etc. But there is little reason to suppose that the Saxons were so poverty-stricken and oppressed as not to be able to eat beef, mutton, or pork. The French names for the dressed meats were taken over because they were the polite names, and the Saxon when he had prepared his ox or his sheep for the table would himself be pleased to call it beef and mutton.

It would be difficult to go through the whole list of borrowed words and classify them exactly, so as to show just what ideas the language tended to express in French to the exclusion of English. As has already been stated, words of all kinds, the most simple as well as the most polite, were taken over, many of them maintaining only a temporary place in the language, but most of them persisting to the present day. These words we no longer feel as French in origin, and we use them in the same way as we use all other words of the language. They have become indeed an essential and inseparable part of the language, and any attempt to distinguish and to discriminate against words of French origin of this period is artificial and vain.

As illustrations of short and simple words of French origin borrowed in the Middle English period, we may cite the following: *able, age, air, boil, card, chair, course, cry, debt, doubt, ease, engine, face, flower, fruit, hasty, hour, hulk, jolly, move, pass, oust, peck, river, soil, table, use,* etc. These simple words, the number of which could be increased indefinitely, are exactly on the same plane as the popular words of Scandinavian origin cited previously, and native words of Teutonic origin. They are completely amalgamated with the rest of the language, and have become thus to all intents and purposes identical with the popular native element. It is, therefore, not this part of the borrowed French strand in the English vocabulary that is most characteristic, so far at least as the style of English is concerned, of the influence of French upon English.

Besides these simple, commonplace words there is another large group of words of French origin which is specially significant of the relations which existed between French and English in this period, a group of words which clearly reflects the attitude of mind of the English of the thirteenth and fourteenth centuries both towards their own and towards the French language. This difference is well illustrated by lines 45, 46 in Chaucer's *Prolog* to *The Canterbury Tales*, in which he describes the virtues practiced by the knight:

> he lovede chivalrye,
> Trouthe and honour, fredom and curteisye.

Of these five nouns, the second and the fourth are English words, the first, the third, and the fifth are French. The English words, *truth* and *freedom*, are the names of two simple manly virtues, fundamental virtues in English character.[19] The French words, *chivalry, honor*, and *courtesy*, name virtues of a different kind, courtly virtues, such as only those who are bred under certain conditions can know and practice. Honor and courtesy are determined by a code of conduct, a code which has been made elastic enough to permit a gambling debt being called a "debt of honor." But truth and freedom are not names for varying rules of conduct, but are names for permanent essential traits of character.

It would be easy of course to make too much of this distinction, especially if we should attempt to show that French words, as is sometimes supposed, were generally borrowed to designate the shallower and more artificial ideas and sentiments. A truer statement would be that the French element has often the qualities of courtliness and grace, these words themselves, *courtliness* and *grace*, being French words, and the ideas for which they stand being largely French ideas. To the French the Middle English period was indebted for those standards of conduct which we usually group under the broad head of chivalry.

Anglo-Saxon society may have been simple, earnest, and sincere, but it can hardly be said to have been light or graceful. The characteristics of charm and fancy, of polish and lightness,

---

[19] It should be noted, however, that *freedom* in this context meant 'liberality, generosity,' and that *truth* was closer to the idea of keeping the faith than to mere verbal accuracy. A.H.M.

196

do not appear prominently in English literature, and probably did not exist in any considerable extent in English life, until after the period of French influence.

It is the polite part of the English vocabulary, taken over from French at this time, that constitutes the striking difference between the language of the Middle English and the Old English period. This is illustrated by borrowed words which have to do with eating and table-manners, as, for example, the words *dine, dinner, supper, table* (for Old English *board*), *plate, napkin, pasty, feast,* besides many names of edibles, of kitchen utensils, and of ways of preparing food, such as *roast, broil, boil,* and others.

Costume and dress also changed and became much more elaborate in the Middle English period, French words here again often taking the place of English ones. Examples are *coat, cloak, gown, boot, cap,* etc., also many names of cloths. Words of address were taken from the French, such as *sir, madam, master, mistress,* as well as many from the high titles, like *prince, duke, duchess, marquis, baron, captain, sergeant, colonel, officer,* etc. Names of relationship, except the immediate relationships of the family, were expressed by French words, as *uncle, aunt, nephew, niece,* and *cousin;* but *father, mother, brother, sister* remained English.

Accomplishments were usually French, both in words and fact. Four of the six talents mentioned by Chaucer in the following couplet descriptive of the gallant Squire in *The Canterbury Tales* require French words to name them:

> He koude songes make and wel *endite,*
> *Juste* and eek *daunce* and weel *purtreye* and write.[20]

Many of the terms of sport, especially hawking and hunting, were taken from the French, and naturally also a great many words connected with the higher official life, as, for example, *crown, state, realm, royal, country, nation, power,* etc.; words connected with war and military affairs in general, as *arms, peace, battle,*

---

[20] *Prolog*, ll. 95, 96. *Endite* = compose; *juste* = joust; *eek* = also.

armor, banner, siege, and a great many others; words pertaining to the law courts and the administration of justice, as, for example, *judge, justice, court, suit, plea, plead,* etc.; numerous words of ecclesiastical meaning, as *service, savior, relic, cloister, preach, prayer, clergy, clerk,* etc.

But most important of all, perhaps, is the long list of words of more or less abstract value denoting chivalric ideas or matters of general conduct. The words *honor* and *courtesy* have already been cited from Chaucer. To them should be added the word *villainy,* in Chaucer's well-known line descriptive of the Knight in the *Prolog* to *The Canterbury Tales*:

> He nevere yet no vileynye ne sayde.

The word means in Chaucer not quite what it does in Modern English. In its earlier sense it signified any conduct not befitting a gentleman. Other words of this kind are, *duty, fame, virtue, gentle, valor, chivalry, courage, liege, degree, rank, standard, noble, grace, favor, simple, pleasant, agreeable, amiable manner, dignity, reverence, piteous, dainty, dalliance, familiar, vaunt, adventure, coward, charm, chastity, beauty, benign, oblige, fault, majesty.*

It is a significant fact that it would be extremely difficult to find an Old English equivalent to many of these words, the reason being that the exact shade of thought or feeling expressed by the French words was not a part of Anglo-Saxon experience. The life of the English people in the fourteenth century was much richer and more varied than it had been in the ninth or tenth centuries, and this growth in richness and variety, largely due as it was to their contact with French life and civilization, is also largely expressed in words of French origin.

18 ✐ Renaissance Borrowings in English

The borrowing of French words, which has been described in the foregoing paragraphs, continued with but little diminution down through the fifteenth century. Towards the end of this century the tendency to import words of both French and Latin origin was greatly strengthened by the general drift of the Renaissance movement, that revival of learning and of interest in literature, both classical Latin and Greek and English vernacular, which, in its results upon language, was hardly less important than the period of French influence of which we have just spoken.

The effect of the Renaissance upon English is interesting and remarkable also because it was almost altogether the result of conscious effort. In preceding periods, any changes which affected the language took place largely without the conscious knowledge of the people who spoke the language. Words were borrowed from Scandinavian or French words. But there was no avowed theory that it would be a good thing to add to the English vocabulary by borrowing from these languages, words being taken as the need for them arose in the social intercourse of daily life.

In the Renaissance period, however, there arose a perfectly conscious movement, on the part of scholars and authors, to extend the limits of the English vocabulary by direct borrowing from other languages. This was quite in keeping with the general spirit of the Renaissance, one of its most characteristic aspects being a deep and general interest in questions of language. From their study of the classical authors, the Renaissance scholars were naturally led to the consideration of the matter of style in literature, the ability of a language to express all the various shades of thought and feeling of the human mind and heart. The perfect models of style they thought were to be found in such writers as Cicero and Vergil, and though a modern vernacular such as English could never hope to rival the classical languages, these latter were nevertheless the ideals towards which the modern languages were to strive. A modern language could not be as good as Latin, but it ought to strive to be as like as possible to Latin.

There arose thus the idea of "improving" the language, of "augmenting" it, of making it richer and fuller, and more capable

199

of expressing what the Latin language could express so well. The desire to translate the monuments of classical literature into English also encouraged the belief that English should be improved. Obviously there could be no adequate translation into English until that language should be at least approximately as expressive as the language from which translation was to be made. The great endeavor, therefore, of the Renaissance reformers was to enrich the vocabulary and to make the language more expressive mainly as a medium of artistic, literary expression.

As is true of all reform movements. the positive or radical party is sure to beget a reactionary or conservative party. In this movement also the enrichers or improvers had to contend with the opposition of the conservatives, who maintained that English should not borrow words from other languages, but should try to develop her own native resources. The conservatives contended that if English needed new words they should be taken from the earlier periods of her own language, rather than from foreign languages. Both of these bodies of theorists in the end helped towards the enrichment of the language, the one by external borrowing and imitation, the other by internal development.

The Renaissance in England is characterized by two events, both of them of the greatest importance in the history of the language. The first of these is the revival of learning, meaning thereby the study of Greek and Latin Literature; the second is the introduction of printing.

There was very little knowledge of Greek in England during the Old and the Middle English periods. The first Englishman to acquire proficiency in Greek in the Renaissance period was William Tilly of Selling, near Canterbury, a Benedictine monk, who died in 1491. Others who succeeded him were his nephew, Thomas Linacre (1460–1524), William Grocyn (1446–1519), and William Latimer (d. 1545). Sir Thomas More (1480–1535) was also a student of Greek, and the great Dutch scholar, Erasmus, lived for several years in England, and gave instruction in Greek at the University of Cambridge. To these names may also be added that of William Lily, first High-Master of St. Paul's School in London, and author of the Latin grammar which Shakespeare, as well as most of his contemporaries, used as a schoolboy.

The direct influence of Greek upon English in the Renaissance period was, however, very slight as compared with the influence of Latin and French. The study and the knowledge of Greek were more important as expressive of a deep and enthusiastic interest in language as language, rather than as affecting directly the feeling for, and the use of, the English language.

The introduction of printing into England was due to William Caxton, an Englishman born in Kent about 1415. He lived on the Continent a number of years and during his residence in the Low Countries learned the printer's trade. On his return to England he set up a press of his own, and on November 18, 1477, the first dated book printed in England issued from his press. His work was very favorably received by the nobility in England, and thereafter Caxton's press was kept busy. To find material for publication, he himself became a translator. His first translation was a summary of the stories centering about the Trojan war, called *Recuyell of the Historyes of Troy*; other translations which he made were of *Reynard the Fox*; Jacobus deVoragine's *Golden Legend*; a modernization of Trevisa's English version of Higden's *Polychronicon*; a form of the story of the *Æneid* called *Eneydos*; and many others.

As author and translator Caxton was deeply impressed by the beauty and expressiveness of the Latin and the French languages, and was desirous of making English the equal of these languages. To attain this end he treated English with a freedom not always approved by his readers, who were sometimes puzzled by the strange words with which he confronted them.

Thus in the preface to his *Eneydos*, which was published in 1490, he says he was attracted to the French book "by cause of the fayr and honest termes and wordes in frenshe"; and having

201

decided to translate it into English, he "wrote a leef or tweyne" as sample. Then he adds:

and whan I sawe the fayr and straunge termes therin/ I doubted that it sholde not please some gentylmen whiche late blamed me, sayeng that in my translacyons I had ouer curyous termes whiche coude not be understande of comyn peple/ and desired me to vse olde and homely termes in my translacyons. And fayn wolde I satysfye euery man/ and so to doo, toke an olde boke and redde therein/ and certaynly the englysshe was so rude and brood that I coude not wele vnderstande it. And also my lorde abbot of westmynster ded do shewe to me late certayn euidences wryton in olde englysshe, for to reduce it into our englysshe now vsid/ and certaynly it was wreton in such wyse that it was more lyke to dutche than englysshe; I coude not reduce ne brynge it to be vnderstonden/ And certaynly our langage now vsed varyeth ferre from that whiche was vsed and spoken whan I was borne/ For we englysshe men/ ben borne vnder the domynacyon of the mone, whiche is neuer stedfaste/ but euer wauerynge/ wexynge one season/ and waneth & dyscreaseth another season.[21]

Caxton then adds that his book is not translated "for a rude uplondyssh man to laboure therein," but for the clerk and gentleman, and if these do not understand his words, let them go read Vergil and the other Latin writers, and then they shall lightly understand all. It is plain from what he says here that Caxton's sympathies were with the enrichers rather than with the conservatives.

As a further illustration of Caxton's method of Latinizing and Gallicizing English, we may quote the following extract from the *Eneydos*:

For to here/ opene/ and declare the matere of whiche hereafter shall be made mencyon/ It behoueth to presuppose that Troye, the grete capytall cyte/ and thexcellentest of alle the cytees of the countre & regyon of Asye, was constructe and edefyed by the ryght puyssaunt

---

[21] *Comyn* = common; *brood* = broad; *ferre* = far. The crossbar, used in the passage above, is found in manuscripts and early printed books as a kind of punctuation, standing either for a period or a comma. It is not, however, very consistently employed.

& renomed kyng Pryamus, sone of laomedon, descended of thauncyen stocke of Dardanus by many degrees/ whiche was sone of Jubyter & of Electra his wyf, after the fyctions poetyque/ And the fyrste orygynall begynnynge of the genealogye of kynges. And the sayd Troye was enuyronned in fourme of siege/ and of excidyon by Agamenon, kynge in grece, brother of menelaus/ whiche was husbonde to helayne. The whiche agamenon, assembled and accompanyed wyth many kynges, dukes/ erles/ and grete quantyte of other princes & grekes innumerable, hadde the magystracyon and vnyuersall gouernaunce of all thexcersite and hoost to-fore Troye.[22]

The words in this passage which would likely have seemed strange to an unlearned Englishman of Caxton's day are the following: declare; matere = matter; mencyon = mention; presuppose; capytall; thexcellentest = the excellentest; regyoun = region; constructe (from Latin *constructum*); edefyed = (from Latin *aedifico*, I build); puyssaunt; renomed = renowned; descended; thauncyen = the ancient; degrees; fyctions; poetyque; orygynall; genealogye; enuyronned; fourme = form; excidyon (from *excidium* = siege); assembled; accompanyed; quantyte; innumerable; magistracyon = magistracy; vnyuersall; gouernaunce; thexcersite = the excersite (from Latin *exercitus*, army).

Of these it is interesting to observe that only two, *excidyon* and *excersite*, are altogether unknown to the Modern English reader, and that most of the rest are perfectly familiar to any adult person of average education. One or two are used in somewhat unusual senses, as, for example, *edefyed* in the sense of 'built' (but cf. Modern English 'edifice'); but the meanings seem strange because our Modern English words have ceased to be used with the strict etymological value that Caxton gives them.

It is interesting to observe also that Caxton endeavors often to explain and define his new and strange words by coupling them with words of similar meaning and familiar form, as, for example, *opene and declare*; *countre & regyon*; *first orygynall begynnynge*; *of siege and of excidyon*; *excersite and hoost*. But sometimes also he puts two

[22] *Eneydos*, pp. 10–11.

new words together, trusting perhaps that they will explain each other, as *constructe*[23] *and edefyed*; *puyssaunt & renomed*; *assembled and accompanyed*.

Caxton gives credit to Chaucer as a pioneer in this attempt to enrich the English language which he carries on. In the Proem, or Preface, to his edition of *The Canterbury Tales* he praises Chaucer in the following terms, which indeed carry the methods of the enrichment to the limits of absurdity:

> For to-fore that he [i.e., Chaucer] by labour embellished, ornated and made fair our English, in this realm was had rude speech and incongruous, as yet it appeareth by old books, which at this day ought not to have place ne be compared among, ne to, his beauteous volumes and ornate writings, of whom he made many books and treatises of many a noble history, as well in metre as in rhyme and prose; and them so craftily made that he comprehended his matters in short, quick, and high sentences, eschewing prolixity, casting away the chaff of superfluity, and shewing the picked grain of sentence uttered by crafty and sugared eloquence.[24]

Caxton, however, was somewhat inaccurate in counting Chaucer among the conscious enrichers of the language. Chaucer, to be sure, used a great many words which were not in the English vocabulary before the period of French influence. But the words which he used were almost all of them words which had acquired citizenship in the English language of his time. He used them because in the centuries which had followed the Conquest they had come to be standard English words.

---

[23] The form *constructe* is a past participle formed from the Latin past participle *constructum*, the present form of which is *construo*, 'I build or construct.' It could be appreciated as a past participle only by those who were aware of this etymology; for the normal English feeling for a past participle demanded a participial *-ed* ending. As the word came to be accepted into general use, it took the past participial form *constructed*. In legal phraseology, however, the form *situate* (without the *-ed*) is still used as a past participle, being of the same formation as Caxton's *constructe*. The present form of Latin *construo* appears in English *construe*, the past participle of which is no longer felt to be *construct* but *construed*.

[24] See Pollard, *Fifteenth Century Prose and Verse*, p. 232.

Another scholar and author of this period who was extremely zealous in his efforts to enrich the language was Sir Thomas Elyot (1490?–1546). Among Elyot's numerous books written in English, the most interesting and important is *The Boke named the Gouernour*, published in 1531, a book on general political philosophy and the theory of education. Convinced of the poverty of the Old English, or native, vocabulary as compared with the Latin, Greek, and French, Elyot set about the task of augmenting or enriching his English vocabulary. Naturally, his strange words met with the same opposition that Caxton's had found. "Diuers men," he says, "rather scornyng my benefite than receyuing it thankfully, doo shewe them selfes offended (as they say) with my strange termes."

He was gratified, however, that his work should meet with the approval of the king, Henry VIII, and he expresses the purpose of his reforms as follows:

His Highnesse benignely receyuynge my boke, whiche I named *The Gouernour*, in the redynge therof sone perceyued that I intended to augment our Englyshe tongue whereby men shulde as well expresse more abundantly the thynge that they conceyued in theyr hartis (wherefore language was ordeyned), hauynge wordes apte for the pourpose, as also interprete out of greke, latyn or any other tonge into Englysshe, as sufficiently as out of any one of the said tongues into an other. His Grace also perceyued that throughout the boke there was no terme new made by me of a latin or frenche worde, but it is there declared so playnly by one mene or other to a diligent reder, that no sentence is thereby made derke or harde to be understande.[25]

Among the examples of what were regarded as "strange termes" in his day, but which have now become generally accepted as commonplace words in the language, Elyot mentions *industry, magnanimity, maturity, sobriety,* and *temperance.* Thomas Nashe, a few years later, finds much to criticize in the vocabulary of his literary enemy, Gabriel Harvey. Among the words and

[25] Crofts, *The Boke named the Gouernour*, p. lxvi.

phrases used by Harvey which sound strange today may be cited the following: *canicular tales*; *effectuate*; *addoulce his melodie*; *polimechany*. But by far the greater number of those words mentioned by Nashe are good, if somewhat learned English today; a few may be given in modern spelling: *ingenuity*; *putative opinions*; *artificiality*; *cordial liquor*; *perfunctory discourses*; *the gracious law of amnesty*; *amicable end*; *extensively employed*; *notoriety*; *negotiation*; *mechanician*.

Like Caxton, Nashe is of the opinion that Chaucer was a great innovator in the use of words, but declares that if Chaucer had lived to his time, he would have discarded the harsher sort of his strange words. They were, he says, the ooze "which ouerflowing barbarisme, withdrawne to her Scottish Northren chanell, had left behind her. Art, like yong grasse in the spring of Chaucers florishing, was glad to peepe vp through any slime of corruption, to be beholding to she car'd not whome for apparaile, trauailing in those colde countries."[26] Yet Nashe himself is very fond of a learned word, and in reading any of his or his contemporary's works one is surprised to find how many of their Latin words have made their way into accepted use. There are, to be sure, many words which were probably never again used after the immediate occasion which called them into being.

As we might expect, when a scholarly author sets to work with the avowed intent of enriching the language, he is sure to be led into numerous extravagances. And the extremists among the Latinists, or enrichers, were undoubtedly fair game for such satire as that of Thomas Wilson, in his *Three Orations of Demosthenes*, 1570, where he gives the following high-sounding letter, purporting to have come to him from an old schoolfellow: "Pondering, expending, and revoluting with myself your ingent affability and ingenious capacity for mundane affairs, I cannot but celebrate and extol your magnificent dexterity above all other. . . . I doubt not but you will adjuvate such poor adnichilate orphans as

[26] *Works*, ed. McKerrow, I, 317. The work in which this passage appeared was first printed in 1592.

whilom condisciples with you and of antique familiarity in Lincolnshire."[27]

Another satire on extravagance in the use of big words is to be found in the character of Rombus, the schoolmaster, in Sir Philip Sidney's mask *The Lady of May*. Rombus addresses his ignorant companions in language like the following: "Why, you brute nebulons, have you had my corpusculum so long among you, and cannot yet tell how to edify an argument? Attend and throw your ears to me . . . till I have endoctrinated your plumbeous cerebrosities!"[28] With the character of Rombus should also be compared the three artificial characters in Shakespeare's *Love's Labour's Lost*, the Spanish Knight, Don Armado, with "a mint of phrases in his brain," Sir Nathaniel, the curate, and the pedantic schoolmaster, Holofernes.

The extravagances of these satirical characters expressing (as they undoubtedly do) to a certain extent the methods of the augmenters of English, it will be readily seen that the conservatives and opponents of the introduction of new words had an important and necessary duty to perform. If the Latinists had been allowed full sway, they would practically have turned English into a sort of mongrel Latin dialect.

The conservatives, or the Saxonists as we may call them to distinguish them from the Latinists, therefore had considerable justice on their side, and indeed defended their cause with ability. Yet it is interesting to see that even the most conservative of the Saxonists are driven unconsciously to use many words of recent introduction from Latin. The language needed these words to express the ideas which both Saxonists and Latinists wanted to express; it needed them to become the cosmopolitan and universal language which even the Saxonists would have it to be; though they were conservatives, they could not be altogether reactionary and unprogressive.

[27] Quoted in Raleigh's *Introduction to Hoby's Courtier*, p. xliii.

[28] *Miscellaneous Works of Sidney*, ed. Gray, p. 274.

The head of this conservative faction may be regarded as Sir John Cheke, first Regius Professor of Greek in Cambridge University (1540), who lays down the principles of his school in a letter to his "loving frind Mayster Thomas Hoby," which Hoby prefixes to his translation of Castiglione's *Courtier*. His statement is as follows:

I am of this opinion that our tung should be written cleane and pure, unmixt and unmangeled with borrowing of other tunges, wherein we take not heed by tijm, ever borrowing and never payeng, she shall be fain to keep her house as bankrupt. For then doth our tung naturallie and praisablie utter her meaning, when she bouroweth no counterfeitness of other tunges to attire her self withall, but useth plainlie her own, with such shift as nature, craft, experiens and following excellent doth lead her unto, and if she want at ani tijm (as being unperfight she must), yet let her borow with such bashfulness that it mai appeer, that if either the mould of our own tung could serve us to fascion a woord of our own, or if the old denisoned wordes could content and ease this neede, we wold not boldly venture of unknowen wordes.

In his *Toxophilus*, published in 1545, Roger Ascham also ranges himself under the banner of the conservatives:

He that wyll wryte well in any tongue must folowe thys council of Aristotle, to speake as the comon people do, to think as wise men do. Many English writers haue not done so, but usinge straunge wordes as latin, french, and Italian, do make all thinges darke and harde. Ones I communed with a man whiche reasoned the englyshe tongue to be enryched and encreased thereby, saying: Who wyll not prayse that feaste, where a man shall drinke at a diner bothe wyne, ale, and beere? Truely, quod I, they be all good, euery one taken by hym selfe alone, but if you putte Malmesye and sacke, read wyne and whyte, ale and beere, and al in one pot, you shall make a drynke neyther easie to be knowen nor yet holsom for the body.

A similar argument is made by Wilson, in his *Arte of Rhetorike* (1553):

Some seke so far for outlandishe English, that they forget altogether their mother's language—and yet these fine English clerks will saie they speke in their mother tongue, if a man should charge them for counter-feyting the king's English. He that cometh lately out of France, will talke Frenche Englishe, and never blush at the matter. Another choppes in with English Italianated, and applieth the Italian phrase to our English speaking . . . I know them that thinke Rhetorike to stand wholie upon darke wordes; and he that can catche an ynkehorne term by the tail, hym they compt[29] to be a fine Englishman and good rhetorician.

The same side is taken by Gascoigne in his *Posies*, published in 1575. He declares that he has "always bene of opinion that it is not unpossible eyther in Poemes or in Prose too write both compendiously and perfectly in our English tongue. And there-fore, although I chalenge not unto my selfe the name of an English Poet, yet may the Reader finde oute in my wrytings, that I have more faulted in keeping the olde English words (*quam-vis iam obsoleta*) than in borrowing of other such Epithetes and Adjectives as smell of the Inkhorne."[30] And, to quote one more of these scholar-critics, we find Puttenham, in his *Arte of Poesie* (1589), joining the chorus: "We finde in our English writers many wordes and speaches amendable; and ye shall see in some many inkhorne termes so ill affected, brought in by men of learnyng, as preachers and schoolemasters: and many straunge termes of other languages, by secretaries and marchaunts and travailours, and many darke wordes, and not usual nor well sounding, though they be daily spoken in court."

But these complaints and cautionings of the conservatives were largely in vain. The result of the conflict between the Latinists and the Saxonists was a virtual victory for the Latinists. The whole situation is admirably summed up in the following passage from a contemporary writer, who is rebutting the argument of those conservatives who maintained that English had lost its

[29] From Latin *computo* = Modern English 'count.'

[30] *The Posies*, edited by Cunliffe, Vol. I, p. 5. Elsewhere he adds that he has rather "regarde to make our native language commendable in it selfe, than gay with the feathers of straunge birdes."

credit and become completely bankrupt as result of wholesale borrowing:

"I mervaile how our English tongue hath crackt it credit, that it may not borrow of the Latine as wel as other tongues; and if it have broken[31] it is but of late, for it is not unknowen to all men, how many wordes we have fetcht from thence within these few yeeres, which if they should be all counted ink-pot tearmes, I know not how we shall speake anie thing without blacking our mouthes with inke: for what word can be more plain than this word (plain), and yet what can come more neere to the Latine? What more manifest than (manifest)? and yet in a manner Latine: what more commune than (rare), or lesse rare than (commune), and yet both of them comming of the Latine? But you will saie, long use hath made these wordes currant: and why may not use doe as much for those wordes which we shall now devise? Why should we not doe as much for the posteritie as we have received of the antiquitie? ... But how hardlie soever you deale with youre tongue, how barbarous soever you count it, how little soever you esteeme it, I durst myselfe undertake (if I were furnished with learning otherwise) to write in it as copiouslie for varietie, as compendiously for brevitie, as choicely for words, as pithilie for sentences, as pleasantlie for figures, and everie waie as eloquentlie, as anie writer should do in anie vulgar tongue whatsoever."[32]

To be sure not all the words, or perhaps even most of them, which the enrichers attempted to add to the English vocabulary were accepted into general use. But the principle of their contention was accepted by all, and of course a great many of their specific recommendations. It was felt that the English language to be a fitting medium for the expression of all the thought of Europe, of all that the Greek, the Latin, the Italian, and the French had expressed, needed to extend its resources. The result was not a wholesale and violent importation of foreign words, but rather a tendency towards a generous liberalism which allowed

[31] That is, if it has become bankrupt.

[32] From *The Civile Conservation of M. Stephen Guazzo ... translated by G. Pettie out of French* (1586), quoted by Raleigh, Hoby's *Courtier*, pp. xlv–xlvi.

a writer to introduce whatever words he could make good use of.

Naturally these additions to the vocabulary were largely learned or semi-learned words. There was no reason why common objects should receive new names, since they already had perfectly adequate terms to designate them; but ideas of a more or less abstract character, descriptive words often, and words designating actions, these frequently required the invention of a new term. Even when the language already possessed a fairly adequate word, the invention of a new and synonymous one often enabled a writer to express himself more exactly or more musically and rhythmically.

It is of course absurd to give a single reason for so complex an appearance as the Elizabethan period of English literature, with its unequaled throng of poets and dramatists, Shakespeare at their head. But it is perhaps not unreasonable to suppose that the broadening and extending of the English language in the Renaissance period, through its assimilation to itself of all the preceding culture of Europe, was a necessary preliminary to the appearance of a world-poet like Shakespeare in England. There is, to be sure, no telling that Shakespeare might not have been born and expressed himself just as powerfully and with just as universal an appeal if the language had not been subjected to the critical examination and augmentation of the Latinist theorizers, if it had remained practically as it was at the end of the fifteenth century. We cannot prove that this would not have been true, but we can fairly doubt it.

We can point out that no other Teutonic nation has produced a figure to be compared with Shakespeare, with the possible exception of Goethe, in Germany, and that even Goethe, who lived and died two centuries after Shakespeare, must yield to the great Elizabethan when we consider both from the side of their cosmopolitan appeal. Goethe is the greatest poet of Germany, but Goethe is not known and admired in Italy, France, and England as Shakespeare is in Italy, France, and Germany. The

211

French influence of the Middle English period, followed by the classical influence of the Renaissance period, both working upon the solid and constant Teutonic base, these are the great influences which have made the English language what it is. They gave it a variety, a richness, and an adaptability that enabled a great poet like Shakespeare to use it as the measure, not only of all English thought, but of the thought of the Western world.

19 ✒ Word-pairs in English

Before passing on to the consideration of later borrowings in English, one question relating to the earlier borrowings frequently misstated and misunderstood must be given a moment's attention. This is the question of the use of words in pairs by the English writers of the Middle English and Renaissance periods, as in the following examples from the Prayer Book (1549): *pray and beseech*; *dissemble nor cloak*; *vanquish and overcome*; *defender and keeper*; *dearth and scarcity*, etc. It is often mistakenly supposed that this habit of using two synonymous words for one idea arose in the Middle English period as a result of the bilingual development of English at that time. It is assumed that a writer when he used a word of French origin would join with it an explaining word of similar meaning of English origin, and, *vice versa*, a word of English origin would be explained by a word of French origin.

An examination of actual usage, however, does not support the theory, since it is found that words occur in pairs without reference to their etymological origin. In Chaucer's *Prolog*, for example, occur sixteen word-pairs consisting of one French and one English word, thirteen in which both are English, and nine in which both are French, making a total of twenty-two in which the theory of bilingualism is not illustrated as opposed to sixteen in which it might be illustrated.[33]

[33] See Emerson, *Modern Language Notes*, VIII, 202–206.

But there are other good reasons besides this testimony of actual practice for disbelieving that their etymological origin had anything to do with the coupling of words together in pairs. An examination of earlier English literature before the time of French influence, and consequently before any bilingual tendencies can be supposed to operate, shows the same custom in the use of synonymous word-pairs. In the *Blickling Homilies*, for example, written towards the end of the tenth century, in the Alfredian translation of Bede's *Ecclesiastical History*, and elsewhere, we find word-pairs very abundantly used, both words necessarily being English. Moreover, it would be easy to find illustrations of the same device of expression in other languages than English, for example, in the Latin of Cicero, in which the theory of bilingualism could not possibly enter.

In short, the real explanation of the use of words in pairs is rhetorical and oratorical rather than etymological. By the use of two words a writer often gets a richer cadence, an oratorical amplification of the expression that may seem to him more effective than the use of a single word would be. A language rich in synonyms, as, for example, Modern English, is peculiarly liable to an abuse of this rhetorical device; it is an easy one, and young writers are much given to the use of two parallel words where one would answer as well. This is due less to a desire for clearness than "to that craving for symmetry which finds expression in all varieties of antitheses and balance. . . . Mr. Swinburne's adjectives and substantives hunt in fierce couples through the rich jungle of his prose. The taste for pairs, once acquired, like all the tastes of the wealthy, is hard to put off." [34]

Although the origin and the use of word-pairs is due to some such rhetorical or oratorical cause as has been mentioned, it should not be overlooked that in the period of the Renaissance, with its more or less conscious attitude towards vocabulary, the doctrine of bilingualism is a little more to the point in explaining

[34] Raleigh, Introduction to Hoby's *Courtier*, p. lviii.

213

the use of word-pairs. Undoubtedly a strange word was often explained by coupling with it a familiar word, and both Caxton and Sir Thomas Elyot expressly state that such was their custom.

Translators were especially given to the use of several words in translating a single word of their original. Lord Berners' translation of Froissart, for example, has such groups as the following: "they show, open, manifest and declare to the reader"; "what we should inquire, desire and follow"; "with what labors, dangers and perils," etc. Caxton, also, in order to make sure that he is expressing the meaning of his original fully, often uses two synonymous words, without reference however to etymology, when the French or Latin from which he is translating uses but a single word.[35]

20 ▨ Later Borrowings in English

No later period of English has borrowed words so freely from other languages as did the Middle English and the Renaissance periods. By the beginning of the seventeenth century the English vocabulary in its main outlines was fixed once and for all. Consequently in reading Shakespeare, although there are occasional words which have become obsolete, or which are now used in somewhat different senses from Shakespeare's, we nevertheless feel that in general the dramatist's vocabulary is Modern English. It is no longer in an experimental stage, as, for example, Caxton's is, but is the definitely fixed and settled vocabulary of the English language. This does not mean that no new words have been added to English since Shakespeare's time. On the contrary, the language has been continually receiving new words; it does so today, and will doubtless continue to borrow from other languages as long as native speakers of English are thrown into contact with other peoples.

[35] For further discussion of these points, see Raleigh, as above; Griffin, in the *Publications of the Modern Language Association*, xv, 172, note; Hart, "Rhetoric in the Translation of Bede," in *An English Miscellany, presented to Dr. Furnivall*, pp. 150–154.

21 ✒ Later Borrowings from French

French words have continued to filter into English in modern times beginning with the late seventeenth and eighteenth centuries, the so-called Augustan or Classical period of English literature. At this time French again came to be regarded in England as a polite language. This was partly due to the influence of Charles II, who, having acquired French tastes during his residence in France, transferred his French habits and preferences to the English court on his restoration to the English throne in 1660. It became a fashionable custom of the time to interlard one's speech with French words and phrases, a custom which is frequently satirized in the comedies of the period.

Nevertheless a good number of the faddish and fashionable words thus introduced seemed to be needed, since they have persisted in the language, and have now become everyday words in the vocabulary. Examples are words like *cadet, caprice, caress, coquet, dessert, festoon, gazette, grimace, grotesque, guitar*. It should be noted that many of the French words introduced in this period have the accent on the second syllable, following thus the French rule of accent, whereas words of French origin introduced in the earlier periods have all changed the accent from the second to the first syllable, following the English rule, as, for example, *palace* (French *palais'*), *courage* (French *courage'*). In general it is a safe rule that when a word of French origin bears an accent on the second syllable the word is of late introduction into English.

In contemporary English, French words of several kinds have been borrowed. We have, for example, a number of words which constitute what might be called hotel French, such as *menu, entrée, carafe, chef, demi-tasse, suite* (of rooms), *table d'hôte, à la carte*, etc. Another group comes under the head of milliner's and dressmaker's French, words like *toilette, habit* (meaning *dress*), *coiffure, manteau, couturier*, etc.; and another might be called society French, words like *début, fiancée, née, soirée, musicale*, etc. The interest of the French early in the twentieth century in

215

automobiles and mechanical invention in general has resulted in the common use of a number of words which may be called engineer's French, e.g., *aeronaut, aerostat, caisson, chauffeur, garage, tonneau,* etc.

It is interesting to note that the balance between Modern English borrowings from French and Modern French borrowings from English inclines rather in favor of the English. Some of the English words taken over into French in the last two centuries are the following: *redingote* (English riding coat), *jockey, rhum* (English rum), *rosbif* (roast beef), *ponche* (punch), *coquetel* (cocktail), *pique-nique* (picnic), *boulingrin* (bowling green), *club, boghei* (buggy), *dogcart, tramway, cricket, football, boule-dogue* (bulldog), *lawn tennis, bifteck* (beefsteak), *pannequet* (pancake), *sandwich, châle* (shawl), *black-bouler* (to blackball), *fifoclock* (five o'clock), *higlif* (high life), *toast, home*.[36]

22 ▨ Borrowings from German

English has never shown a strong tendency to borrow from German, and the number of German words in the English vocabulary is consequently small. Some of those which have been taken, however, are very characteristic words, like *waltz, carouse, poodle, meerschaum*; a few words naming objects or foods, like *pretzel, stein* (a drinking-mug), *sauerkraut, mangel-wurzel* (the name of a vegetable). A number of words naming minerals, *bismuth, blende, cobalt, quartz, shale, zinc,* etc. are from German, illustrating the fact that "it was in Germany that mineralogy first attained the rank of a science."[37] The word *carouse*, from German *gar aus*, that is, 'all out,' was taken over in the early Elizabethan period. It designated originally a drinking custom

[36] See Nyrop, *Grammaire historique de la Langue Française*, Vol. I, pp. 75, 84–85. Nyrop remarks, p. 84, that "the language which unquestionably has furnished and which continues to furnish the largest number of borrowed words to modern French is English." The words are especially those connected with "commerce, manufacturing, sport, and fashion."

[37] Bradley, *Making of English*, p. 103.

similar to that known as drinking *super nagulum*—"which is, after a man hath turnd vp the bottom of the cup to drop it on hys naile and make a pearle with that is left; which, if it slide, and he cannot mak stand on, by reason thers too much, he must drinke againe for his penance."[38]

A few words are more or less used in their German form, though they can hardly be said to have been adopted into English. Examples are *heimweh*, 'homesickness'; *zeitgeist*, literally 'time-spirit,' that is, 'the spirit of the age'; *weltschmerz*, literally 'world-pain,' 'weariness of the world'; *vaterland*, 'fatherland'; *hinterland*, meaning the region or land back of a seaport necessary to support it; and *wunderkind*, literally 'wonder child,' but applied specifically to a musical prodigy. The word *kindergarten* came into English with the thing itself, which originated in Germany. The Second World War brought *blitzkrieg* (often in the simplified form *blitz*, used as both noun and verb), *panzer*, and *ersatz*, 'substitute,' to the English lexicon.

On the other hand, the Germans, like the French, have borrowed, and continue to borrow, freely from English, especially of recent years. The words which they have taken over are of many different kinds. Many words of more or less fashionable character have been borrowed, showing the German admiration for English social customs and conduct. A few such words are the following: *butler, groom, nurse, porter, gentleman, four-in-hand, schlips* (meaning necktie, and adapted from English *slip*, which, of course, never meant necktie; the Germans, however, confused the word with their own native word for necktie, i.e., *Schleife*); *smoking* (for Tuxedo coat, being an abbreviation of *smoking jacket*); *knock-about* (a soft felt hat); *Raglan, Redingote, Mackintosh, Spenzer* (English Spencer), *Ulster*, all these being names of different kinds of coats.

Numerous words were taken over into what the Germans call "sport," meaning thereby usually field-sports after the English

---

[38] Nashe, *Pierce Penilesse*, ed. Grosart, II, 78.

fashion. Examples are *cricket, croquet, lawn tennis* (with all the terminology of tennis), *goal, golf, handicap, rekord* (English record), *sweater, trainer, turf, jockei* (jockey), *finish, robber* (i.e., rubber, in bridge), etc.

Words of nautical and seafaring character in general have also been borrowed, e.g., *brigg* (brig), *chartern* (to charter), *driften* (to drift), *ballast, jacht* (yacht), *sloop, steward, tender, top* (of mast), *trimmen* (to trim, i.e., sails, etc.), *kommodore* (commodore), *schmack* (smack), etc. A few further miscellaneous illustrations are the following: *bombast, essay, slang, clown, punch, humbug, lift* (i.e., elevator), *dschungel* (jungle, Kipling's *Jungle Book* being called *Dschungelbuch*), *scheck* (check), *stocks, store, streik, streiken* (strike, to strike), *kake* (cake), etc.

23 ◾ Various Borrowings in English

From Italian Modern English has borrowed a number of words, chiefly relating to music and the fine arts, as, for example, *piano, opera, studio, fresco*. Words of Spanish origin are *matador, ambuscade, grandee*, and in the United States, *ranch, adobe, lariat, mustang, vigilante*, among others. From Russian have come *knout, steppe, verst, vodka, ikon, pogrom*, etc. Modern Dutch has given a number of nautical terms, e.g., *boom, dock, hull, sloop, yacht, skipper*. A few words have entered Modern English from the Scandinavian languages, e.g., *floe, fiord, viking, troll, saga, geyser, gantlet, ski*.

As a result of the English occupation of India, a number of words of East Indian origin have made their way into English; examples are *bandanna, chutney* (a kind of sauce), *loot, indigo, rajah, rupee*, etc. From the American Indians we have borrowed *squaw, wigwam, wampum, hickory, moose, toboggan, moccasin, pemmican*, besides, of course, many place names. From Malay have come *gingham, gong, gutta-percha, orangoutang, amuck*, and *ketchup*.[39]

[39] Bradley, *Making of English*, p. 104. See also A. H. Marckwardt, *American English*, Chapter III.

From Chinese have come *tea, mandarin, ginseng*; from the Philippines, *datto, manila*; from the Polynesian languages *taboo, tattoo*; and *lanai* and *luau* from Hawaii.

Perhaps there is no people with which the English have come in contact for any length of time that has not added a word or two to the language. These words are all interesting as showing the kinds of relations which existed between the English and the various other peoples. But relatively their number must always be small. Modern English has not felt the need of any very extensive borrowing, and with one exception, to be noted in the next paragraph, has managed to get along satisfactorily on its inherited resources.

Foreign words are sometimes taken into the language temporarily. They are used as long as the special circumstances which called them into prominence are present, but afterwards they pass completely out of use. Thus, during the Spanish-American War a number of words became familiar to the American public through their use in the newspapers, words like *pronunciamento, machete, reconcentrado*; and during the Boer War a number of South African words gained considerable currency, as, for example, *kopje* (hill), *trek, laager, Uitlander*. During the period of the Hitler regime in Germany, we became familiar with *gauleiter*. Recent events in South Africa have given us *apartheid*. But such terms might be called "occasional words." They do not respond to any permanent need of the people, and after the occasion which brings them into use, they tend to disappear altogether from the language.

The one instance in which Modern English continues to borrow freely from foreign languages is in its scientific and pseudo-scientific vocabulary. Here the general tendency is to name all new inventions and discoveries by Latin or Greek words, usually the former, either separately or in composition. Thus Lord Rayleigh, the discover of the new element argon some years ago, made up the name for it from the two Greek elements α-, a prefix with a negative value, like English *in-*, and ἔργον, *work*, the whole

219

meaning 'not working,' or 'inactive,' the significance of the name being found in the fact that argon does not readily combine with other elements. The discovery of the Roentgen rays also brought to light the substance, *radium*, the name of which was taken from the Latin *radium*, 'ray,' the characteristic of the substance being the emission of rays of light.

Some of the applications of science to practical purposes have carried with them their classical terminology. The word *telephone*, for example, is made up of two Greek elements, τηλε-, 'far,' and φωνή, 'sound.' Words like *telegram*, *telegraph*, *television* are similar compounds. The word *phonograph* is made up of Greek φωνή, 'sound,' and the root γραφ-, meaning 'to write,' the whole word thus meaning literally 'sound-writer.' *Automobile* is a hybrid compound, that is, its two elements are taken from different languages, *auto-* being from Greek αὐτόν, 'self,' and *mobile* from the Latin word of the same form, meaning 'moving,' the whole compound meaning therefore 'self-moving.' Other words entirely from Latin are *carbon*, from Latin *carbo*; *insulation* from *insulate*, which is a past participle from the Latin verb *insulare*, formed from the noun *insula*, 'island' (cf. isolate); *calcium* from Latin *calx*; *spectrum*, from the Latin word of the same form.

Commercial terms are also often made of Latin or Greek words, as, for example, the names of products like *glucose*, *oleomargarine*. Any number of tooth powders, pastes and mouth washes employ the greek root ὀδόντ-, 'tooth.'

24 ✐ Etymology

Since the English vocabulary is derived from so many different sources, it will be readily seen that the study of etymology, which is the study of the origin and history of words, is one of peculiar importance to those whose native speech is English. It is not always, or indeed generally, necessary to know the etymology of a word in order to use it correctly. Words mean today exactly the ideas which they convey from one person to another, and any forcible attempt to make their present use conform to their etymological meaning is pedantic and vain.

Thus the word *villain* etymologically is related to village, and meant originally a serf, or person who was bound to the land. From the meaning of 'serf' or 'villager,' through the stages 'ignorant,' then 'degraded,' the word has come to its present meaning, an evil or wicked person. Its value therefore in Modern English must be determined by its use, not by its etymological history.

Nevertheless, as one's knowledge of the history and origins of one's vocabulary increases, in the same degree one's use of words will grow in definiteness and certainly of meaning, and in richness of content. Many great writers have been earnest etymologists; they have striven to give their words as full and rich a meaning as they would hold, and the reader, on his side, can get as much meaning out of them only when his knowledge equals that of his author.

Etymology, however, is something more than mere guesswork. Because two words look alike, it is not always safe to infer that they are forms of the same word. In Old English there are two words *god* and *gōd*, the first with a short vowel, giving Modern English *god*, the second, with the long vowel, giving Modern English *good*. But the two words are etymologically altogether distinct; one is not derived from the other, and the etymology which one used to hear sometimes from the lips of well meaning but linguistically naive preachers, "God is good," is altogether false.

In Modern English the adverb *gingerly*, as in the phrase "to touch something gingerly with the tips of the fingers," looks as though it had some connection with the noun *ginger*—certainly not an obvious connection, although with ingenuity one might be able to hammer it out. In fact, however, the word *gingerly* is not etymologically related to *ginger*, but to *gentle*, *gentry*, etc., and the similarity in form does not indicate any relationship in meaning.

This method of explaining the etymologies of words by their general apparent similarities to other words was the one in common use until the comparatively recent results of the exact study of language, especially phonetics, enabled scholars to formulate the rules of etymologizing in a systematic and scientific way. Thus Chaucer, in his version of the life of St. Cecilia in *The Canterbury Tales*, following the custom of his period, gives a half dozen different etymologies of the name Cecilia, all of them pure guesses and all of them wrong. Shakespeare, in *Cymbeline*,[40] gives a similarly fanciful etymology of the Latin word *mulier*, 'woman,' from *mollis aer*.

Two writers of the nineteenth century who were particularly given to the vicious habit of careless etymologizing are Carlyle[41] and Ruskin. In illustration of Ruskin's method we may quote the following passage: "What do you think the beautiful word 'wife' comes from? It is the great word in which the English and Latin languages conquer the French or Greek. I hope the French will some day get a word for it instead of their *femme*. But what do you think it comes from? The great value of the Saxon words is that they mean something. 'Wife' means weaver.[42] You must be either house-wives or house-moths, remember that. In the deep sense, you must either weave men's fortunes and embroider them, or feed upon them and bring them to decay." The absurdity of this is obvious. Whatever the word *wife* may at one time have meant, it certainly does not now mean *weaver*, and all of Ruskin's fine sentiment is based upon a manifest falsehood.

The grave defect of all such etymologizing is that it takes account only of the mere surface similarities that exist between words, similarities which may or may not be indications of a real relationship, but which are never systematically tested or

---

[40] See *Cymbeline*, ACT v, v. 446; also v, iv, 140, and v, v, 437.

[41] See *Sartor Resartus*, Chapter vii, where Carlyle gives the often-repeated but false etymology of *king* from *kenning* (cunning), 'canning,' 'the one who can,' or 'is able.'

[42] Presumably because *wife* and *weaver* have initial *w* in common, and the two somewhat similar sounds *f* and *v*.

examined. The weakness usually lies in the insufficient knowledge and observation of the etymologizer. Legitimate and sound etymologizing is not, indeed, work for novices. It is a science that follows a method; it has its rules and tests, and is not dependent only on clever guessing and imagination.

The tests of a reasonable etymology are these: 1. it must be in accord with the phonetic relationships which have been established; 2. it must agree with common sense on the side of any change in meaning which the etymology supposes; and 3. in the case of borrowed words, it must agree with probability on the side of geographical and ethnological relationships. Thus, if we find a similarity between a Hottentot word and an English one of Chaucer's day, it must be shown that English might have borrowed from Hottentot, or *vice versa*, before an etymology deriving one from the other can become even probable. Until one has had considerable practice in the principles involved, the safest method to follow in matters of etymology is to trust to the authority of reputable dictionaries and special works on that subject.

A considerable number of words, it should be observed, have been taken over into English in exactly the forms in which they occur in their original languages. The problem of etymology is here a very simple one, since the words suffer no change of form in transmission. Examples from German and French have been cited above. But the language from which such direct borrowings have been most frequently made is Latin. The following is a list of a few words in common use which have exactly the same form in both languages: *animal, apex, bonus, dogma* (originally Greek), *excursus, exit, extra, fungus, genius, index, odium, omen, onyx, opium, pastor, pauper, premium, series, species, spectrum, terminus, transit.*

It was remarked above that the meaning of a word in Modern English is dependent on its present use, and not on its etymology, a point which should not be overlooked. The historical meanings of words and their contemporary meanings are often the same; but when the meaning which Shakespeare or Chaucer gave to a

223

word is different from the meaning which men give it today, the earlier meaning cannot impose itself on the modern meaning. People often say that a word *ought* to mean so and so, because its etymology is this or that. They forget that language is not determined by theories of what ought to be or what might be, but by the conditions of its actual use today.

Jeremy Taylor, for example, speaks of "holy and innocent idiots, or plain easy people of the laity." A plain person might well resent being called an idiot today, because the word, originally from Greek ἰδιώτης, 'a private person,' hence a layman, as distinguished from a clerk, has developed very far away from its primary meaning. The word *lewd* has had a similar history. It is derived from Old English *lǣwed*, meaning simply a layman; like *idiot* it developed in an unfavorable direction, first into the meaning ignorant, then into its present uncomplimentary significance.

To take another illustration, the word *mischief* now applies only to wrongful or vicious acts; it comes, however, from an Old French word which formerly meant merely 'misfortune,' 'that which ends badly.' *The Book of the Knight of the Tour Landry*, a work of good counsel which a father wrote for the use of his daughters at the end of the fourteenth century, and which was soon translated from the original French into English, uses the word in its old sense when it advises the daughters to be charitable, "in the same wise as seint Elizabeth, seint Luce, seint Cecile, and many other ladyes that were charitables. They gauen the most parte of thayre good vnto pore peple that were in necessite and mischeef."[43] The same book speaks of robbery, extortion, tyranny, murder, "and mani other inconueniencies."[44] To class robbery and murder together as inconveniences seems a little odd until we realize the original meaning of the word, which was 'that which is not fitting,' 'wrong,' from the Latin negative prefix *in-*, united to the present participle of *convenire*, 'to be fitting or proper.'

[43] Early English Text Society, Vol. xxxiii, p. 152.

[44] Ibid., p. 92.

224

Certain words have persisted in English in occasional uses as faded, traditional survivals. They preserve the older forms of the words, but have lost the older meaning without supplying a definite new meaning. Thus we speak of a person as "wading through blood," or "wading in his own blood." One need only visualize the picture suggested by the modern sense of "wade" to see how ridiculous these phrases would seem if the word were given its literal meaning. But the word *wade* in these uses is only a colorless survival from its older sense, where it means merely 'to go, walk,' as in the following line:

Beholde how he wadeþ yn hys owne blod![45]

Another illustration is the phrase *time and tide*. The word *tide*, in the sense of "ocean tide," fairly fits its use in the familiar proverb, in which alone the phrase is used; but the idea of ocean tide may or may not be in the minds of speakers when they utter the proverb. The word *tide* in the phrase really has no definite meaning, although originally it had the same meaning as *time*, a sense which is still preserved in compounds like Christmastide, Whitsuntide, etc. In the proverb, therefore, it is merely a colorless survival, like *wade*.

Occasional words of this nature are at times used in an affected way in modern literary style. Thus one now and then meets the phrase "hark back" in the sense "return to," as in the sentence "He harked back to the subject of his former discourse," or "He was continually harking back to the experiences of the preceding summer." It is often vaguely used also in the sense of "imitate," as when one poet is said to hark back to another. The phrase has necessarily become somewhat vague and unnatural, since its primary significance is lost, and no new definite meaning has been given to it. Originally it was a term in hunting, and was used of the hounds returning "along the course taken when the scent has been lost, till it is found again."[46] As long as this literal

---

[45] *Meditations on the Passion*, Early English Text Society, Vol. LX, p. 17.

[46] See *Oxford English Dictionary*, under "hark back."

meaning was clear, the figurative sense of the phrase was intelligible; but with the loss of literal significance, it has become merely a traditional survival.

Another phrase of the same kind is "at first blush," as in the sentence, "At first blush it would seem that the poets were little concerned with the practical affairs of life." The word "blush" has now no meaning which can make this phrase seem reasonable. Its earlier and primary meaning, however, was 'look,' 'glance,' and the phrase meant 'at the first glance.' Writers who use it nowadays do not often have any sense of its meaning, but affect it merely because they have read it in the works of someone else.

25 ▨ Proportion of the Elements of the English Vocabulary

Although the English vocabulary has never ceased to open its doors for the introduction of foreign words, it must not be forgotten that it has always remained fundamentally and predominatingly English. The number of words of foreign origin used by different writers naturally varies with the style and manner of the writers. The same writer also uses sometimes more and sometimes fewer foreign words, depending largely upon the subject matter of his composition.

It has been estimated that the proportion of native words to foreign, counting each word every time it occurs, is in Shakespeare 90 to 10; in the King James translation of the Bible, 94 to 6; in the writings of Dr. Johnson, 80 to 20; of the historian Gibbon, 70 to 30; of Tennyson, 88 to 12. In the normal colloquial English of an average educated person the proportion of words of foreign origin probably never rises above ten per cent.

This low percentage of foreign words does not mean, however, that they are ineffective and unnoticeable in style. Of the ninety per cent of native words, a large part is made up of colorless words, like the articles, prepositions, conjunctions, etc. Often the words which really give quality and tone to a passage in

226

writing, or a phrase in speech, are just these occasional and somewhat exceptional words of foreign origin.

By far the greater part of the borrowed element in English is derived from Latin and Greek, either directly or through the medium of a French form. Some idea of the extent of this classical element in English can be formed from the fact that we have in English in common use, not counting the few occasional technical and scientific terms, words derived from about 450 Latin rootforms. Each of these root-forms is represented in English by a varying number of differentiated words. Thus the Latin root *ped-*, meaning 'foot,' appears at least in twelve common English words derived from it: *biped, expedite, impede, pawn* (a figure in the game of chess), *peon, pedal, pedestrian, pedicel, pedigree, pediment, pioneer, quadruped*. Other roots are represented by even more words in English. The root *duc-*, for example, as in Latin *ducere*, 'to lead,' appears in 27 words in English; *fac-*, as in Latin *facere*, 'to do,' appears in 39 words; and *pon-*, as in *ponere*, 'to place,' appears in 36 words.

The number of English words derived from Greek roots is not so numerous as those derived from Latin, the total number of root-forms used with any frequency falling below a hundred. An example of a Greek root that has been abundantly productive in English is the root contained in the words λόγος, 'a saying,' and λέγειν, 'to speak,' which appears in all the following words: *analogy, apolog* (or *apologue*), *apology, catalog* (or *catalogue*), *decalog* (or *decalogue*), *dialect, dialog* (or *dialogue*), *eclectic, eclog* (or *eclogue*), *epilog* (or *epilogue*), *eulogy, lexicon, logarithm, logic, monolog* (or *monologue*), *prolog* (or *prologue*), *syllogism*, and in all words in *-logy*, as *astrology, biology, neurology*, etc.

26 ▨ Purity of Vocabulary

The question of purity of vocabulary is one of constant recurrence. According to the usual understanding of the term, that vocabulary is said to be " pure " which is made up altogether, or almost exclusively, from words of a single native stock. We have seen that the vocabulary of the Old English period, as compared with that of the Modern English period, is relatively very "pure." For although Old English borrowed a few words from Latin in order to name objects which were brought to England and ideas which were given currency by the Roman missionaries, in general the language was sparing in its use of new words. It preferred when necessary, to adapt an old word to a new meaning rather than borrow a new word outright. Later, however, first through the Scandinavian conquest, then through the French influence, then the Renaissance, and finally the modern interest in science, learning, and commerce, English has borrowed a vast number of words. From a "pure," a unilingual tongue, it has come to be a polyglot language, one made up of elements from a variety of languages.

Now it happens that this polyglot character of Modern English carries with it, to some minds, the connotation of "impurity." If a language made up of entirely native elements is "pure," they argue, then one made up of divers elements is "impure," and, to that extent, less admirable than the other. This feeling for the purity of the language is partly based upon patriotic sentiment, a reverence for the native idiom as such, a feeling perhaps praiseworthy in itself, but not one which alone should be allowed to determine all questions of vocabulary. Of infinitely more importance is the matter of the effectiveness of the language in use. It is from this point of view that we shall consider briefly the question of purity.

Typical of the defense usually made for the pure, or Saxon, vocabulary is an essay written some time ago by Herbert Spencer entitled *The Philosophy of Style*. Spencer argued for the "greater forcibleness of Saxon English, or rather non-Latin English." The reasons why he regarded the Saxon, or native, vocabulary as more forcible than the foreign, were, first, early association, "the child's vocabulary being almost wholly Saxon"; and, second, the brevity of Saxon words as compared with words of foreign origin. Spencer further added that we should endeavor to use concrete and specific words, which are usually of native origin, rather than abstract and general words, which are usually of foreign origin. Thus, he said, we should avoid such sentences as the following: "In proportion as the manners, customs, and amusements of a nation are cruel and barbarous, the regulations of their penal code will be severe." Instead of this we should write: "In proportion as men delight in battles, bull-fights, and combats of gladiators, will they punish by hanging, burning, and the rack."

With these two sentences we may compare a sample of Spencer's own style, taken from the body of this same essay, the foreign words being italicized: "As we do not think in *generals* but in *particulars*—as, whenever any *class* of things is *referred* to, we *represent* it to ourselves by calling to mind *individual members* of it; it follows that when an *abstract* word is *used*, the hearer has to choose from his stock of *images*, one or more, by which he may *figure* to himself the *genus mentioned*."

Mr. Spencer's own style is in large measure the answer to his criticism. In the above passage of 66 words, there are 13 words of Latin origin, a proportion of $19\frac{2}{3}$ per cent, which is the proportion of foreign words in the writings of Dr. Johnson. Moreover, the sentence quoted is an admirable illustration of general, or abstract, statement; it does not follow Mr. Spencer's own rule of always speaking in concrete terms—as indeed it should not, since the purpose of the sentence is to make a generalized statement, and not to give a group of concrete instances. Again, the words are not such as one usually finds in the vocabulary of children, nor are they remarkable for their brevity. One word, *genus*, is distinctly a learned word.

Yet, in spite of the fact that the sentence, which is fairly representative of Mr. Spencer's style, breaks all the rules which he himself gives for a good style, it is nevertheless a good sentence. It has those qualities of clearness, definiteness, and simplicity which were general characteristics of Mr. Spencer's writings, even when he wrote on difficult and subtle matters of philosophy. It serves its purpose well, and if so, can anything more be asked of it? In short, the question of the proper and effective use of words is not dependent upon their length or their origin and history, but upon their immediate, contemporary value; and their value is always determined by the purpose which the person speaking or writing has in mind.

Sometimes it is effective to use short words—if one wishes to produce the effect which short words produce. But long words also have their place, and the poetry of Milton shows that they can be used to good effect. All that we can say, therefore, as to the choice of words, is that we should use the words which fit the thought, whether they are Saxon or Latin. A Saxon word, because it is a Saxon word, has no special claims or special powers, nor, on the other hand, has a Latin word. A word is justified, or is not justified, by its effectiveness in expressing the thought or feeling of the person who uses it, and any considerations beyond this are vain theorizings.

There is one group of words of partial foreign origin that is often regarded with special disfavor or by those who are governed by theories of the purity of language. This is the class of words known as hybrids. These are compound or derived words, the elements of which are taken from two different languages, one element from Greek, Latin or French, and the other from English, or at any rate from a language other than that represented by the first element in the combination. A number of such combinations are in common use in English, so common in fact that no one in natural speech is ever conscious that they are hybrids. Thus the word *because* is made up of the English preposition *be-* and the Latin (through the French) *causa*; *around* is compounded of English *a-* and French *round*; *plentiful*, of French *plenti-* and English *-ful*; *outcry*, of English *out* and French *cry*; and so with a great many words. In general these hybrids have become so much a part of the language that it never occurs to anyone to question them because of the manner of their formation.

The hybrids which are picked out to bear the burden of the disapproval of the purists seem indeed to be rather arbitrarily chosen. Thus it has been assumed that the Latin suffix -al should be united only to words of obviously Latin origin, as in *regal* from Latin *regalis*; *legal* from *legalis*; *communal* from *communalis*, etc. One word which violated this rule, and which was therefore branded as incorrect at the beginning of the century, is the adjective *racial*, compounded of *race* and -al.[47] That there is anything wrong or blameworthy, however, in combining -al with a root not obviously Latin is disproved by such words as *tidal*, from English *tide* and -al; *postal*, from French *post* and -al, etc., which have been taken into accepted and general good use. Since then *racial* has been taken into good use, there is no reason, so far as its compositional elements are concerned, why it should not have been.

Likewise the suffix -*ist*, which is ultimately of Greek origin, would be restricted by some theorists to composition only with words of Greek origin, as *chemist, atheist, monist,* etc. They would, therefore, disapprove of that free extension of the use of -*ist* by which it is united to words of Latin, English, or other origin, as, for example, words like *scientist, florist, druggist, dentist, tobacconist, contortionist, publicist, folklorist, tourist, typist, elocutionist, canoeist,* etc. Certainly these words are in good, reputable use,[48] and the fact that they are has nothing to do with the elements of which they are composed.

In short, the true guide to the use of hybrid combinations is to be found, not in the history of their etymology, but in their actual value in general use. If a hybrid compound expresses an

---

[47] The following is typical of the objections which were raised: "The word *racial* is an ugly word, the strangeness of which is due to our instinctive feeling that the termination -*al* has no business at the end of a word that is not obviously Latin." *The King's English*, London, 1906, p. 22.

[48] How far the attitude toward words of this nature has changed in the last sixty years is indicated by the fact that in the original edition of this book the author conceded that, "It may be that certain of these hybrids cited have not been accepted into good use, among which we may perhaps include *typist, canoeist, educationalist, conversationalist,* and others."

idea adequately, it is in itself as good a word as any which is not a hybrid, since the so-called "pure" word cannot do any more. This is all the justification which a hybrid combination, or any other word for that matter, needs to make it a reputable word; and the acceptance or rejection of a word of whatever kind is a matter almost altogether independent of its etymology.

27 ⌀ Profit and Loss in Word-borrowing

The question naturally arises, after a consideration of the elements of the English vocabulary, whether or not the language has been altogether the gainer by word-borrowing. That the introduction of foreign words has been advantageous in many ways is of course unquestioned. The language has not become bankrupt as a result of word-borrowing, as many of its Renaissance critics feared it would. New ideas have been appropriated, new standards of thinking and conduct, and, as the English-speaking peoples have grown in cosmopolitan spirit, their vocabulary has kept pace with them.

Another gain from word-borrowing is to be found in the variety of the English vocabulary, especially its richness in synonyms. These synonyms, or approximately synonymous words, for language does not often preserve two words of exactly the same value, enable the discriminating writer to express extremely subtle shades of thought and feeling. In illustration of such terms we may cite word-pairs like the following: *science, knowledge*; *information, wisdom*; *virtue, goodness*; *malevolence, wickedness*; *benevolence, goodwill*; *regal* or *royal, kingly*; *infant, child* or *baby*; *adults, elders*, etc. Sometimes we have four or five words with closely related meanings, as *still, placid, quiet, calm, peaceful*; or *vast, great, large, big*. Yet each of these has its own special uses. A big man is not the same as a great man.

Another advantage which the English vocabulary has by reason of its large number of words of foreign origin, especially of Latin origin, is that the language has at its disposal two widely different styles of expression, two planes of utterance, the one learned or elevated, the other simple and popular. Perhaps this is not to be regarded as an unmixed advantage. Possibly it would be better if the most learned and elevated ideas should be all expressed in our simplest vocabulary. Certainly it is true that the learned vocabulary of big words is a dangerous instrument for the inexperienced writer to work with, and of these dangers we shall have more to say later. But properly managed, the learned and high-sounding Latinized vocabulary serves a very useful purpose.

For one thing, it enables the writer to give variety to the cadence of his phrasing. Long words may vary and alternate with short ones, according as the thought or mood of a passage changes. Certain effects of dignity and stateliness can be attained in style only by the judicious use of words which by their mere bulk and volume of sound are stately and dignified, and such words, it generally happens, are of Latin origin. The language is like a great organ, and the various classes of words are like its stops. The more stops, that is, the greater the number of kinds of words, the more varied and the richer are the effects which can be produced by the artist who is capable of playing upon the language.

An author who was specially successful in his use of the high-sounding word, of the rotund, oratorical style, was Sir Thomas Browne. His writings have the dignity and the stately eloquence that one associates with the monumental classic style. In illustration, a single sentence may be quoted from his *Hydriotaphia*, or *Urne-Buriall*, the first edition of which appeared in 1658. He is discussing the comparative advantages of burning and of burying as a means of disposing of the dead, and says: "Some being of the opinion of *Thales*, that water was the original of all things, thought it most equal to submit unto the principle of putrefaction, and conclude in a moist relentment." An illustration of somewhat unpleasant subject matter was chosen to show how the author's style rises superior to his subject. "To submit unto the principle of putrefaction," and "to conclude in a moist relentment" almost reconcile one to the thought of mortal decay. The expression, it must be confessed, is somewhat remote from the fact, and one is a little inclined to forget the matter of the sentence in dwelling on the cadence of its phrasing.

Indeed the same question that troubled the minds of the conservative Renaissance critics of English arises now in considering the style of Sir Thomas Browne and is continually arising in the consideration of Modern English style. English is always in danger of falling into a toploftical manner of expression which soon degenerates into empty mannerism. Perhaps it is not necessary to point out the fascination which the "grand style" often has for the unskilled writer. We may admire it in the pages of a master of the method, like Sir Thomas Browne, without setting it up as a general model of English style.

But the long words of the vocabulary lend themselves to other effects than those which are dignified and stately. By contrast with the simple vocabulary, the long word playfully used often has humorous value. This sort of humor, polysyllabic humor as it may be called, also has its dangers; it is an easy trick, and, like most easy tricks, tends to be overworked. Always to speak of one's house as "a domicile," or of a horse as "an equine quadruped," is as cheap and tiresome a form of humor as constant punning. Sparingly used, however, the polysyllable is not without a touch of quaintness and charm. Charles Lamb was fond of this humorous device, though he also was occasionally guilty of a too abundant use of it. As an instance of his more successful manner, we may quote the following paragraph from the opening of his essay on *The Praise of Chimney Sweeps*: "I like to meet a sweep—understand me—not a grown sweeper—old chimney-sweepers are by no means attractive—but one of those tender novices, blooming through their first nigritude, the maternal washings not quite effaced from the cheek—such as come forth with the dawn, or somewhat earlier, with their little professional notes sounding like the *peep-peep* of a young sparrow; or liker to the matin lark should I pronounce them, in their aërial ascents not seldom anticipating the sunrise?"

234

By restating the ideas of this sentence in short words of native origin, one sees how much the flavor of it is dependent on just the words which Lamb has chosen. In a simple native vocabulary one would miss the occasional playful contrast between the loftiness of the diction and the lowliness of the subject, which lends it its chief charm.

Another advantage which the language has in its learned borrowed words consists in the fact that it can thus give to scientific objects and ideas names which have not been traditionally attached to other objects and ideas, and which have not acquired through long use a group of connotations and meanings which the scientific word should not have. Thus, the word *zoölogy*, a compound word of Greek origin, according to the meaning of its elements might be translated literally as 'life-lore,' a meaning which is decidedly too wide for zoölogy, that science being concerned only with the forms of animal life. So also 'star-lore' as a name for astronomy is not a good name, since it connotes a great many popular notions and astrological superstitions that astronomy is not concerned with. The word *inoculate* means a very definite process in medicine. Etymologically it comes from Latin *in-*, the preposition, compounded with the noun *oculus*, 'eye,' also 'bud of a plant.' Its original meaning in English was to graft by budding, from which the meaning of imparting the germs of a disease for the purpose of preventing the disease is a metaphorical derivation. In Modern English, however, *inoculate* is a word with a single, specific value, the best kind of word that science could have. And so often it would be extremely difficult to find simple native words as names for scientific ideas that would not connote either more or less than it was necessary to express.

Borrowed words, being without the connotations which come of long and familiar use, can often be employed for new ideas with less danger of prejudice or misunderstanding than the native words of the vocabulary. Thus it is an advantage to have the word "conductor" to name the person in command of a train, the corresponding English word "leader" not answering the purpose, and "captain" being limited to the commander of a ship. So also we may speak of a "regent" of a university, for example, whereas the word "ruler" would imply a kind of authority not intended. Manufacturers of commercial products have seen the value of this use of foreign words, and frequently avoid prejudice against their wares merely by giving strange names for familiar objects. Thus the product known as "cottolene," a substitute for lard made from the cotton seed, means simple "cotton oil."

Sometimes, however, the use of a big word for a familiar idea or object is due to affectation or to a desire to glorify the commonplace, as when one speaks of a fee as an *honorarium*, or of wages as *salary* or *emolument*. Just when wages reach the dignity of being properly called *salary* is doubtless a matter of opinion; but each word has its proper place, and the fault of using either for the other is equally great. It is hardly necessary to speak of a barber as a "tonsorial artist." And all perhaps except the proprietor would agree that the sign "Horse-shoeing Parlours," which for many years adorned the window of a New York blacksmith's shop, was a little more elegant than the occasion required.

On the other hand, it is certain that the large Latin element in the English vocabulary creates certain problems in the use of English. In the first place, there is the possibility of losing the sense of an intimate knowledge of the meaning of words. Borrowed words often do not have the familiar associations, the certainty of effect, and the precision and exactness of meaning which native words are likely to have.[49] Often they seem not to be

---

[49] English in this respect does not compare favorably with German. "There is nothing which cannot be expressed in German by a native word, homely, picturesque, appealing straight to the intelligence alike of learned and unlearned. The phraseology of abstract thought is concrete here [i.e., in German]; it is also of native growth, not imported from Greek or Latin. Instead of 'incarnation,' Germans speak of *Fleischwerden* or *Verfleischung*. Instead of 'relation,' 'definition,' they use *Verhältniss, Bestimmung*; instead of 'concept,' *Begriff*. Some of their philosophical expressions, such, for instance, as *Weltanschauung* [literally world beholding, i.e., philosophy of life], display an inimitable aptitude. Even the terms of physical science are not remote from common life. *Schwefelsäure* explains itself more easily than Acidus Sulphuricus [i.e., sulphuric acid]." Symonds, *Essays, Speculative and Suggestive*, Vol. I, p. 313.

completely assimilated, and are thus used with a looseness and vagueness not characteristic of the native words. This results at times in shifts in meaning which at first often cause considerable annoyance to those who are sufficiently familiar with Latin to know how the words were used in that language. An instance of this occurred some years ago with the word *aggravate* (from Latin *ad* and *gravis*), which etymologically meant 'to make worse,' but which came to be used in the more general sense of 'to annoy.' The authors of books on usage and manuals of style protested vehemently, but in the long run to no avail. Every current dictionary gives 'to annoy' as an accepted meaning.

Other instances of shifts from the etymological meaning which have become common are *incisive*, generalized from 'cutting' to 'to the point'; *predicament* in the sense of 'plight'; *oblivious*, strictly 'forgetful,' used in the sense 'unaware of'; *stupendous* used as though it simply meant 'large'; *unique*, shifting from 'the only one of its kind,' to 'extraordinary, unusual'; *balance* becoming equivalent to 'remainder.' Each of these ran into some controversy at the outset but has ultimately gained at least a degree of acceptance.

A more recent illustration of the same tendency is to be found in the use of *transpire* in the sense of 'to happen, occur.' It is worthwhile tracing the development of this word in some detail, not only to show how the process of change takes place, but to describe as well the strong feelings that are sometimes generated by these semantic shifts. The word first came into English in the sixteenth century. It occurred in a translation of a French work on surgery, and no doubt the translator lifted it bodily from the French original, where it obviously had been taken from the Latin. It was used in its strict etymological sense, 'to breath through,' and referred to the exhalation of vapors through tissue.

The second stage in its development was a figurative extension of meaning, referring to news or information that had leaked out from its source. Thus, if one said, "It transpired that Mr. Smith intended to buy the property," the inference was that the information, once confidential in nature, had become common knowledge. This usage is wholly approved today, even by those persons who object to the use of *transpire* in the more general sense of 'happen, occur.' What they do not know is that *transpire* in the sense of 'become known, leak out,' was denounced by Dr. Johnson as an illustration of the deleterious effect of Gallicisms upon the language.

Early in the nineteenth century, *transpire* acquired the sense 'happen, occur,' which, from one point of view, could be looked at as a further extension of meaning. It was used on both sides of the Atlantic, by such writers as Dickens, Hawthorne, and Froude. At the beginning it excited no comment, but in the 1870's and '80's objections to it began to appear, possibly as the usage became more general. For almost a century it was roundly condemned, but recent editions of authoritative dictionaries have recorded it without comment, citing its use in current writers. Nevertheless, this is still avoided by many careful speakers and writers, but they will undoubtedly diminish in numbers as time goes on.

Fortunately not every Latin borrowing undergoes a series of changes in meaning. For every word like *aggravate* or *transpire* there are scores, even hundreds, which pose no problems about the propriety of their use. Where we seemed to have failed, however, is in developing some reasonable set of limits to the application of the etymological principle. We rarely appeal to etymology in connection with the meanings of words drawn from languages wholly unlike our own. It would be futile, for example, to insist that *squash*, the American word for a gourd-like vegetable, be used in its etymological sense of 'that which is eaten green,' or that *moose* be applied to any animal that paws or scratches. Yet in the case of Latin, some well-meaning zealots have gone so far as to maintain that *dilapidated* can properly apply only to a stone structure because *lapis* means 'stone.' This kind of extremism may serve to retard the development of a reasonable attitude toward semantic change and the growth of a sense of style and proportion with respect to the use of the Latin element in our vocabulary.

There is, of course, always a real danger in using more or less unfamiliar words in vague and indefinite senses, the danger of thinking and speaking in loose and general terms instead of in the exactly fitting terms. Closely related to this is an abuse of the language already mentioned which the young writer is likely to be guilty of, that is, the use of words for themselves alone. There are so many "fine" words, so many learned words, in the English vocabulary, that one sometimes runs the risk of becoming enamored of words for their own sake, of using them because they sound well, even though they mean nothing, or are entirely inappropriate to what one is speaking or writing about.

In works on composition this use of big words is given the ironical name of "fine writing." Stylistically the use of "fine" words is ineffective because writing of this nature calls attention to itself rather than to the ideas the author wishes to convey. Such methods are comparable to those of a painter trying to paint a pink flower by using his most brilliant crimson color. He not only does not paint his pink flower, but he has no color left when he wishes to produce his strongest effects. As has been stated, it is usually the inexperienced writer who is liable to fall into this error. For a writer to persist in the use of "fine" words out of their proper places is to convict himself of insensibility to the effects produced by language. He must learn that one who is always striving to be fine succeeds chiefly in being cheap, tawdry, and vulgar. To know when not to use the big word in English is, therefore, one of the best safeguards a writer can have. Indeed, it may be set down as a rule: Never use a long word when a shorter one will do as well.

Whereas so-called "fine" writing generally reveals inexperience and a lack of linguistic sophistication, there is another kind of overuse of long words and complex sentence structure which is often encountered in the writing emanating from official or semi-official sources: government bureaus, college and business

239

administrative offices, professional organizations and groups. It is the kind of language to which U. S. Representative Maury Maverick applied the term *gobbledygook* some years ago, and against which Sir Ernest Gowers, the reviser of Fowler's *Current English Usage*, has consistently inveighed.

A typical example reads as follows: "There is a large loss of educational talent prior to the application of college entrance examinations; and the profession at large is not in agreement on or even well informed about why this loss occurs or under what varieties of circumstances it begins to occur." What this somewhat cumbersome sentence means to convey is that many bright students drop out of high school before they graduate, and their teachers don't know why they do it.

A sentence such as this is not the product of inexperience, but rather of long addiction to Latinate diction and complex structure. What is in origin an attempt at precision results in the habitual · use of set and ornate phrases even when they are more formal, complex, and indirect than the situation demands. Apparently, about the middle of the nineteenth century, some newspaper writing became similarly inflated. It was satirized by James Russell Lowell in his Introduction to the Second Series of *The Biglow Papers*. According to him, "A great crowd came to see," became in the journalese of that time, "A vast concourse was assembled to witness." "Man fell" was transformed into "Individual was precipitated," and "Sent for the doctor," would appear as "Called into requisition the services of the family physician."

Today it is the bureaucrat rather than the journalist who most often transgresses on this score. The English of current newspapers is generally direct and to the point, except for a few clichés and a cautious manner of statement dictated by the necessity of avoiding suits for libel or defamation of character. Nevertheless, the problem of style in English with respect to the Latinized vocabulary is essentially the same, whether we look at it from the point of view of bureaucratic English, of literary style, or of conversation.

An anecdote concerning Dr. Johnson, recorded by Boswell, is especially apropos here, showing clearly the tendency of mind which every English writer has to struggle against. According to Boswell, Dr. Johnson was speaking of Buckingham's satirical play *The Rehearsal* and said, "It has not wit enough to keep it sweet," adding after a moment's reflection, "It has not vitality enough to preserve it from putrefaction."

7

ENGLISH GRAMMAR

1   Modern English Grammar

The word grammar, as it is understood by the scientific student of language, is a term of wide inclusion. The grammar of a language, in the broadest sense, includes a consideration of all the facts of the language,—sounds, inflections, syntax, excepting only vocabulary. Indeed, many scientific grammars never get beyond the consideration of sounds and inflections. There is, however, a less general and more popular sense of the word grammar, which is the meaning intended in its use in the present chapter. This is a use of the word which makes it practically equivalent in meaning to correct syntax. We say a person speaks grammatically when he uses such syntax as is accepted as standard use, and he speaks ungrammatically when he departs from standard custom.

In modern times the tendency of grammar in this sense has been towards an increasing rigidity in many aspects of the grammatical system. This applies both to written and to spoken English. In both, the limits of permissible variation in usage are narrower today than they ever have been before. The custom of the language has tended to establish one "standard" or "correct" form for each grammatical category, and then to adhere to this form.

The difference between present and earlier usage can be seen by comparing Modern English with the English of Shakespeare. In Modern English we have, for example, only one form for the third plural present of verbs. Shakespeare, however, though he generally used what we now regard as the standard form, could also form plurals in -*s*, as in *Tempest*, v, i, 16: "His tears runs down his beard." He also formed third plurals in -*en*, as in *Midsummer-Night's Dream*, ii, i, 56:

> And then the whole quire hold their hips and laugh,
> And *waxen* in their mirth.

And occasionally we find third plurals in -*th*. Shakespeare thus had four ways of forming his third plurals, and these various forms he was at liberty to choose from apparently much as the need of the moment impelled him.

A similar freedom exists with respect to many other grammatical categories. These various forms are generally historical, but where later English has chosen one of a number of historical forms to the exclusion of the rest, earlier English frequently employs several different forms side by side.[1]

Sometimes the discarded earlier form of expression persists in Modern English, but is regarded as characteristic of the popular or uneducated speech. Thus the double comparative is now frequently heard in the speech of the uneducated and of children. In Shakespeare, as in *Merchant of Venice*, iv, i, 251, "How much more elder art thou than thy looks," it was a construction in as good standing as our so-called "correct" single comparative. In substandard English we also have the verb *learn* used transitively, in the sense of 'to teach.' In Elizabethan English *learn* could be either intransitive or transitive, an illustration of the

---

[1] Attention has been called above (see pp. 76 ff.) to the earlier use of the two forms of the pronoun *thou* and *you*, Modern English having limited itself, to its own disadvantage, almost entirely to the second form.

243

latter use being found in the King James translation of the Bible, Psalm CXIX, 66: "O learn me true understanding and knowledge."

It is interesting, also, to compare the standards of spoken English of earlier periods with that of Modern English. For this purpose the comedies of the seventeenth and early eighteenth centuries offer abundant material. The dialogue in these comedies is very realistic, coming as near to being an actual transcript of the speech and manners of its times as English literature has ever done. Perhaps, also, no later period of English literature except that of our own day has equaled this dialogue in its vivacity, its ease, and its truthfulness. Yet the characters, even when we use for illustration only such as represent educated and cultivated persons, are very free indeed in their treatment of Standard English.

In the works of Sir George Etherege occur such constructions as the following: *'Tis them*; *It must be them*; *It may be him*; *let you and I*, and *let thee and I*; *all you'll ha' me*, for 'all you will have me.'[2] In Farquhar's *Beaux Strategem*, ACT II, we have: *Then I, Sir, tips me the Verger with half a crown*. Frequently the same author uses abbreviations like *a'n't we*, or *a'n't I*, for the full forms *are we not* and *am not I*. The full form for *I have not* is contracted into *I han't*. A few further illustrations may be cited from the comedies of Vanbrugh. In a passage of serious prose, one of his prefaces,[3] we find forms like the following: *they'll*, *I'm*, *'t was*, *find 'em*. These, of course, are common enough in Modern English colloquial speech, but are now practically never used in written style. In the dialogue of the comedies themselves the following may be noted: *'Tis well, admit 'em*; *a purpose*, for "on purpose"; *on't*, for 'on it'; *These shoes an't ugly, but they don't fit me*; *I han't*, for 'I haven't'; *don't* as third singular present, frequently; *'twixt you and I*; *in these kind of matters*; *ben't*, for 'be not'; *by who*, for 'by whom'; *sha't*, for 'shalt'; *blow'd*, for the preterit of the verb; *with my Lord Rake and I*; *but was ye never in love, sir? nor is it me he exposes*.

---

[2] *The Works of Sir George Etherege*, ed. A. Wilson Verity, London, 1888.

[3] *Vanbrugh*, ed. W. C. Wood, Vol. I, pp. 7–9.

Many of these usages are such as exist today in the popular speech. They are not cited here as indicating a low general tone of cultivation in the comedies from which they are taken. On the contrary, conversation was never more brisk and effective than it is in these comedies; wit and satire have never been expressed more deftly than here. The examples have been cited merely to show the change which has come over English speech. Conversation now tends to be more precise and formal, or at least it admits fewer contracted forms and alternative constructions. Mere correctness or regularity counts with many people for more than it formerly did. That there has been, however, a corresponding gain in vivacity, lightness, and spontaneity, one would hesitate to say.

2 ⊠ Inflectional Change

With the setting up of a more rigid system of grammar, naturally the tendencies towards inflectional change, which are so characteristic of earlier periods of English, have been almost completely checked. The most important contemporary change is that which is affecting the subjunctive mood. One of the few constructions in Modern English, in which the subjunctive is in living, natural use is in the condition contrary to fact: "If I *were* you, I wouldn't do it." Even here, however, the indicative form is used in a surprisingly large number of instances in authors whose language must be considered as exemplifying standard English. A few instances may be cited: "It poured all night as if the sky *was* coming down" (Matthew Arnold). "I should feel more sympathy with Germany if it *was* only a question of its being welded together" (Life and Letters of Dean Church). Such usages, which indeed seem perfectly natural, lead one to doubt whether the subjunctive will be able to maintain itself even in this almost final stronghold of the condition contrary to fact.

The other situation where the subjunctive maintains a firm hold, at least in American English, is the reporting of actions, decisions, conclusions, etc., of a more or less formal nature. "The committee voted that the expenditure *be* authorized." "It was decided that action *be* deferred until a more suitable time." In sentences of this kind, British English leans toward the use of such periphrastic constructions as *should be*, but the inflectional form is common in the United States. In certain other constructions, although the subjunctive may still be employed with some subtle distinction of thought, there is always a trace of consciousness in its use; it has a more or less literary, or archaic, or affected flavor.

Occasional variation in the principal parts of verbs is also to be observed. The principal parts of *get* are *get, got, got,* or *gotten.* Neither *got* nor *gotten* is historically the normal or regular form for the past participle, which should be *geten.* But the vowels of the past participle and the past tense, as frequently happened, have been leveled under one form; and in the case of *got* as past participle, the leveling has been extended to the *-en* ending. The form *gotten* is often criticized as an Americanism, and it is undoubtedly a more general American use than British. The authentic story is told of an American who sent a telegram to a friend saying that he had gotten tickets for the theater that night, which the British operator transmitted "Have got ten tickets for the theater tonight," to the confusion of the ten when they came to occupy two seats.

But it has already been pointed out that the *-en* ending is historically correct. It is supported, moreover, by the forms *forgotten, begotten, ill-gotten,* etc. Unless one arbitrarily elevates one section of English usage to the position of standard, there seems to be no reason why the form *gotten* should even be questioned. It is as natural in that word as are such past participles as *driven, ridden, written,* etc. There are some constructions, however, in which the form *got* is the only one in customary use. We say "I've got to go," never "I've gotten to go," as the British critic sometimes asserts. Moreover, the currency of both *got* and *gotten* in American English leads to the useful distinction between, "We've got tickets," and "We've gotten tickets," in short the distinction between 'possess' and 'obtain, acquire.' There is of course no reason why *got* should not be used as the past participle of the verb when the natural custom of the language calls for it— and the same may be said of *gotten.*

The past participle of the verb *drink* is variously given as *drank* and *drunk.* Historically *drunk* is the regular form, following the class of *begin, began, begun; sing, sang, sung; run, ran, run,* and other verbs. The form *drunk,* however, runs into a verbal taboo because it suggests the adjective use of the word. In spite of this, the weight of usage still favors the form *drunk* as past participle.

Although there is considerable uncertainty in the popular speech with respect to the forms of a number of past tenses, the past of *blow* being often made *blowed,* of *begin* being made *begun,* of *catch* being made *catched,* etc., such forms are now considered as departures from the standard speech. Where formerly there was liberty of choice, as, for example, *began* or *begun,* for the past tense of *begin,* standard Modern English has recognized only one correct form, due in no small part to the influence of the grammatical preface to Dr. Johnson's dictionary.

It is a fact, however, that the rule of the grammarians is not always followed in practice by good speakers and writers. The past tense of the verb *dive* is conventionally *dived;* but the form *dove* is also in very general use, especially among persons not held in restraint by academic traditions. The former is the convention- ally "correct" form, but the latter, following the analogy of *drive, drove, ride, rode,* etc., is a natural formation and, in spoken use at least, is perhaps more frequently heard than the former. An example may be cited: "The little animal . . . struck out at him like an angry cat, *dove* into the bushes, and was seen no more" (T. Roosevelt, *Hunting the Grisly,* p. 111).

As H. A. Gleason has pointed out, "English dialects," and here he means different varieties of Standard English rather than dialect in the conventional sense, "do not agree in their choice of past tense forms for some of these verbs. Some use *sprang,* other *sprung;* some use *swam,* others *swum.* The alignment

247

of dialects is different for each verb. Moreover, in a few dialects both forms occur, sometimes associated with different keys, sometimes carrying different meanings. I would say: *The boat sank. He sunk the boat.* Some others would distinguish: *The bucket sprung a leak. He sprang to the rescue.*" [4]

Traditional grammar has attempted to regulate, according to a strict system, the use of *shall* and *will* in future and other verb-phrases, but not with complete success. The conventional rule, in a somewhat simplified form, is that *shall* is used in the first person, present tense, singular and plural for the expression of simple futurity and *will* in the second and third persons, present tense, singular and plural for the same purpose. Conversely, *will* in the first person and *shall* in the second and third are employed to express determination. It is also assumed that *should* and *would* respectively are used in the past tense where *shall* and *will* are used in the present.

There are several things wrong with this attempt to legislate language usage. That the rule does not faithfully reflect the facts of actual usage was clearly demonstrated some years ago by Charles C. Fries in his monograph, "The Periphrastic Future with *Shall* and *Will*." [5] Fries's study, historical as well as descriptive in scope, indicated unmistakably that over the past four centuries *will* has gained ground at the expense of *shall*. Even a casual comparison of Middle, Early Modern, and Modern English versions of the Bible will point to the same conclusion. In the Middle English version, verbs appearing in the Latin Vulgate with the future tense inflection are almost invariably translated as *shall*. In the King James version, many of them appear as *will*, and recent modernizations show an increase in the tendency.

Among other things this observation negates the claim, made from time to time by grammarians, that the Scotch, Irish, and Americans recognize no distinction between the two auxiliaries. If this were true, *shall* would appear in place of *will* as often as

---

[4] *Linguistics and English Grammar*, pp. 404–5.

[5] *Publications of the Modern Language Association*, XL (1925), 963–1024.

will occurs when *shall* seems to be demanded. As far as American English is concerned, Fries's monograph definitely shows that this is not the case. Moreover, it is by no means certain that *should* and *would* follow the same distributional pattern as *shall* and *will*. They are by no means limited in function to indicating the future perfect but have a number of modal uses, such as the expression of condition, contingency, obligation, etc.

It is true that in certain restricted communities, there is a body of speakers who tend to use these words in their conventionally recognized standard form. But even they, in ordinary conversation, naturally employ the contracted *I'll, you'll, he'll*, etc. In these reduced forms, the distinction between *shall* and *will* is largely obscured. Thus *I'll, you'll, he'll* may as well represent *I will*, etc., as *I shall*, etc.

Aside from the fact that it is not an accurate reflection of standard usage, the traditional rule is at fault on two other counts. First of all, by attempting to distinguish between futurity on the one hand and determination on the other, it creates a false dichotomy. Futurity is a matter of time, determination one of modality, of attitude. Almost any expression of an action which is to take place in the future represents as well some degree of intention. "Pure" futurity, totally divorced from volition or intent is difficult to conceive. Conversely, any expression of determination would seem to project the action in question into future time, either near or remote. It is reasonable to demand that grammatical categories reflect a consistent basis of classification.

In addition, the *shall–will* rule, and the presentation of verb conjugations based on it, often leaves the erroneous impression that the only way to indicate future time in English is by the use of these two auxiliaries. This is by no means the case, nor has it been at any time within the recorded history of English. In Old English the present tense was regularly used to indicate future time. It is still so used when an indication of the time of action is specified: "He leaves for England next March." "He gives his book report this afternoon."

Even more prevalent is the *going to* future, a construction which arose in the late sixteenth century and has been increasing in frequency ever since. Such expressions as "He's going to study" or "We're going to play ball" carry no implication of movement as far as the verb *go* is concerned, as the double use, "They're going to go," clearly indicates. Still another mechanism for future time is the construction *am (are, is) to*: "He is to speak at the church." "You are to return the book when you have finished." It appears to carry with it a somewhat greater suggestion of formality or compulsion than some of the other future constructions, and possibly approaches *shall* more closely in this respect.

The whole question of the future tense points to the necessity of restudying many of the conventional grammatical rules, first of all from the point of view of the actual usage of the standard language in all parts of the English-speaking world, and second in terms of the rule as a rule: is it not only an accurate but a complete, consistent, and economical description of the patterns of the language. The *shall–will* rule falls short on the scores of completeness and consistency as well as accuracy.

In the noun the only inflectional changes of importance are those affecting plurals of foreign origin. Here there is more or less tendency to give the foreign plurals the form of English words, with the regular *-s*, *-es*, endings of plurals. Thus the plurals of *index, appendix, focus, antenna,* may be either the foreign forms *indices, appendices, foci, antennae* or the English forms *indexes, appendixes, focuses, antennas.* In some words, like *gymnasium, bandit, cherub,* the English plurals *gymnasiums, bandits,* and *cherubs,* instead of *gymnasia, banditti,* and *cherubim* (used only with reference to the Biblical cherubim), are the only ones generally used. In general the tendency to substitute English for foreign plurals is one which increases in strength as words pass from the learned and technical spheres of the vocabulary into common usage, as has been the case with *antenna.*

In the instance of the word *data,* a Latin plural from a little used singular *datum*, the strong popular tendency is to take the word as a singular. This tendency is helped by the fact that the word has no corresponding singular in general use. It is consequently understood as a singular, equivalent in meaning to 'information,' as in the sentence, "This data has been furnished on the understanding that it will not be published." Although historically inexact, the meaning has become so general among those who employ the word in colloquial speech that it must be regarded as an established usage and is so recorded in current dictionaries.

There is a similar tendency to use the plurals *phenomena* and *criteria* as singulars, upon which new plurals, *phenomenas* and *criterias*, are then formed. This tendency is held well in check, however, by the learned character of the words. As they become more popular, an increasing use of the plural forms as singular may be expected.[6]

3 ▨ Word Order

To take the place of the older method of binding the parts of the sentence together by means of concord in inflectional endings, Modern English, having lost almost all its inflectional endings, has been compelled to substitute instead the order of the words in the sentence. The principles determining the word order of Modern English are two; first, that ideas shall be expressed in the order of their logical succession, or at least what appears so to a native speaker of the language; and second, that related ideas shall stand in close proximity to each other.

By the first principle English has settled upon an almost invariable succession of the main parts in the structure of the sentence. The main scheme of subject + verb + object is but little

---

[6] For examples of *phenomena* as a singular and *phenomenas* as plural, see the *Oxford English Dictionary* under *phenomenon*. In the case of the word *opera*, which is etymologically the plural of the Latin neuter noun *opus*, both the popular and the standard speech accept the plural form as singular, forming a new plural *operas* after the common analogy of English words.

obscured by the insertion of modifying parts and is not departed from except in occasional interrogative and exclamatory sentences. In colloquial speech, where the sentences are naturally shorter and simpler than in the more conscious literary style, the simple subject + verb + object structure is almost the only one employed. It is, in fact, the only one that can be employed; for even in sentences in which the forms of the words indicate their cases, for example, *I saw him* and *Him saw I*, that rigid feeling for one set form which is generally characteristic of Modern English permits only the first, or natural, order of words.

The second principle requiring that related ideas shall be expressed in close proximity to each other is a necessary result of the importance of word order and of the leading part which logic of situation plays in Modern English. If the interrelations of words in a group are to be determined by the logic of the ideas which they express, naturally those ideas which are closely related must be brought close to each other in expression, since the logical connection would otherwise be obscured by the introduction of extraneous ideas. We thus demand that adjectives stand near their nouns, usually immediately before them; that pronouns stand near their antecedents; that adverbs stand close to the words they modify; and that verbs stand as near as possible to the subjects which determine their number and person.

In the ordering of phrases and clauses also, the parts must be arranged in the order of their logical sequence. Humorous illustrations (for example, "Piano to rent by a lady with solid mahogany legs") of the result of not heeding this rule abound in the grammars and rhetorics. But the fact that we find such departures from a fixed word order ludicrous, even when the logic of the situation makes the meaning perfectly clear, as in the above example, shows what a strong hold mere proximity and order of words have acquired in Modern English speech.

This feeling for order of words in some instances comes into conflict with certain traditional grammatical rules. A stock illustration of this is the split infinitive. It is one of the traditional rules of Modern English grammar that nothing shall stand between the infinitive and its sign *to*. But it is difficult to see the logical justification for this rule. By origin the sign *to* is a preposition, and the infinitive which follows it is by origin a verbal noun, which, in the inflectional stage of the language, was inflected, like any other noun, for the dative case after its preposition. Moreover, in the similar construction of the infinitive in *-ing* after a preposition, no question is ever raised. If one may say "His plan *for heavily taxing* the people did not meet with approval," why may not one as well say "It is difficult *to quickly convert* these securities into cash"?

Indeed the principle of Modern English grammar that a modifying word shall stand as near to the modified word as possible often favors the insertion of an adverb between the infinitive and its sign. This is especially true when the adverb might as appropriately or logically modify the main verb as the following infinitive construction. The following sentence will serve as a case in point: "The newly-formed board of directors had unanimously decided *to quickly develop* a new process for making nitrates out of sea water." If *quickly* is to be interpreted as modifying *develop* rather than *had . . . decided*, there is scarcely any place for it except within the infinitive construction. To place it before the infinitive runs the risk of ambiguity. To place it anywhere after the infinitive results in an awkward insertion between verb and object or between noun and modifying phrases. To put it at the end results again in ambiguity since it could be interpreted as modifying the verbal noun *making*.

The best writers have always availed themselves of the privilege of placing an adverb before the infinitive when the effective exposition of their thought required it. In contemporary speech the split infinitive is most frequently heard in the usage of those speakers who give much attention to the precise definition and expression of their thought, especially lawyers, but who are not too much restrained by the injunctions of the academic grammarian. By the test of actual use and by the test of the feeling for the Modern English idiom, the split infinitive is not only a natural, but often an admirable, form of expression.[7]

The pressure of word order sometimes results in the use of case forms contrary to the usual rules of grammar. Thus from early times the nominative form of the interrogative pronoun, instead of the grammatical objective, has been used in sentences like "Who do you mean?" Shakespeare, in *Coriolanus*, II, i, 8, writes: *Who does the wolf love?* where the context shows that *Who* is to be taken as the object of *love*. Examples are frequent in colloquial English of all later periods. According to the rules of conventional grammar, they are of course simply incorrect. They violate the rule that the object of a verb must be in the objective case, and the objective case of *who* is *whom*.

But is nothing to be said for "Who do you mean?" The justification of the construction, so far as it goes, is to be found in the explanation of its origin. The type-form of the English sentence, as has been stated, follows the scheme of subject + verb + object. The general feeling thus comes to be that the word which precedes the verb is the subject word, or at least the subject form, and that which follows, the object. It is an instinctive tendency, therefore, to make all sentences adapt themselves to this typical structure.

Naturally enough, *who*, when it comes first in interrogative sentences, is given the subject form, not only in those many sentences in which it is the grammatical subject, as in "Who called yesterday?" but also in sentences in which it is the grammatical object, as in "Who did you call?" Since this latter construction follows the logical tendency of modern grammar, by that test it is acceptable; and since, moreover, it is in wide colloquial use, it can be condemned in practice only by the believer in a rigid and unrealistic system of grammar.

Another instance in which order of words has been influential

---

[7] For a full discussion, with numerous examples, of the split infinitive, see Lounsbury, *The Standard of Usage in English*, pp. 240–268; Hall, *American Journal of Philosophy*, III, No. 9, 1882; Borst, *Englische Studien*, XXXVII, 286–393; Bryant, *Current American Usage*, pp. 194–197.

in determining the form of a case is the construction "It is me." This usage may be said to have fairly won its way, at least into good colloquial speech. Other similar forms, like "It is her, him, them," have perhaps not been quite so successful, although they follow the same tendency. In these sentences the type-form, subject + verb + object, has caused even the word after the copulative verb to assume the objective form. So strong is this feeling for the objective as the case of all words after the verb that the traditionally correct "It is I" has come to be regarded as somewhat pedantic and affected.

An interesting conflict of tendencies arises in such sentences as "I had no expectation of him doing that," or "I had no expectation of his doing that." Both usages are widely current in colloquial speech, although the traditional grammarian prefers to consider the forms with the genitive, that is, "of his doing that," the only correct form. This is especially true when the -*ing* word is preceded by a pronoun.

Otherwise, even in good literary style, one finds the non-genitive, that is the common case form frequently used, as in the following examples: "This impossibility of one *man producing* work in exactly the same manner as another makes all deliberate attempts at imitation assume the form of parody or caricature" (Symonds, *Essays Speculative and Suggestive*, II, 7); "I can only suggest a reason for the *effect being* so much greater in my own case" (Hudson, *Idle Days in Patagonia*, p. 226); "He points out the necessity of *style being fashioned* to the matter" (G. Gregory Smith, *Elizabethan Critical Essays*, p. xlii); "the fact is that, strictly speaking, there is no such thing as a *language becoming* corrupt" (Lounsbury, *The Standard of Usage*, p. 57); "there had been a scene between his father and himself, which ended in his *father disinheriting* him" (*New York Times*); "the shortness of his left leg prevented *him running*" (ibid.).

The logical origin of the two forms of expression, the one with the genitive, the other with the common case form of noun or pronoun, is not difficult to see. In a sentence like "I was used to him being so excited," the instinctive feeling is that the preposition *to* should be followed by an adjective case, *him*, especially so since the word which follows *him* is not a simple noun, but that peculiar kind of noun which we call a verbal, a noun that possesses as much the value of verb as of noun. Even when the substantive which governs the gerund is not preceded by a preposition, the particular focus of the sentence may result in different constructions. In the final example cited in the foregoing paragraph, for example, the constructions *prevented him running* and *prevented his running* are by no means identical in meaning. In the first the emphasis is upon the actor, in the second upon the action. On logical grounds, therefore, both constructions are acceptable.

The choice of the construction should, accordingly, be governed by considerations of logic and emphasis rather than by an incomplete and not wholly accurate statement of the custom of the language. As has been stated, there has been an academic tendency to regard the form of construction with the objective as popular English, and to elevate the construction with the genitive as the sole standard form of the construction. The examples given above, however, are sufficient to indicate that a hard and fast rule requiring the genitive before the verbal in *-ing* is not a description of the real facts.

There are indeed some instances in which the genitive is never found, some even where it would be impossible. Spoken English does not distinguish between the genitive plural and the plural of the common case. Consequently, in this kind of construction the apostrophe, as an indication of the genitive plural, seldom appears in writing. One would not be likely to write *Protestants'* in the following: "This has arisen in good measure from Protestants not knowing the force of theological terms" (Newman, *Apologia*, p. 352); or *authorities'* in "She laughed at the idea of the authorities holding her" (*New York Times*). In a sentence like "We had not thought of *that being* his real occupation," a possessive form *that's* is out of the question; the pronoun must be in the common or non-possessive form. Moreover, when a phrase or clause used substantively, rather than a single noun, governs the verbal, no inflection is added. Note: "He could not conceive of *the end of the war* coming so soon." "They could not understand *John who was now eighteen* wanting to leave home." The same is true of nouns in apposition or in a coördinate construction. "I was concerned about *Harry and Dorothy* coming too late." "People seldom hear about *Bryant, the poet*, having been a journalist."

It seems then that only when the verbal is preceded by a personal pronoun or the name of a person is there any strong feeling that the genitive form is necessary. The hostility towards a sentence like the following, "History has no record of a *city existing* under such circumstances," is decidedly less than it is towards a sentence like, "No one ever heard of *Lincoln making* such a speech." But sentences like this second are common enough even in good writers, and the dogmatic assertion of the grammarian, here as ever, must be taken with liberal allowance.

4 ⊠ Concord

The triumph of the logic of meaning over form is frequently illustrated by the concord of verb and subject in Modern English. A sentence, for example, like "The whole car were laughing," is acceptable, although it contains a singular subject and a plural verb. By "car," however, one of course means "all the people in the car," and this idea has more value in determining the number of the verb than the singular form of the mere word. Likewise we may have two related ideas, connected by the coördinating *and*, which stand as the subject of a singular verb because they are thought of as practically one idea. An illustration is Kipling's line, "The shouting and the tumult dies." Strictly interpreted, we should of course have "die"; but again the logic of ideas rises superior to the rules of formal grammar.

Autograph of Milton's "Lycidas," ll. 165–193
(For description, see Appendix, p. 290)

The same principle applies to the varying treatment of collective nouns. We may say "The jury were of one mind," in which the component parts of the jury is the thought uppermost in the mind; or we may say "The jury was selected without difficulty," where the jury is thought of as a whole.

A plural verb is often used in constructions in which we have a singular subject to which is united a prepositional phrase which has all the value of a coördinate subject. Thus the following sentence is part of the inscription on a tablet erected in memory of the novelist Blackmore: *This tablet with the window above are a tribute of admiration*, etc. This construction is very old, being found abundantly as far back as Old English. Again it is the logic of the situation which determines the concord, "This tablet with the window" being logically, though not grammatically, equivalent to "This tablet and the window."

In a similar way a plural demonstrative adjective is often used before the singular noun, in constructions like "These kind of apples are hard to get," or "Those sort of people are not often met with." This is very general colloquial usage, and sufficient examples may be cited from good authors to show that it is not impossible literary usage. Again it is the general logic of the situation which determines the plural forms *these, those*. The words *kind* and *sort* are themselves collective nouns and imply the idea of plurality. They are, moreover, usually followed in this idiom by the plural of the whole of which the word *kind* or *sort* is a part, as in the above examples, *of apples* and *of people*. The predominant thought of the whole group of words is consequently a plural idea, and the demonstrative naturally takes the plural form. The grammar of such constructions is determined by the logic of general situation, not by the rules of formal concord.

Another familiar illustration of the importance of general situation as compared with grammatical concord is to be found in the construction known as "dangling" or "unrelated participle." The traditional rule of the grammars and rhetorics is that the participle must not be used without definite and expressed indication of the word which it modifies. With unskilled writers this is a reasonable and necessary warning, since often ridiculous blunders are made by neglect to follow it. The loose construction often results also when the writer has not taken the trouble to think out clearly what he has to say. A sentence like "Standing on the hilltop the valley stretched away for miles" is unacceptable, not merely because the participle "standing" has no word to modify, but because the general situation is not adequately expressed.

At the same time it must be acknowledged that as a rigid rule admitting no exceptions, the prohibition against the dangling participle is also a dogma of the theoretician which is contrary to actual practice. Sentences like the following from Carlyle, "Speaking in quite unofficial language, what is the net purpose and upshot of war?" can be readily paralleled, not only in colloquial speech, but also in the more formal literary style. The following is from Robert Louis Stevenson, whom one can hardly regard as a careless writer: "Thence, *looking* up and however far, each fir stands separate against the sky no bigger than an eyelash, and all together lend a fringed aspect to the hills" (*Silverado Squatters*).

Such sentences are indeed quite in harmony with the general and laudable tendency of English towards contracted and elliptical forms of expression. After all, contractions are means of indicating ease and informality; ellipsis helps us to avoid tiresome redundancy. So long as the meaning is clearly conveyed, we do not usually trouble ourselves much about questions of completeness. It is only when the meaning is obscure, or when some unsuitable grouping of ideas is brought about by the failure to build a sentence on sound structural principles, that we have recourse to the formal rule of grammar to correct the situation. In other words, grammatical correctness in the rigid and traditional sense is in many instances in Modern English not a positive, not even a necessary, virtue, but rather a safeguard to prevent misleading or inadequate forms of statement.

5 ▨ Meaning and Function

Attention has already been called to the ease and frequency with which words of one part of speech pass over into another. This again is partly due to the importance of meaning as distinguished from form in Modern English. Since words in Modern English usually stand for ideas, without formal restrictions as to the way these ideas shall be expressed, they easily lend themselves to a great variety of uses. The function, or part of speech, of a word can thus be determined in Modern English only by the logic of its use, the key to which is often its position in relation to other words.

The words *out, in, then* are usually adverbs, but in phrases like "the out voyage," "the in voyage," "In the then condition of my mind" (Dickens), they are plainly adjectives. Similarly the word *so*, in the sentence, "He was poor but honestly so," can hardly be disposed of as an adverb. Its function rather is similar to that of the pronoun, although the word which it here stands in place of is the adjective *poor*, an equivalent form of the sentence being "He was poor but honestly poor."

In some instances the loss of older inflectional forms has resulted in a feeling of some uncertainty with respect to the classification of words into the traditional part-of-speech categories. Thus the old dative adverb formed by the addition of the inflectional -*e* to the adjective, by the loss of final -*e* has become exactly like the adjective in form (see above, p. 61). Some grammarians therefore have been inclined to regard such constructions as "go slow," as in "The need of going slow in astronomical science we have urged many times on its practitioners" (*New York Times*), or "I can't walk fast," etc., as incorrect, substituting what they regard as the correct adverbial forms, "go slowly," or "I can't walk rapidly." They thus strive to establish a rigid and unequivocal form for adjective and adverb.

This, as we have endeavored to point out, is contrary to the spirit of Modern English grammar, which makes logical meaning rather than form the test of value of a word, and if *slow* and *fast* are used as adverbs, they are adverbs and nothing else. On this basis the word *evenings*, in the sentence "The library will close evenings at eight o'clock," is a pure adverb, equivalent in meaning to the adverbial prepositional phrase "in the evening." In origin it is indeed derived from an older adverbial genitive in *-es* (a construction which still exists in Modern German), with which in later times was confused the idea of the plural. But logically, and therefore grammatically, its function is adverbial in Modern English whether it is regarded as a singular or a plural, and the construction is to be accepted as a natural idiom of the language.

Such adverbial ideas as extent of time and space are also expressed without inflection for adverbial form. Thus *hours* in "I walked two hours," and *miles* in "I walked two miles" are both adverbs. They are sometimes called "adverbial objectives," because this adverbial function was expressed in the Old English period by inflection for the accusative case. In Modern English, however, there is no thought of case connected with the words, and their function is determinable merely by their logical meaning. In one instance, in the construction "I am going home," we have the word *home* preserved in what was originally a locative case of a noun; but here also the feeling for case has disappeared, and the word is to be regarded simply as an adverb.

Another adverb which in origin is derived from an inflectional form, but which has become even more obscured than those cited, is the adverb *the* in such expressions as "The more the merrier"; "The sooner you do this, the better it will be for you." The word *the* in the inflectional Old English period of the language was, in this construction, an instrumental case of the demonstrative pronoun, its form being *þȳ*; in meaning it was equivalent to a prepositional phrase "by this," or "by that." Our Modern English "The more, the merrier" might be paraphrased, therefore, as "more by this, merrier by that," in which of course *by this* and *by that* are adverbial phrases modifying the adjectives *more* and *merrier*. From this analysis it will be seen that the word *the* in such constructions as *the more*, etc., since it has the function of an adverb, is to be treated as such, even though in form it seems very remote from everything that we connect with the idea of adverb. It is not possible to dismiss the construction, as is often done, merely as an "idiom," incapable of analysis. An easy but unjustifiable way of evading grammatical difficulties has been to group them together as idioms, understanding by that term peculiar, illogical, and inexplicable constructions which have found their way into the language in some mysterious manner beyond the power of man to discover. There is little reason in the concept of idiom as a confession of failure on the part of the student of language. True enough, there are many constructions which are difficult to account for on the basis of a purely descriptive approach to the language, but a knowledge of its historical development will shed light on many of these.

The term "idiom" is needed for better uses than to serve as a designation for something which the grammarian finds difficult to explain. It is needed to designate those methods of expression which are peculiar to one language as distinguished from another. Thus it is proper to speak of an English, a German, or a French idiom. To write or to speak English idiomatically means to write or speak it with due understanding of and regard for those specific forms of expression by virtue of which English is English as distinguished from all other languages.

An interesting development of Modern English grammar is the extension of the class of copulative verbs. A copulative verb may be defined as a verb of weakened predication or assertion. It serves as a colorless link-word rather than to make a positive declaration. Its commonest, and apparently oldest form, is the verb *to be*, which in its most positive significance expresses merely the fact of existence. Closely related to *to be* are such words as *to become*, *to appear*, *to seem*, etc. Syntactically these copulative verbs have to be put into a class apart from the transitive verbs, because when they are followed by a substantive word, noun or pronoun, this word is in the nominative, or predicate nominative,

263

case, and also because, unlike the transitive verbs, they may be followed by predicate adjectives, as in "I am glad," or "He seems happy."

It is in this second construction, in cases in which the copulative verb is followed by the predicate adjective, that the extension of its use has occurred. The forms of the verb *to be* have remained the only ones which may be followed by a nominative case of the pronoun. But the number of verbs which may be followed by predicate adjectives has been largely increased. Examples are *turn*, as in "The milk turned sour"; *look*, as in "he looks sad"; *feel*, as in "I feel sick"; *smell*, as in "it smells sweet"; *sound*, as in "the horn sounds loud"; *flush*, as in "he flushed red"; and a great many others.

Instances occur abundantly in literary English. Jeffries (*The Open Air*) has: "There was a coat of fallen needles under the firs an inch thick, and beneath it the dry earth *touched warm*." With the novelist Meredith it developed almost into a mannerism of style. Almost every page will furnish illustrations, of which one or two from the early pages of his *Vittoria* may be cited: "Luigi's blood *shot purple*"; "In his sight she *looked a dark Madonna*, with the sun *shining bright gold* through the edges of the summer hat."

Many of these verbs have quite as much asserting value as most intransitive verbs, and if it were not for the predicative adjectives which accompany them, we might classify them simply as intransitive verbs. That these words which stand after the verbs are true adjectives and not adverbs is determined by our feeling for the logic of the statements. Sentences like "The flower smells sweet" or "The earth touched warm" do not describe the manner of action of the verb. They are rather equivalent to the paraphrases, "The flower is sweet to the smell," and "The earth was warm to the touch." They combine, therefore, the function of the copulative and the intransitive verb, and are characteristic of Modern English in their vigorous compression of statement.

The same feeling for compact, strong expression which leads

264

to the direct formation of verbs from nouns, as, for example, *to bell a cat*, instead of the weaker "to put a bell on a cat," or *to house the poor*, instead of "to provide houses for the poor," will help to explain also such elliptical and strongly expressive uses of the verb as *The earth touched warm*, instead of "The earth was warm to the touch."

6 ✍ Function-groups

One result of the loss of inflections in English and the consequent tendency of the words of the language to assume generalized forms, each word becoming a completely independent word-unit, has been the formation of what may be called function-groups. In a completely inflectional language, such things as function-groups would not exist; for the language would have for every grammatical function which it wished to express an appropriate inflectional form.

In English, however, many of the grammatical functions can be expressed only by means of groups of words. Thus English has no true inflectional passive voice, and has not had any since the earliest recorded periods of its existence. The passive voice has to be expressed by a group of words, consisting of a form of the verb *to be* united to the past participle. Likewise most of the tenses in Modern English, e.g., *I have gone, I had gone, I shall go*, etc., have to be expressed by function-groups, not by inflections. If we were strictly logical, we should write the parts of a function-group together as one word, since it has but a single value; or at the very least we should connect them by hyphens, *I had-gone, I shall-go*, etc. As a matter of fact we do this in some instances, but in others we do not. We write *blue-collar* and *blue-sky* with hyphens, *bluebird, bluegrass*, and *bluenose* as single words, but such groups as *blue book, blue spruce*, and *blue note* are not united at all.

The usage of the printed and written language in this respect is altogether inconsistent. Certain compound prepositions, like *into, beside*, etc., are written together as one word, but others are not only not written together, but may not be written together, such as *out of*, *alongside of*, *because of*, by reason of the artificial distinction established by conventional usage. This diversity of printed and written forms is, however, purely accidental and external. The function of *out of* and *into* are identical in the sentence, "He fell out of the boat into the water," even though they do differ in form.

A few further illustrations may be cited. The words *head on*, in "The ships struck head on" is an adverbial function-group modifying *struck*. In the sentence, "The shores were steep to all around" (Conrad, *Nostromo*, Chapter I) *steep to* is a predicate adjective. The verb in the sentence, "It is all over with me" is the function-group *is over*, which is modified by the adverb *all*. The value of *burst open* as a function-group is clearly brought out in the following sentence, where the words are once used as a verb and then as an adjective: "The cottonfields themselves when the bolls *burst open*, seem almost as if whitened by snow, and the red and white flowers, interspersed among the *burst-open* pods, make the whole field beautiful" (T. Roosevelt, "In the Louisiana Canebrakes"). In the sentence "I will look into it," the verb is the group *will look into*; in "The ball went flying through the air," the verb is the group *went flying*. In "He ran up a bill," the verb is *ran up*, in direct contrast to, "He ran up the street," where the verb is merely *ran*. Many other illustrations might be cited, but those given are sufficient to show that not every separate word by itself has grammatical function in Modern English grammar, but that words must often be taken together as constituting function-groups. In such cases it is contrary to the structure of the language to try to analyze the groups into their constituent parts so as to give every word, standing alone, a clearly defined functional value.

So far has this feeling for the function-group developed that often we have a kind of group inflection. Thus in a phrase like "The governor of California's policy," the genitive inflection should strictly go with *governor*. The whole phrase, however, *the governor of California*, is felt to belong together and to serve as a genitive modifier of *policy*, and the inflection is consequently attached to the group as a whole. This use is capable of almost indefinite extension. In groups of two or more words in names or titles, as, for example, *Beaumont and Fletcher's Works*, the *Chicago and Alton's rolling stock*, etc., the genitive inflection ends the group. In two appositive nouns the genitive inflection is added only to the second, as in "We stopped at Mr. Barton, the clergyman's house, for a drink of water."

In popular speech a sentence like "That's the man we saw yesterday's hat" is not only quite intelligible but is felt to be quite idiomatic. It is equivalent to "That is the hat of the man whom we saw yesterday." This, however, is very formal English, the phrase "the hat of the man" being unusual spoken idiom and somewhat awkward as well. One would more naturally say "That is the man's hat whom," but this is open to the criticism of misplaced modification. In the sentence as first given the kernel of the sentence is simply "That is the hat." The rest of the sentence is felt to be merely a genitive modifier of *hat*, and the mark of the genitive relation is consequently added to the last word of the group preceding the modified word.

7 ⬚ Mixed Syntax

Occasional questions of grammar arise in which the source of the difficulty lies in the mixing of two forms of construction. This may be illustrated by the expression *different than*. It is generally condemned in composition textbooks and is likely to be questioned by careful editors. Yet, for the past two centuries it has appeared with a fair amount of regularity in the writings of standard authors; a catalogue of those who have used it could almost serve as a reading list for prose fiction from the eighteenth century on, although it occurs possibly not more than fifteen percent of the time in any one writer. American authorities prefer *different from*; *different to* is the more usual form in Britain.

267

As far as the *different than* construction itself is concerned, it would seem to have arisen from a blending of *different from* (*to*) and *other than*. Both *different* and *other* have the sense 'not the same, apart from, not classifiable with.' The comparative degree of the adjective, similar in its tendency to place the thing or object outside the general class, also employs *than*: (*greater than*, *warmer than*, etc.). It is reasonable to suppose that the use of *than* with comparatives and especially with *other* explains in good part the use of the same connective with *different*. Unquestionably, the construction appears more often in familiar speech than in careful writing, where it is still a minority form. On the one hand, there is little to recommend its use; on the other, it can scarcely be said that it is unclear or imprecise. It is a confusion of structure rather than a violation of logic.

Another illustration of mixed syntax is to be found in a construction like "The reason is because . . . ." Here the objection rests on the grounds of redundancy: either *The reason is* . . . or *Because* . . . would constitute a sufficient introduction to an explanatory statement. Several factors may be involved in the development of this questionable expression. One is the relative rarity, in the spoken language, of initial adverbial clauses beginning with *because*. A second is that either one of them might constitute a so-called short-answer reply to a question: "Why were you so late?" "Because I overslept," or "The reason is (that) I overslept." The blending of both into a single construction may reflect a desire for emphasis. Moreover, in the event that a number of fairly long modifiers follow *reason*, it is possible that the speaker loses sight of the original thread of the construction: "The reason for my having been so late this morning when I promised that I would get here early is . . . ." and at this point *because* takes over instead of the *that* which logic would normally demand. These constructions are of interest not so much in terms of what is or is not acceptable, but rather as illustrations of the means and processes of syntactic change.

An old linguistic superstition which is now happily passing

out of existence ran to the effect that sentences must not end with prepositions. The rule was maintained in face of the fact that in actual speech and in writing, sentences do end with prepositions, and historically, from the Old English period down, have always ended with prepositions in certain constructions. It is more than likely that the composite elements of the word *preposition* itself (*pre*+*position*) had something to do with the development of the idea.

It is immediately obvious that in sentences containing a relative clause with the relative pronoun omitted, the sentence cannot end otherwise than with a preposition, as in "Where is the boy you are to play with?" or "This is the house I was born in." Moreover, many of those who were zealous in their condemnation of the *preposition* in final position tried to extend it as well to words like *up*, *down*, *in*, *out*, and *with* when these were functioning not as prepositions but as second members of a composite verb construction: *call up*, 'telephone'; *call down*, 'reprimand.' Even with the relative pronoun present in the construction, any position for *up* except a final one is impossible in "Mr. Jones is the man (whom) they called up." The superstition was given a shattering blow by Winston Churchill's response when someone called his use into question: "That is a piece of nonsense up with which I will not put!" but even so, it lingers on to a slight degree.

The English language is notable for its failure to develop a really satisfactory impersonal pronoun. The form cognate with German *man* was lost during the Middle English period; the form equivalent to French *on* has never been naturalized to the point of easy informal use. As a result, in casual, conversational English we are often driven to the use of personal pronouns in an impersonal sense: "You can't buy anything in England on Sunday." "They don't make shoes as well as they used to."

But these seem somewhat inappropriate in formal written English, so we are driven to the use of *one* instead. Here the problem of multiple reference arises, and Americans, unlike the British,

269

feel the repeated use of *one* to be somewhat awkward and artificial: "If *one* should do that, *one* would soon find that *one's* reputation would suffer." At the same time they have an uncomfortable suspicion that the substitution of *he* and *his* for the second and third occurrences is somewhat questionable. Never was the American dilemma on this score better illustrated than in the survey by S. A. Leonard, *Current English Usage*, where a sentence such as the one quoted above was criticized as being too stilted, but one in which *he* and *his* were substituted was given only qualified approval. It is quite likely that the tendency, in much of our formal writing, towards overuse of the passive voice has its origin in our lack of an easily functioning impersonal pronoun.

The prohibition against the use of *like* is of interest because it demonstrates the importance of attitudes toward languages as well as the mere facts of usage. There are people for whom it serves as an index of refinement, their dislike of the construction having been heightened by its use in a slogan advertising a popular brand of cigarette.

The use of *like* as a conjunction developed in the sixteenth century as an ellipsis of a fuller form *likeas*, sometimes spelled as a single word, sometimes written as two. Thus we have in the Psalms, "Like as a father pitieth his children," etc. In the simplification of this double conjunction, at times one element persisted, at times the other. The one which won complete approval on the part of the traditional grammarians was the second element of the combination, namely *as*. In precisely the same manner, the current use of *like* goes back to a persistence of the first element in certain sectors of the language, and from a strictly rational point of view, there is little to choose between the two processes.

Reliable surveys of current usage show that *like* appears more frequently in speech and informal writing than in formal prose. The *Oxford English Dictionary*, though reporting that the usage was generally condemned as vulgar or slovenly, felt impelled to add that "examples may be found in recent writers of standing."

The argument that *like* is indefensible because it represents a change of function from preposition to conjunction can easily be countered by the reminder that *as* is a reduced form of Old English *ealswā*, originally an adverb. In this same connection, it may be observed that on the very same grounds as the objection to *like*, the employment of *but* as a coördinating conjunction might be condemned with equal justification, for it represents a functional shift from a preposition as well.

With respect to this question, the concluding statement in the original edition of this book is still apropos: A colloquialism *like* as conjunction may be, but indefensible it certainly is not. It is first of all a widespread custom of the speech, it has arisen naturally and in the same way that *as* has, and unless one starts from the *a priori* position that there is only one legitimate form of expression for every idea in speech, it makes as strong a bid for favor as the conjunction *as*.

8 ▨ Book Grammar

The study of systematic, or technical, or formal grammar, as it is variously called, has shifted about considerably in modern times. It was once a part of every elementary and high school course of instruction, and was even sometimes carried over into the college. In earlier periods the development of the feeling for the customary forms of expression was left almost entirely to natural habit, as developed in the home and in general social intercourse. Somewhat later, partly through the elevation of a more rigid standard of uniformity in usage, but mainly through the wide extension of popular education, there was an effort to make grammar as conscious and systematic a study as history or mathematics.

This tendency began only in the middle and latter part of the eighteenth century. One of the earliest grammars of the modern type was that of Bishop Lowth, published in London in 1767. In the preface to this volume, the author declares that "the

271

principal design of a Grammar of any language is to teach us
to express ourselves with propriety in that language, and to
enable us to judge of every phrase and form of construction,
whether it be right or not. The plain way of doing this is to lay
down rules, and to illustrate them by examples. But, besides
showing what is right, the matter may be further explained
by pointing out what is wrong." And so the greater part of
Lowth's grammar is taken up with pointing out what he thinks
to be right and what he thinks to be wrong in the writings of Pope,
Dryden, Prior, and other authors of his period whom we now regard as classic.

Grammars were also written, about this time, for the instruction of "young Gentlemen," and especially for the use of "the
fair Sex," whose defective education in grammar, spelling, and
composition is the subject of frequent satirical comment in the
writings of the period. These grammars are significant of a
change which was coming over English education at that time.
Formerly it had been regarded as sufficient linguistic attainment
for a gentleman if he was able to sign his name to a document,
and many a lady famous in English history could not boast even
of this accomplishment. Now, however, a new test of education
or cultivation began to assume prominence, the test of ability to
express one's self in the conventional or standardized forms of
expression, both in speech and in writing. The tendency towards
a fixed spelling and a fixed grammar went hand in hand, and so far
has this tendency advanced that today deviations from the established and conventional orthography and grammar serve as convenient and frequently applied rough tests, if not of culture, at
least of education and social position.

The importance which modern education has assigned to
language competence had its first result in the development of
what we have called "book grammar." Acceptable usage having
been made one of the essentials of acceptable conduct it was
felt necessary to have books giving the rules of correct grammar.
To supply this need, those speakers of the language who were

convinced that they knew what the established usage of the language was provided such books with amazing abundance. These books were, of course, nothing more than the record of the customary use of the language as observed or imagined by the authors of them, and at times their observations were limited and their imaginations were fertile.

The hold, however, which the dicta of the professed grammarian have acquired over the average user of the language is peculiar. In the proper pursuit of his craft the grammarian merely records the social habits or customs of the speech of his community. Yet many persons who in other ways determine their social habits or customs by their own observation, give to the grammar the power of a final authority. The rules of personal conduct, for example, behavior at table, or the forms of politeness, are learned by the process of social intercourse. No one of any social experience governs his conduct by, or defers to, the authority of the rules of any book of good manners. For such he usually has the greatest contempt, preferring to follow the guide of personal experience and observation. But the customs of speech are also merely the regularized habits of the speech of a community. Why, then, should not the speaker depend as much upon the authority of his personal experience and observation here as in the other social relations of life?

If the discussions of the preceding pages have been followed, it will be evident that it is the author's opinion that he should. Grammars are sometimes helpful in enabling a speaker or writer to broaden the field of his personal observation. In recent years, moreover, the available records of usage have improved considerably in the accuracy and range of their observations. The general dictionaries are more conscious and complete in their coverage of the current language than they were at the beginning of the century, and there are several carefully compiled manuals dealing with moot problems of vocabulary and grammar. Even so, they must be carefully read and properly interpreted in the light of their editorial policies, the sector of the language which they cover, the terminology they employ, and the manner in which their conclusions are presented.

When all is said and done, however, the real guide to acceptable use of the language in all respects is to be found in the living speech. And only he whose experience and observation of the living speech are sufficiently broad to enable him to employ it with perfect ease and confidence can be said to have realized the spirit, the idiom of the language.

8

CONCLUSION

In the discussions of the preceding pages a good deal has been said here and there concerning good English and that which, for one reason or another, is unacceptable. It may be of advantage to gather together, by way of conclusion, the various threads of these discussions, and to endeavor to present some connected answer to the ever-recurring question, What is good English?

It is plain that the question of good English may arise with reference to any of the different sides of language. Thus the point to be determined may be one of sound, or pronunciation; of words, or vocabulary; or one of grammar in the narrower sense, the way in which the sounds and words of the language are united for the expression of thought. But the principles which govern the answer to all questions of good English, whether of pronunciation, or vocabulary, or grammar, are the same. The feeling which underlies the distinctions of right and wrong, of good and bad, is a general feeling for the language as a whole, and the threefold division that has been made is only of practical value as a convenient way of ordering the various kinds of detail which come up for discussion.

In the first place, there should be a clear understanding of the difference between "good English" and "conventional" or "standard English." Standard English is likely to be good English, but all good English is not necessarily standard English. What, then, is good English? The purpose of language being the satisfactory communication of thought and feeling, that is good English which performs this function satisfactorily. Such a definition of good English, it will be observed, is purely utilitarian and practical. It defines good English only in the terms of its activity or function, without reference to any theoretical and abstract conceptions of its value or significance.

Whenever two minds come into satisfactory contact with each other, through the medium of language, we have then, so far as each instance taken by itself is concerned, a good use of language. The rustic with his dialect, and in his own homogeneous dialect community, realizes as much the purpose of language as the most polished speaker in the "best society" of the city. Each expresses himself satisfactorily and is understood satisfactorily, and more than this language at its best cannot do.

Our definition of good English is, therefore, very simple. Any English that hits the mark with force and precision is good English. To hit the mark in the center, it must express exactly what the speaker or writer wishes to express, in such linguistic terms as will convey to the hearer or reader exactly those impressions which it is intended that he shall receive. Anything less than this fails to meet the test.

When we come to analyze the situation a little more closely, however, we find that there are various kinds of good English, that the question of "bad English" usually arises when one kind of English is used in circumstances which require a different kind, when one has tried to hit the mark with the wrong arrow, and has missed the bull's-eye as a consequence. Thus there is that form of English which is known as "popular English." This is the speech of those, who usually through limited experience and education, are unacquainted with the usage which the community in general regards as the better social custom.

Sometimes, as in the poetry of Burns, it is made the vehicle for literary expression. Usually, however, it is a purely colloquial speech.

Naturally, the limits of popular English are not absolutely defined, but are largely a matter of opinion. The term often carries with it some unfavorable connotations. Popular English is the English characteristic of the unschooled and the unskilled in our society. But just how one establishes the dividing line between the skilled and unskilled, the educated and the unschooled, the cultured and the uncultivated is difficult to determine. A positive test of culture, outside the dogmatic opinion of individuals, has never yet been discovered. Certainly it can hardly be said that the person who has received the conventional education is, by and for that reason solely, a more highly cultivated person than one who has not.

A second kind of English is called "colloquial English." This is the speech of the commonplace concerns of daily life and of less serious conversation, a speech freer and less conscious than formal speech, but not carrying with it the suggestion of illiteracy which characterizes popular speech. It has been characterized as the language of well-bred ease. The degree of colloquialism which is likely to occur in one's own speech or in that of others depends on the subject of conversation, on the intimacy of the acquaintanceship of the persons speaking, and in general on all the attendant circumstances.

A third kind of English is "formal or literary English." This is the English of public speaking, or more formal conversation, and of printed and written literature. It varies widely in the degree of its formality, the style of a philosophic treatise being appropriately more formal than that of a light essay. There is also one manner of speaking for the pulpit and another for the lecture platform, one manner for the judge in court and another for the stump orator. The line of demarcation between formal and colloquial English is not sharp, just as it is not between colloquial and popular English. The style of some authors or public speakers, for example, is decidedly more colloquial, more familiar, than that of others.

With all, however, whatever the degree of formality, the dependence of the literary speech upon the colloquial speech of natural intercourse is necessary. It is from the colloquial speech that the literary speech has its vitality. If left to itself, its tendency would be to develop into a highly specialized and artificial form of expression—a special high-caste language for literature that would grow less and less real and expressive as it detached itself more and more from the colloquial speech in which the common human concerns of life and death find their most intimate expression.

It is perhaps better, therefore, to speak of these three kinds of speech, popular, colloquial, and literary, not as three distinct and separate species, but rather as three varieties of directions of development of what is at bottom one speech, and that a popular speech, in the sense that it comes directly from the experiences of men and women, in the immediate affairs of life. Language, as Walt Whitman says, "is something arising out of the work, needs, ties, joys, affections, tastes, of long generations of humanity, and has its bases broad and low, close to the ground. Its final decisions are made by the masses, people nearest the concrete, having most to do with actual land and sea."

Each of these three varieties of English speech has its appropriate uses. They are three kinds of arrows with which different speakers at different moments strive to hit the mark of good English. To hit the mark of the serious literary style, one does not use the arrow of the obviously colloquial speech, and still less of popular speech. To hit the mark in colloquial conversation, one does not use the arrow of the formal speech, nor, among cultivated persons, of the popular speech. The popular speech naturally does not often come into conflict with the colloquial speech of polite conversation, or with the formal speech, since the characteristic of the popular speaker is his lack of contact with the other forms of speech. In general it is assumed "that a man of taste and ability will modify his use of language to meet the special requirements of the task proposed. He will have learned by study to distinguish between different tones and values in the instrument of speech, and will have acquired by exercise the power of touching that mighty organ of expression to various issues." [1]

It thus appears, if the above statements are true, that language which may be adequately expressive, and therefore good, under one set of circumstances, under a different set of circumstances becomes inadequately expressive, because it says more or less than the speaker intended, and so becomes bad English. One learns thus the lesson of the relativity of language, that language is valuable only as it effects the purpose one wishes to attain, that what is good at one time may be bad at another, and what is bad at one time may be good at another.

But something further must be said about that variety of English which results in what is known as the conventional, or standard, English. It is not necessary to discuss here why mankind strives to formulate customs and habits into a fixed system. The fact itself is obvious. Through this natural instinct, as we may call it, in all our social customs, of daily manners, of dress, of morals, of speech, more or less regularized systems of conduct grow up.

In language, each community, whether it is large or small, has a general understanding that this or that pronunciation, or, this or that rule of grammar, is the accepted standard, or conventional, one. This general understanding is arrived at in a purely voluntary, and often at first unconscious, way. Nobody imposes, nobody has the power to impose, any rules of standard speech on a community. As we have before pointed out, a rule is merely the statement of the general custom of a community. We might, consequently, speak of the standard popular, the

[1] Symonds, *Essays, Speculative and Suggestive*, Vol. I, p. 267.

standard colloquial, and the standard literary speech of this or that geographical community.

Usually, however, the term is understood in a somewhat more limited sense. It is used to signify not merely the customary use of a community, but especially that use when it is recognized and acknowledged as the approved use of that community. Any usage which is thus given its patent of acceptability is regarded as standard use. It is customary use raised to the position of conscious legalized use.

Of course the question of standard does not arise until there is some conflict of standards. As in the case of civil law, no customary practice is legalized, or standardized, until doubts are raised with respect to it, until some one attempts to depart from the customary practice. Then it is necessary to come to some agreement as to what shall be recognized as the accepted practice. In the case of civil law this is done either through the passing of a formal law by some legislative body, or through the decisions handed down by judges in passing upon disputed cases of customary and accepted practice in the dealings of men with each other.

In matters of language the legal or standard practice cannot be so easily determined. Owing to the fact that there is no legislative body in language, no specified court of appeal, there is occasionally lack of agreement as to what shall and what shall not be recognized as the accepted use of the language. The government of the language is not as fully and as definitely organized as is the government of the business and other overt acts of men. In many instances, or rather in most instances, there is unanimity of opinion, and then we have an unquestioned and general standard use. The great body of English usage is thus made up of forms of language with respect to which there is practically no difference of opinion.

Sometimes, however, due to various causes, such as the coming together of two speakers from two different geographical or social speech communities, instances occur in which there arises difference of opinion. In one community or one group, *coal oil* as a term for 'kerosene,' *greasy* pronounced to rhyme with *easy*, *woken* as the past participle of *wake*, or *I will* for the future, will be accepted as the conventional, standard speech of the community. When they are used in this community or this group, they express their thought completely, and carry with them no connotation to the discredit of the speaker. In another geographical community, or by certain speakers within a community, one or another of these usages will be condemned as not standard, therefore as not satisfactorily expressive because they call attention to themselves at the expense of the idea or message they are intended to convey.

Who shall decide? Nothing can decide but the observation of custom. What is defended as customary use by a community, or even by a single speaker, to carry the matter to its final analysis, is standard, or conventional, in that community or for that speaker. The question of correctness and incorrectness, that is, of standard, can only arise when a conflict of opinion arises, and this conflict can only be decided by such an extension of the field of observation of customary use, on the particular question, as will determine finally what the true custom is.

That this is often a difficult matter is not to be denied. It is, however, only one of the many ways in which man is driven to an observation of his surroundings and to a continual adaption of his conduct to these surroundings. The importance of standard speech for the welfare of the community should also be recognized. It is only by the acceptance of general custom that speech can be made effective at all, and it is every speaker's duty to follow the best custom of the speech as he views it. Not idiosyncrasy, not singularity, should be the ideal in speech, but a wise adjustment to and harmony with the general custom of the speech.

Standard, and in that sense conventional and "correct," English is consequently not altogether the same thing as good English. We have said that standard English is the customary use of a community when it is recognized and accepted as the customary use of the community. Beyond this, however, is the larger field of good English, any English that justifies itself by accomplishing its end, by hitting the mark with precision and force. It is plain that standard English must continually refresh itself by accepting the creations of good English. It has always been so in the past, and so it is in the present.

If the standardizing tendency were carried to its fullest extent, it would result in a complete fixity of language. If by following standard use one should have to follow customary use, it is plain that there could be no place in the standard speech for innovation —all would be summed up in the simple formula, Follow custom. Language would thus soon cease to be positively expressive; it would soon come to have no more personal value than an algebraic formula. But fortunately the standardizing tendency can never be carried out to its completest development, and opposed to it, or at least complementing it, will always be the ideal of good English in the broadest sense of the words. All that the standardizing tendency can do is to fix a somewhat general outline of the language. This indeed is necessary and valuable to prevent a complete chaos of pronunciation, of vocabulary, and of grammar.

But within these vague limits there is broad freedom. Poets and prose writers, lively imaginations of all kinds, in speech as in literature, are continually widening the bounds of the conventional and standard language by adding to it something that was not there before. They must do so if speech is ever to rise above the dead level of the commonplace. "Justice of perception consists in knowing how and when and where to deviate from the beaten track." But deviation there must be, and the persons who attain an individual style in the use of language are those who seize their opportunities as they present themselves. To them the prime and necessary virtue in language is expressiveness, and, as complementing this, there should correspond on the part of the hearer the willingness to receive the expression as fully as it was intended.

Again, however, we insist on the continual application of the *test* of good English—it must be satisfactorily expressive. If it does not justify itself by accomplishing its purpose, if it shocks the prejudices, or the traditions, of the person to whom it is directed, or if it be unintelligible, if in any way it fails to secure a satisfactory and unhindered transmission of the thought, then to the extent of this failure it is bad English. And it is bad not because it has failed to satisfy any condition of theoretical, ideal excellence, any notions of standard, but because in the actual employment of language as a social tool it has failed to produce the result for which that tool exists.

APPENDIX

▨ The Old English Chronicle, Laud, 636

The manuscript of which the opening page is reproduced on page 23 was written in the early part of the twelfth century. This is of course relatively late in the Old English period. Owing, however, to the literary conservatism of the writers and compilers of the *Chronicle*, the English which we have here differs little in style of handwriting and in the forms of language from the English of the two centuries preceding. The transcription of this passage, with interlinear translation, is as follows:

Of Britain the island is eight hundred of miles long
1 Brittene igland is ehta hund mila lang

two hundred broad here are in this
2 and[1] twa hund brad. And her sind on þis

island five languages English
3 iglande fif geþeode, englisc and

British Welsh Scotch Pictish
4 brittisc and wilsc and scyttisc and pyhtisc and

Latin First were inhabitants of this land
5 bocleden.[2] Erest weron bugend þises landes

---

[1] *and*. The manuscript has here, as frequently, an abbreviation for the conjunction.
[2] *bocleden*. Literally 'book-Latin,' meaning the Latin of the learned classes.

     the British These   came   from Armorica   settled
6 brittes. Þa coman of armenia[3] and gesætan

     southward   Britain   first.   Then befell it that the
7 suðewearde bryttene ærost. Þa gelamp hit þæt[4] pyh-

     Picts came   from the south from Scithia(?) with   long   ships
8 tas coman   suþan   of Scithian mid langum[5] scipum

     not   many   they came   first   to north Hibernia
9 na manegum. And þa coman ærost on norþ ybernian

          there asked of the Irish   they there   might   dwell   But
10 up, and þær bædon[6] scottas[7] þæt hi ðer moston wunian. ac

     they would not them permit   for   they   said   the Irish
11 hi noldan heom lyfan, forðan hi cwædon, þa scottas:

     you   may   though   counsel teach   know
12 we eow magon þeah hwaðere[8] ræd gelæron. We witan

     another island here to the east   ye   may   dwell   if
13 oþer egland her be easton. Þer ge magon eardian, gif

     will   any one you   opposes   assist
14 ge willað. And gif hwa eow wiðstent, we eow fultumiað

          may   conquer. Then fared
15 þæt ge hit magon gegangan. Ða ferdon þa pihtas and ge-

     acquired   northwards   southwards it had
16 ferdon þis land norþanweard, and suþanweard hit hef-

     the British as   before said   for themselves
17 don brittas, swa we ær cwedon. And þa pyhtas   heom

     obtained wives of the Irish   the condition   would choose their
18 abædon wif æt scottum on þa gerad þaet hi gecuron heora

     royal-kin ever   woman side   they held   so   long
19 kyne cinn aa on þa wif healfa. Þæt hi heoldon swa lange

---

[3] *armenia*. The manuscript reading must be a mistake for Armorica, on the Continent.
[4] *þæt*. Here again, as frequently, the conjunction *þæt* is abbreviated by giving only the first letter.   [5] *langum*. The manuscript writes *langu*, but the stroke over the *u* indicates an abbreviation.   [6] *bædon*. The manuscript has *bædo*, the *n* being omitted by mistake.
[7] *scottas*. The Scotch in the early periods of English were the inhabitants of Ireland or Hibernia.   [8] *þeah hwaðere*. Equivalent to 'however,' although literally the words are 'though whether.'

afterwards   then   befell   it   after of years the course
20 syððan. And þa gelamp hit imbe geara   rina,   þaet

of the Irish some deal   went from Hibernia to   Britain   there
21 scotta   sum dæl gewat of ybernian on brittene and þer lan-

land some deal conquered   was   their   leader   Reoda
22 des sum dæl geeodon. And wes heora heratoga reoda ge-

called   this one they are   named   Dælreodi Six-
23 haten. From þam heo sind genemnode dælreodi. Six-

ty   winters ere that   Christ was   born   Gaius Julius
24 tigum wintrum ær þam þe criste were acenned, gaius iulius

of the Romans cæsar with   eighty   ships sought (i.e., visited)
25 romana   kasere mid hund ehtatigum scipum   gesohte

Britain   was first   afflicted with   grim
26 brytene. Þer he wes ærost geswenced mid grimmum

battle   much of his army led astray   then
27 gefeohte and micelne his heres forlædde. And þa he

In order to indicate the relatively fixed or "classic" character of the Old English period, it may be interesting to point out the forms of this text as they would have been given two hundred years before the time at which the text was written. It will be observed that the changes are comparatively few in number and in themselves not very striking. In line 1, *ehta* would probably have been written *eahta*; in l. 5, *erest* and *weron* would have been *ærest* and *wæron*. In l. 11, *forðan* in earlier Old English would have been *forðam*; in l. 16, *hefdon* would have been *hæfdon*; in l. 17, *cwedon* would have been *cwædon*; in l. 21, *þer* would have been *þær*; in l. 22, *wes* would have been *wæs*.

By the time of this text, moreover, there was already entering some feeling of uncertainty with respect to the vowels of unstressed syllables. In l. 6, *brittes* would have been *brittas*, as it is in l. 17; in the same line, *coman* and *gesætan* would have been *comon* and *gesæton*. In l. 18, *gecuron*, an indicative form, would have been *gecuren*, an optative or subjunctive form; in l. 22 *heratoga* would have been *heretoga*, etc.

These changes are very rarely of sufficient importance to

obscure the grammatical relationships of the words. In popular speech doubtless the changes were much more extensive. The language of the *Chronicle* is conservative, literary Old English, such as was preserved in the seclusion of the monasteries and libraries of England. When this conservative literary culture was destroyed by the Norman Conquest and its consequences, the only English which was left was of course the popular, unliterary English, in which changes had taken place at a much more rapid rate. It is from this popular English that the language of the Middle English period is largely derived.

✒ Chaucer's Pardoner's Tale

(From Ellesmere Manuscript, fol. 144ʳ)

This manuscript was completed not later than 1410, just a decade after the death of Chaucer. It was written by one of the professional lay scribes who by this time had largely replaced the earlier monastic scribes. A black and white reproduction does not begin to reveal the extraordinary beauty of its rich illumination. The manuscript is named after one of its former owners, the Earl of Ellesmere. It was acquired in 1917 by the American collector Henry E. Huntington and is now in the possession of the Huntington Library in San Marino, California.

> Heere bigynneth the Pardoners tale.
> In fflaundres whilom was a compaignye
> Of yonge folk that haunteden folye,
> As riot, hasard, stywes, and tauernes
> Where as with harpes, lutes, and gyternes
> They daunce and pleyen at dees bothe day and nyght,
> And eten also and drynken over hir myght,
> Thurgh which they doon the deuel sacrifise
> With inne that deueles temple in cursed wise
> By superfluytee abhomynable.
> Hir othes been so grete and so dampnable
> That it is grisly for to heere hem swere.

Oure blissed lordes body they totere;
Hem thoughte þat Jewes rente hym noght ynough,
And ech of hem at otheres synne lough.
And right anon thanne comen tombesteres,
Ffetys and smale, and yonge ffrutesteres,
Syngeres with harpes, baudes, wafereres,
Whiche been the verray deueles officeres
To kyndle and blowe the fyr of lecherye
That is annexed unto glotonye;
The hooly writ take I to my witnesse,
That luxurie is in wyn and dronkenesse.

In the interests of legibility, only half of the page has been reproduced in this illustration. There were fourteen lines of the Pardoner's Prologue preceding the tale proper, and there were eight more of the tale following the photographed portion. Letters which in the manuscript are indicated by an abbreviation are printed here in italics. The capital I of the first word is part of the decoration. The following is a literal translation of the passage:

In Flanders there formerly dwelt a company
Of young folk who were given over to folly,
Such as riotous living, gambling, brothels, and taverns,
Where with harps, lutes, and guitars
They dance and play at dice both day and night,
And eat and drink also, beyond their capacity,
Through which they do sacrifice to the devil
Within the devil's temple, in a cursed manner
By abominable excess.
Their oaths are so great and damnable
That it is grisly to hear them swear.
They tear our blessed Lord's body to pieces.
It seemed to them that the Jews did not tear Him enough.
And each of them laughed at the others' sin.
And thereupon come dancing girls,
Shapely and slender, and young fruit vendors,
Singers with harps, bawds, confectioners,

Who are the very devil's officers
To kindle and blow the fire of lechery,
Which is closely related to gluttony.
I take the Holy Writ as my witness,
That there is licentiousness in wine and drunkenness.

A phonetic transcription of the passage follows:

ɪn flaʊndərs hwiːlɔm was ə kʊmpæmiːə
ɔf jʊŋə fɔlk θat haʊntədən fɔliːə
as riːɔt hazard stiuəs and tavɛrnəs
hwɛr as wɪθ harpəs lɪutəs and dʒɪternəs
θæɪ daʊns and plæɪ at deːs bɔːθ dæɪ ənd nɪxt
and æːt alsɔːand drɪŋkən ɔːvrɪr mɪxt
θʊrx hwɪtʃ θæɪ doːn θə dɛvɪl sakrɪfiːzə
wɪðɪn θat dɛvɪls təmpl ɪn kʊrsəd wiːzə
bɪ sɪupərflɪuɪteː əbɔmɪnaːbəl
ɪr ɔːðəs beːn sɔː græːt ənd sɔː damnaːbəl
θat ɪt ɪs grɪzlɪ fɔr toː heːr əm swæːrə
uːr blɪsəd lɔːrdəs bɔdɪ θæɪ toːtæːrə
hɛm θɔuxt θət dʒɪuəs rɛnt ɪm nɔxt ɪnɔːux
and æːtʃ ɔf hɛm at oːðrəs sɪnə lɔːux
and rɪxt anɔːn θan kʊmən tʊmbəsterəs
fɛtɪs and smal and jʊŋə frɪutəsterəs
sɪŋgrəs wɪθ harpəs baʊdəs waːfərerəs
hwɪtʃ beːn θə vɛræɪ dɛvɪls ɔfɪserəs
toː kɪndl and blɔːʊ θə fiːr ɔf lɛtʃəriːə
θət ɪs anɛksəd untoː glʊtɔniːə
θə hɔːlɪ rɪt taːk iː toː mɪ wɪtnesə
θət lʊksɪurɪ ɪs ɪn wiːn ənd drʊŋkənesə

◪ The First Folio of Shakespeare

(*Merchant of Venice*, ɪv.i.119–151)

The First Folio of Shakespeare was printed in the year
1623. The text of the *Merchant of Venice* in the First Folio, which
was the first collected edition of Shakepeare's plays and which was

made up mainly from earlier editions of the separate plays, was taken from a quarto edition published in the year 1600. Our passage represents, consequently, the form which printed literature took in the first quarter of the seventeenth century.

Some of the spellings are noteworthy. In l. 122, *bankrout* represents the older spelling of the word, following French *banqueroute*, from which it was borrowed; our modern spelling *bankrupt* was due to the desire to indicate the ultimate etymology of the second element, from Latin *ruptus*, 'broken.' Shakespeare probably pronounced no *p* in the word.

In l. 123, *soale* and *soule* are spelt differently because at an earlier period there had been a difference in pronunciation. By Shakespeare's time the sounds were probably identical, as they are in Modern English. The spelling still indicates that they are of different etymological origin.

Note the unnecessary letters in such spellings as *kenne, mettall, axe, beare, dogge*, etc. Instead of *inexecrable*, l. 128, many editors read *inexorable*. Note the inconsistent use of capital letters in the passage.

✍ Autograph of Milton's Lycidas, ll. 165–193

This passage from Milton's *Lycidas* is reproduced from a facsimile of the manuscript of Milton's minor poems preserved in the Library of Trinity College, Cambridge. A literal transcription of the passage is as follows, words crossed out by Milton being printed in italics:

LYCIDAS

1 Weepe no more wofull shepherds weepe no more
2 for Lycidas yor sorrow is not dead
3 sunck though he be beneath the watrie floare
4 *so sinks the day starre in the Ocean bed*
5 & yet anon repairs his drooping head.
6 and tricks his beams & wth newspangled ore
7 flams in the forhead of ye morning skie

 8 so Lycidas sunk low but mounted *high* high
 9 through the deare might of him that walkt yᵉ waves:
10 where other groves and other streams along
11 wᵗʰ nectar *pure* pure his oozie locks he laves
12 & heares *listening* the unexpressive nuptiall song
13 in the blest kingdoms meek of joy & love
14 there entertaine him all the Sᵗˢ above
15 in sollemne troops, and sweet societies
16 that sing, & singing in thire glorie move
17 and wipe the teares for ever frō his eyes
18 now Lycidas the shepherds weepe no more
19 henceforth thou art the Genius of yᵉ shoare
20 in thy large recompence, & shalt be good
21 to all that wander in that peril*l*ous flood
22 Thus sung the uncouth swaine to th' oakes & rills
23 while yᵉ still morne went out wᵗʰ sandals gray
24 he toucht the tender stops of various quills
25 wᵗʰ eager thought warbling his Dorick lay
26 and now the Sun had stretcht out all the hills
27 and now was dropt into *westren* the wester'n bay
28 at last he rose and twitcht his mantle blew
29 To morrow to fresh woods and pasturs new

Note the persistence of numerous awkward and uneconomical spellings in Milton's usage, e.g., l. 1, *weepe, wofull*; l. 3, *sunck, watrie, floare*; l. 4, *starre*; l. 9, *deare*; l. 12, *heares, nuptiall*; l. 15, *sollemne*; l. 22, *oakes*, etc. On the other hand, note how Milton, with his free attitude towards spelling, spells phonetically when he is so inclined, e.g., l. 9, *walkt*; l. 24, *toucht*; l. 26, *stretcht*; l. 28, *blew*, to rhyme with *new*.

In line 2, *yoʳ* is an abbreviation for *your*, as in line 6, *wᵗʰ* for *with*, in line 14, *Sᵗˢ* for *Saints*, and line 17, *frō* for *from*. In line 7 *yᵉ* is for *the*, the symbol y being used instead of the older thorn, þ, the Old English representative of th. Of course Milton always pronounced this word as *the* not as *ye*, as is sometimes done by those who are not aware of the fact that the y is merely an orthographic substitution for the older þ.

BIBLIOGRAPHY

This Bibliography gives the titles of only a relatively few representative works under each head. The books named are such as will be found most useful to the student whose special interests are in English.

1 ▨ General Treatises on Language:

BACH, EMMON W. *An Introduction to Transformational Grammars.* New York: Holt, Rinehart & Winston, 1964. A useful introduction to the transformational-generative approach.

GLEASON, HENRY A., JR. *An Introduction to Descriptive Linguistics,* rev. ed. New York: Holt, Rinehart & Winston, 1961. Along with the same author's *Workbook in Descriptive Linguistics,* this is useful as a presentation of the structural method, although other approaches are taken into account.

LEHMANN, WINFRIED P. *Historical Linguistics: An Introduction.* New York: Holt, Rinehart & Winston, 1962.

MARTINET, ANDRÉ. *Elements of General Linguistics.* London: Longmans, Green & Co., 1964. A helpful presentation of the European point of view toward the systematic study of language.

PEDERSEN, HOLGER. *The Discovery of Language.* Translated by John W. Spargo. Bloomington, Ind.: Indiana University Press, 1962. A survey of the development of linguistic science in the nineteenth century.

ROBINS, R. H. *General Linguistics: An Introductory Survey*. London: Longmans, Green & Co., 1964. A good starting point for the layman.

SAPIR, EDWARD. *Language: An Introduction to the Study of Speech*. New York: Harcourt, Brace & World, 1921. One of the early books on the subject; a classic, but still highly readable and useful.

2 ▨ English Origins and Institutions:

BLAIR, PETER H. *An Introduction to Anglo-Saxon England*. Cambridge: Cambridge University Press, 1956.

TREVELYAN, GEORGE M. *History of England*. Vol. I. Garden City, N.Y.: Doubleday & Co., 1953.

WHITELOCK, DOROTHY. *The Beginnings of English Society*. Harmondsworth, Middlesex: Penguin Books, 1952.

3 ▨ General Histories of the English Language:

BAUGH, ALBERT C. *A History of the English Language*, second ed. New York: Appleton-Century-Crofts, 1957.

JESPERSEN, OTTO. *Growth and Structure of the English Language*, ninth ed. Oxford: Basil Blackwell, 1960.

PYLES, THOMAS. *The Origins and Development of the English Language*. New York: Harcourt, Brace & World., 1964.

ROBERTSON, STUART. *The Development of Modern English*, second ed., revised by F. G. Cassidy. Englewood Cliffs, N.J.: Prentice-Hall, 1954.

WYLD, HENRY C. *A History of Modern Colloquial English*, third ed. New York: E. P. Dutton & Co., 1936.

4 ▨ English Grammars:

CHOMSKY, NOAM A. *Syntactic Structures*. 's-Gravenhage: Mouton & Co., 1957. The first statement of the principles of generative grammar.

FRANCIS, W. NELSON. *The Structure of American English*. New York: The Ronald Press Co., 1958.

FRIES, CHARLES C. *American English Grammar.* New York: Appleton-Century-Crofts, 1940.

FRIES, CHARLES C. *The Structure of English.* New York: Harcourt, Brace & World, 1952.

HILL, ARCHIBALD A. *Introduction to Linguistic Structures: From Sound to Sentence in English.* New York: Harcourt, Brace & World, 1958.

JESPERSEN, OTTO. *A Modern English Grammar on Historical Principles.* Copenhagen: Ejnar Munksgaard, 1909–1949.

LONG, RALPH A. *The Sentence and Its Parts: A Grammar of Contemporary English.* Chicago: University of Chicago Press, 1961.

Among the numerous shorter treatises and special monographs, the following may be noted: M. Joos, *The Five Clocks* (1966), *The English Verb, Forms and Meanings* (1964); R. B. Lees, *The Grammar of English Nominalizations* (1960); A. H. Marckwardt, *American English* (1958); R. Quirk, *The Uses of English* (1962); Carroll Reed, *American Dialects* (1967); Barbara Strang, *Modern English Structure* (1962). For a general discussion of the methods and aims in the teaching of grammar and the application of linguistics to the teaching of English, see H. A. Gleason, *Linguistics and English Grammar* (1965) and A. H. Marckwardt, *Linguistics and the Teaching of English* (1966).

5 ▨ English Dictionaries:

The Oxford English Dictionary. Oxford: The Clarendon Press, 1933. A citation dictionary, compiled on the basis of historical principles and in the light of the best scholarship of its time.

The Random House Dictionary of the English Language. New York: Random House, 1966. Somewhat slighter in its coverage than the most complete unabridged dictionaries.

Webster's Third New International Dictionary of the English Language. Springfield, Mass.: G. & C. Merriam Co., 1961.

Dictionary of American English. Chicago: University of Chicago Press, 1938–1944.

Dictionary of Americanisms. Chicago: University of Chicago Press, 1951.

The Oxford Dictionary of English Etymology, ed. C. T. Onions. Oxford: Oxford University Press, 1966.

6 ▨ Manuals of Usage:

BRYANT, MARGARET M. *Current American Usage*. New York: Funk & Wagnalls, 1962.

EVANS, BERGEN M. and CORNELIA. *A Dictionary of Contemporary American Usage*. New York: Random House, 1957.

FOLLETT, WILSON. *Modern American Usage*. New York: Hill & Wang, 1966.

FOWLER, H. *A Dictionary of Modern English Usage*, second ed., revised by Sir Ernest Gowers. Oxford: Oxford University Press, 1965.

LEONARD, S. A. *Current English Usage*. Chicago: Inland Press, 1932.

MARCKWARDT, ALBERT H. and WALCOTT, FRED. *Facts About Current English Usage*. New York: Appleton-Century-Crofts, 1938.

7 ▨ English Sounds:

BRONSTEIN, ARTHUR J. *The Pronunciation of American English, An Introduction to Phonetics*. New York: Appleton-Century-Crofts, 1960.

KURATH, HANS. *A Phonology and Prosody of Modern English*. Ann Arbor, Mich.: University of Michigan Press, 1961

MOORE, SAMUEL. *Historical Outlines of English Sounds and Inflections*, rev. ed. Ann Arbor, Mich.: University of Michigan Press, 1949.

Index of Subjects and Words Cited